WHO DIVORCES?

BARBARA THORNES
and
JEAN COLLARD

Marriage Research Centre
Central Middlesex Hospital

ROUTLEDGE DIRECT EDITIONS

ROUTLEDGE & KEGAN PAUL
London, Boston and Henley

First published in Great Britain in 1979
by Routledge & Kegan Paul Ltd
39 Store Street,
London WC1E 7DD,
Broadway House,
Newtown Road,
Henley-on-Thames,
Oxon RG9 1EN and
9 Park Street,
Boston, Mass. 02108, USA
Printed in Great Britain
by Thomson Litho Ltd, East Kilbride

ISBN 0 7100 0187 8

CONTENTS

PREFACE

The Marriage Research Centre at the Central Middlesex Hospital in London was established in 1970 to examine the present meaning of marriage in our society and to attempt an understanding of the underlying mechanisms of marital satisfaction. The Centre has as its primary aim the undertaking of research in fields relating to contemporary marriage; it also offers a clinical service of marital therapy as well as courses in applied marital studies.

It may seem somewhat paradoxical that the first major research study undertaken by the Centre should be about divorce, rather than about marriage. In the general study of marriage, however, the study of divorce is clearly relevant since knowledge of the factors which influence marital breakdown is crucial for the full understanding of marital relationships.

The present study owes its inception to Dr J Dominian, Director of the Marriage Research Centre, without whose inspiration neither the Centre itself nor this survey would have been envisaged, and upon whose extensive clinical experience much of the questionnaire was based. The entire funding of the study was borne by the Trustees of the Centre, and we pay tribute to their continuing support.

Since our research centre is small and our colleagues few in number, we have needed to call upon them not only for critical response and appraisal, but also for assistance with some of the inevitable clerical chores associated with the writing up of a survey. Our special thanks are due to Penny Mansfield and Margaret Stoneman, who were particularly instrumental in the early stages in enabling the book to take initial shape. We are also grateful to Alan Tait and Julia Brannen who have been generous with their time and expertise.

The successful operationalisation of the survey was in no small measure due to the dedicated efforts of Frances Moir and her stalwart band of interviewers, who worked so uncomplainingly in the field in the depths of winter.

The data-processing was efficiently carried out by Mike Duffy and his colleagues, of Research Surveys of Great Britain Ltd, and it was a matter of regret to us all that necessary economic stringencies severely restricted the multivariate analyses.

We have been fortunate throughout in having the services of the Busy Bee Secretarial Agency, in particular, those of Peggy and

Barbara King, who worked both speedily and unstintingly.

To Robert Chester, of the Department of Social Administration at Hull University, a member of our Academic Board, we owe appreciation for his continuing encouragement and helpful advice.

Others who have contributed to the book in various ways include: Jean Gilbert, Beryl Grix, Theresa Harvey, Wendy Huggett, Jane Perry, Mike Proctor and Trevor Sharot.

And lastly, we must thank our ever-patient husbands, who have endured a great deal.

Barbara Thornes
Jean Collard

GLOSSARY OF TERMS
AND ABBREVIATIONS

CM: Continuing Married (sample of informants whose primary
      marriage was, at the time of fieldwork, still intact)
CMW: Continuing Married Women
CMM: Continuing Married Men
D: Divorced (sample of informants whose primary marriage had
      ended in divorce between September 1970 and March 1972)
DW: Divorced Women
DM: Divorced Men

courtship period:	interval between the first date with, and marriage to that person.
decree absolute:	document subsequent to the decree nisi, making it final and absolute, and declaring that the marriage was dissolved on the date of the decree nisi.
decree nisi:	document recording the decision of the court that the marriage has irretrievably broken down, and that it shall be dissolved in not less than six weeks' time, unless cause is shown why the decree nisi should not be made absolute.
de facto duration:	length of time between date of marriage and the cessation of cohabitation.
de jure duration:	length of time between date of marriage and decree absolute.
divorce rate:	total number of marriages estimated to be in existence in a given year, divided by total number of decrees absolute granted for that year.
family of marriage:	the husband, wife and any children of an informant's marriage.
family of origin:	family into which an informant was born and in which he grew up.
marital dissolution:	legal termination of marriage, leaving partners free to remarry.
Pmd:	pre-marital difficulties: the presence during the courtship period of difficulties serious enough to cause the couple temporarily to break up.

:

Pmp	pre-marital pregnancy: birth of a child within the first seven months of marriage, calculated from date of marriage and date of birth of first child.
Ppd:	post-puerperal depression: depression which follows the birth of a child.
primary marriage:	first marriage i.e. between a spinster and a bachelor.
social class:	based on occupations classified according to the Registrar General's Classification of Occupations (Office of Population Censuses and Surveys, 1970). This distinguishes six 'social class' groups:

    I   Professional, etc. occupations
   II   Intermediate occupations
 III   Skilled occupations
      (Nm)   non-manual
      (M)   manual
  IV   Partly skilled occupations
   V   Unskilled occupations

Chapter 1

INTRODUCTION:
Background and Methodology

Throughout the history of the institution of marriage, societies have generally not regarded divorce as beneficial, either for society, or for the individual; some societies have made divorce illegal or disgraceful, and although others have provided that such dissolution should be legal, none the less the widespread disapproval of divorce has been common. Since marriage in our society is a civil contract whose termination can only be formally effected by law, the divorce rate will obviously be affected by the laws and regulations governing marriage. In recent years in England and Wales there have been a series of changes in such laws leading to the easier availability of divorce, to the extent that no evidence of matrimonial offence has been required since 1971, and divorce by post will shortly become commonplace.

Whilst changes in the laws governing divorce will obviously influence the probability of divorce being sought to end an unsatisfactory marriage, there is some evidence to suggest that divorce rates will also vary directly with the standing that divorcees have within their own society (Goody, 1962), demonstrating that the prevailing social mores regarding marriage will also have an influence upon whether or not divorce is sought, since they will determine the extent to which the lives of individuals after divorce may be either easier or more difficult.

The divorce rate in our own society has increased considerably in the last thirty years, and quite notably following the implementation, in January 1971, of the 1969 Divorce Reform Act. It has recently been calculated by the Office of Population Censuses and Surveys that 22% of all females will divorce at least once by the age of 45 years (OPCS, 1976). Table 1 shows the trend in the divorce statistics in selected years between 1945 and 1976.

INTERPRETATIONS OF THE UPWARD TREND IN THE DIVORCE STATISTICS

Whilst a divorce represents a broken marriage, it is unlikely that the divorce rate itself can be directly equated with the rate of marriage breakdown (as defined by divorce, separation or desertion) in our society. This is because there are not, and never have been,

TABLE 1 The number of decrees absolute (excluding nullity of
marriage) granted in England and Wales in selected years between
1945 and 1976, and the divorce rate (per '000 married population)

Year	Number of decrees absolute	Divorce rate *
1945	15,634	–
1950	30,870	2.8
1955	26,816	2.4
1960	23,868	2.1
1965	37,084	3.1
1970	44,278	4.7
1971	72,895	6.0
1972	117,481	9.5
1973	104,395	8.4
1974	110,068	9.0
1975	117,042	9.6
1976	125,138	10.1

Source: Registrar General
* The divorce rate is calculated by dividing the total number of
  marriages estimated to be in existence in a given year, by the
  total number of decrees absolute granted for that year

any data on desertions and informal separations, and it seems
sensible to suppose that these may have accounted for a substantial
number of marriage breakdowns in the past, especially when divorce
was not easily available, either legally, financially or normatively.
A similar observation was made by Rheinstein (1960), who concluded
that 'in the absence of statistics, we simply cannot know to what
extent the rise in the divorce rate indicates a rise in marriage
instability, or a shift from informal to formalised marriage
termination due to changed social conditions and mores.'
    Nevertheless, some writers do believe that it is possible to
interpret the available statistics in a fairly exact way. For
instance, McGregor (1967) concluded that the trends in the judicial
statistics on divorce, separation, maintenance orders and the like,
may be taken as evidence that the historical increase in divorce
does not represent genuine increases in marriage breakdown but is
largely due to the movement from informal and formal separations to
divorce and mainly results from the easier financial availability of
divorce because of legal aid. The Law Commissioners, in their
report (HMSO, 1966) reached a similar conclusion, as did the
Committee on Statutory Maintenance Limits (HMSO, 1968). However, in
his paper, 'Divorce and Legal Aid: a false hypothesis', Chester
(1972a) reviewed in detail the evidence which was used to account
for the increase in divorce in terms of the facilitating agency of
legal aid and concluded:

The most plausible explanation of the divorce figures for the past two decades is that they reveal a decline from the post-war numbers, followed by a rapid and equally continuing rise which is related to social and cultural changes much more fundamental than amendments to the terms to a somewhat limited welfare scheme.

The extent to which welfare schemes, whether they be prior to the divorce (legal aid), or after the divorce in the form of benefit payments to single parent families, may actually be contributing factors to the increases in the divorce rate is uncertain. There is no evidence to suggest this is so for the UK and the data from the USA on this question is conflicting. Moles (1976) did find that high separation ratios were linked with higher welfare payments since between 1960 and 1970 changes in payment ratios in his sample were directly associated with changes in separation ratios. However, as Moles himself notes, Cutright and Scanzoni (1973) found no effect of benefit levels upon single parent family levels. More importantly, Bane (1975) found that on average welfare payments appeared unrelated to divorce. Similarly, Sawhill (1975) failed to determine any significant effects of welfare benefit levels upon marital instability in low income families. In the light of this conflicting evidence from the USA, Levinger and Moles (1976) have concluded that changes in welfare payments and separation ratios are difficult to interpret in terms of a financial incentive theory.
Other observers of the trends in the divorce statistics tend to comment upon them in terms of the implications that such increases in marriage breakdown may have for society. From such comment two opposing streams of interpretation are evident, with arguments which appear to derive from specific and differing value systems. These two streams, representing wide diversities of public opinion and position, Winch (1971) sees as being broadly divided into groups which he has named 'institutionalists' and 'individualists'. According to him the institutionalists appear to wish to revive an earlier familial form in which the happiness of its members is secondary to the stability and continuity of the overall structure of the family. In contrast, the individualists tend to regard the personal development and happiness of the individual as of paramount importance and do not appear to be alarmed by current changes in family structure since these are perceived as enhancing individual happiness; they further expect that, at some point in the future, consistent with changes that have occurred in other institutions within society, a new form of the family will emerge.
Any speculations regarding the future of marriage are inevitably tentative, and it is open to debate whether the upward trend in the divorce statistics, even if representing increases in absolute marriage breakdown, indicates a dissatisfaction with marriage *per se* (and hence might be said to be signalling its decline in favour of alternative family structures such as no marriage, group marriage, multi-family households and the like), or whether the divorce rate is simply a reflection of the state of the institution of marriage as it presently stands. According to Leach (1968), 'the family with its narrow privacy, and tawdry secrets is the source of all our discontents'; whilst Mead (1971) has stated that the insistence that

'the most flimsy, ill-conceived and unsuitable mating be treated as a sanctified life-long choice' coupled with the idea of divorce as a failure and an index of social disorders, may prevent the development of 'new and appropriate institutions for protecting children from an unrealistic dependence on a situation of life-long marriage between their parents'. Norton and Glick (1976), however, make the point that the divorce rate may simply be reflecting the difficulties of partners in adjusting to a traditional institution (marriage) which is itself in a state of transition. They further postulate that, as time passes, expectations regarding marital roles and relationships should become more consistent with real world experiences, so that when the structural transition is more complete, the adjustment which has to be made by the partners should create less emotional strain. This latter attitude, to a large extent, accords with that held by Dominian (1977), namely that marriage is coming to be viewed less as a legal contract and more as a means whereby the development of a deep and satisfying emotional relationship between a couple can be facilitated, and marriage is therefore likely to persist as an institution, although in a much changed form.

It is, perhaps, important to note that there is at present little reason to suppose that high divorce rates are necessarily inconsistent with a stable society, since in two societies at least, namely the traditional Arab and Japanese, high divorce rates have not led to societal disorganisation. Winch considers that it is more accurate to interpret divorce in these two family systems as reflecting a change in personnel, rather than as indicating disorganisation of the familial system. However, there are two elements in both the traditional Arab and traditional Japanese societies which would serve to cushion the likely functional disadvantages of divorce: there exists in each a strong extended family system, and, additionally, rates of remarriage are very high.

In our own society, rises in the divorce rate are invariably associated with some form of public comment which frequently implies that this upward trend augurs societal as well as familial disorganisation. It is, of course, true that in this century there have been radical changes in family structure within our society, perhaps most evidently typified by the decline of the extended family. None the less, as the annual rates of marriage show, marriage itself remains popular and it has been estimated that over 90% of men and women aged 16 will marry by the time they reach the age of 50 (OPCS, 1976). Additionally, the current remarriage rates of divorcees are high, both here and in the USA, where three-quarters of all divorced women, and five-sixths of all divorced men sooner or later remarry (Norton and Glick, 1976).

The extent to which marriage is presently regarded as a life-long contract is uncertain, although in a recent UK survey, 60% of young single people thought that divorce was something that might happen to them (McCann-Erikson, 1977). Notwithstanding this, marriage would seem to be an important goal in life, for the same survey showed that 91% of both single men and women expected to marry (ibid.), whilst an ISR survey in the USA (1974) demonstrated that 'being married is one of the most important determinants of being satisfied with life'. The available data suggest that there is, in general, a continuing acceptance of the institution of marriage, but there is also a growing acceptance of divorce for 'specific marriages which fail to satisfy individual spouses' (Levinger, 1976).

There is one further interesting augury of change in values, albeit of a slightly different nature, in the public recognition of the making and breaking of contractual relationships. The judgment pronounced by Lord Denning in November 1977, giving a mistress a legal position of right hitherto accorded only to wives, suggests that the law may now be wishing to recognise, and publicly declare, that contractual rights and responsibilities within a cohabiting relationship are accorded a legal equality with those previously restricted to a relationship within a marriage.

THE DIVORCE RATE AND THE CHANGING STATUS OF WOMEN

The upward trend in the divorce statistics has been considered by some observers to be closely related to the changing status of women. It is believed by them that the more freedoms women gain, the less willing they become to accept an unsatisfactory marriage, and as their economic status improves, they have a real alternative to continuing with an unhappy marriage. According to a US Bureau of Census Report (1972) divorced women with a relatively high personal income level tended to delay remarriage or to remain single, whereas those with relatively low incomes tended to remarry within a short time which suggests that economic independence does mean an associated increase in the number of options open to women.

The female share of divorce petitions has generally outnumbered those of men, but has recently shown a striking increase (Annual Judicial Statistics: Lord Chancellor's Office). According to Chester (1978) the explanation of the rising female share of divorce petitions is unclear and the sex distribution of petitions may not necessarily be taken to indicate sex distributions in the 'desire for divorce'. Chester (1970) has shown that the male-female share of petitions varies by such factors as duration of marriage and fertility and he also notes that the issue is further obscured by the effects of the 1969 Divorce Reform Act. It has been suggested that the pattern of petitioning may largely result from agreed arrangements between spouses, but this possibility was not substantiated in recent evidence from Chester's field study (as yet unpublished). A similar historical pattern in the sex distribution of petitions has been noted for the USA, and Goode (1956) has put forward the notion of a 'husband strategy'. According to Goode, even though it is usually the wife who first mentions divorce, the husband is usually the first to desire it, and he will 'engage in behaviour, whose function, if not intent, whose result, if not aim, is to force the other spouse to ask for it first'. Nye and Berardo (1973) point out that the grounds on which divorce proceedings are based tend to be role related and to favour female petitioners, whilst Kephart (1972) maintains that 'it is simply more socially acceptable for the husband to remain in the background and accept the legal and the nominal blame'. A recent finding from the USA (Gunter, 1977), however, noted a complete reversal in the distribution of male-female divorce petitions following the passing of a

marital dissolution law in Florida, which required that irreconcil-
able differences be the only grounds for divorce. Gunter suggests
that if such a pattern persists, it may represent important changes
in the relationship between men and women.

THE CONSEQUENCES OF DIVORCE

Public comment by both the 'institutionalists' and the 'individualists' about the trends in the divorce statistics is implicitly
concerned with the consequences of divorce. Those who deplore the
increase in divorce appear convinced of its overall negative
consequences for society, whilst those who view the divorce rates
with more equanimity point more to the positive benefits divorce may
bring to the individual and hence to society. However, since divorce
on any sizeable scale is relatively recent, little is actually known
about the impact of divorce either upon the marriage partners, their
children or upon society. There is some evidence to suggest that,
following divorce, there can be manifestations of physical and
emotional illness (Goode, 1956; Chester, 1971b; Radloff, 1975). The
suicide rate amongst divorcees is also relatively high (Stengler,
1964), and there may be stigmatisation which can cause severe personal
distress (Hart, 1976). There is presently some debate regarding the
extent to which the breaking of the marriage bond is, in itself,
traumatic. The work of Weiss (1976) has indicated that after the
end of most marriages, whether or not they have been happy and
whether or not the termination was sought, there still persists a
sense of bonding between the spouses which resembles the attachment
bond of children to parents as described by Bowlby (1969). However,
it has to be borne in mind first, that Weiss's observations derive
from the content of his 'seminars for the separated' and second,
that his sample consisted of urban middle-class individuals for whom
separation was, because of their attendance at these seminars, some
sort of problem. The applicability of such findings to a more
general population is an open question.
    It is also important to consider that much of any emotional trauma
following divorce may well result from the lack of a clearly defined
place for divorcees in our society. According to Hart (1976) there
is a gap in the social and institutional provision regarding divorce,
which amounts to an almost total lack of structure in the status
passage from marriage to divorce. If this is so, then the gradual
acceptance of divorcees within our society ought to lead, certainly
to a decline in stigmatisation, and following from this, possibly to
a reduction in other aspects of emotional distress.
    At a more practical level, there can be no doubt that single
parent families, amongst whom there are a substantial number of
divorcees, are financially less well off than most other groups in
society, and this in itself is likely to generate stress for its
members. According to the US Bureau of Census (1975) 51% of female
headed families with children under 18, and 61% of those with
children under 6, fell below the poverty line. The Finer report in
the UK on one-parent families (1974) demonstrated their considerable
financial disadvantage. Notwithstanding economic stresses due to
losses of economies of scale in single parent (usually female headed)

families, in many cases a father's ability to support his children
and ex-wife may be stretched to the limit by remarriage.

Another important aspect of divorce relates to the effects upon
any children of the marriage. In particular, there is the question
of psychological damage caused to the children of broken marriages.
Few would quarrel with the general idea that children are better off
in happy intact homes rather than in unhappy or unstable families,
but debate arises when the relative effects of marital unhappiness
and marital breakdown are considered.

It is widely believed that divorce is bad for children. This
belief is supported by research studies which have suggested that
children from broken homes show relatively more evidence of
delinquency and alcoholism (Otterström, 1952), poor academic
achievement (Douglas *et al.*, 1968), and emotional disorder (Greer
et al., 1966). However, recent reviews of the literature criticise
most of these studies on the grounds that they lacked adequate
controls and asked inappropriate questions (Herzog and Sudia, 1971;
Brandewein *et al.*, 1974). Apparently, studies in which economic
status was adequately controlled do not indicate that divorce is
disastrous for children. Within these seemingly more rigorous
studies, differences between children from one and two parent homes
of comparable economic status, on variables such as school achievement, social adjustment and delinquent behaviour, are small or even
non-existent (Burchinal, 1964; Thomas, 1968; Murchison, 1974).
Furthermore, according to Nye (1957), when comparisons were made
between adolescents from intact but unhappy homes, and those from
divorced homes, those with divorced parents appeared to show less
evidence of psychosomatic illness or delinquent behaviour, had a
better adjustment to parents, and did not differ significantly in
terms of school adjustment. Landis (1960) reported similar findings,
and according to Rutter (1977) the effects of intact but distorted
familial environments appear to be equally or even more damaging for
the children than homes in which the marriage bond has been broken.

There is another possible consequence of divorce which has aroused
some concern, particularly amongst some of the agencies engaged in
marital therapy and counselling. It has been suggested that the
provision of easier divorce may, for some people, prevent the
emotional development and self-discovery which, it is believed,
usually takes place in the context of close, personal, on-going
relationships. It is thus feared that the provision of easier
divorce may in turn make it easier for those with marital difficulties
to avoid discovering that the causes of their marital unhappiness
may well have roots in their own unresolved emotional difficulties
and are not solely caused by living with an unsuitable marriage
partner.

It is certainly a counselling experience that, given time and
support, many couples can be helped through their marital difficulties
to a deeper understanding of themselves and their spouses. What is
not known, and would certainly merit research, are the effects which
the ease or difficulty of termination of the marriage contract has
upon self-development of the individual marriage partners within
marriage, in terms of the extent to which emotional growth might be
promoted or hindered by either.

Some writers have stressed the positive aspects of
divorce for the individual, in particular for the

wife.   Brown, Feldberg *et al.* (1976) show evidence of divorce being
experienced as the start of a new emotional and intellectual freedom
for women.   However, a recent US study (Radloff, 1975) did not find
that, in general, women gain emotional benefits from divorce, since
separated or divorced women had significantly higher depression
scores than did married, single or widowed women.   However, it has
to be borne in mind that studies of this latter kind, since they
have taken place against changing societal views both of divorce
and divorcees, may well be time-bound.

THE AIMS OF THE PRESENT STUDY

There are few research data in the UK about the nature of modern
marriage and of the factors which may lead to its dissolution.   This
present study, which used the survey method as a means of obtaining
a substantial amount of quantitative data in a largely unexplored
field, looked at some of the childhood, adolescent, pre-marital and
marital characteristics and experiences of a sample of people whose
primary marriages had ended in divorce, and compared them with the
characteristics and experiences of a sample of people whose primary
marriages were, at the time of fieldwork, intact.

There were three main aims: first, to discover whether any of the
factors explored in the survey could be considered as high-risk in
the sense of indicating a high probability for divorce; second, to
see the extent to which these factors might delineate, on the one
hand, categories of individuals who were predisposed to divorce,
and on the other, any types of marriages which were not viable;
third, to make use of relevant findings from the project in the
Marriage Research Centre's longitudinal study of the early years of
marriage.

METHODS

The fieldwork took place in a part of the West Midlands.   The
divorced sample was randomly selected from those petitioners who had
obtained a decree nisi between September 1970 and March 1972.   The
original intention had been to carry out a national survey, but this
proved impossible, since no national sampling frame of divorcees was
available, nor could one be compiled by the Marriage Research Centre
because of restrictions placed by The Lord Chancellor on the use of
court records.   It was, however, possible to compile a complete
sampling frame of people divorcing in a part of the West Midlands.
This was because the local newspaper serving this area published the
outcome of each matrimonial causes list, together with the addresses
of all the petitioners involved.   There were three other possible
local areas for which a sampling frame for the divorced could have
been compiled.   None of them was ideal in the sense of likely to be
fully typical (from a socio-economic point of view), of the UK as a
whole, and the one in the West Midlands was finally chosen because
it was administratively the most convenient, and as a standard region
it compared well with the other three standard regions (Appendix I).
It will be seen that the sample of divorced informants includes

both those petitioners who divorced under a law which required
evidence of a matrimonial offence and those who, since they divorced
after the 1969 Divorce Reform Act came into effect in January 1971,
petitioned only on the grounds of irretrievable breakdown of the
marriage. It was originally considered important to sample divorcees
from three time periods, (a) just before the implementation of the
new Act, (b) in the first eight months following its implementation
and (c) from September 1971 to March 1972, when the backlog of people
previously ineligible for divorce was thought to have been dealt
with, to allow for the investigation of any differences between pre-
and post-Act divorcees. In particular, it was expected that
immediately following the working of the new Act, there would be a
relatively high proportion of petitioners who had separated many
years previously but were unable to divorce (because their partner
would not consent to one), and who would now be able to petition for
a divorce under the five year separation clause.

The Judicial Statistics for 1971 did demonstrate that a significant
proportion of petitions between January and December 1971 were
presented on the basis of the five year separation clause. In fact
some 28% of petitions were so based, compared with 18% for 1972, 15%
for 1973, 13% for 1974, 11% for 1975 and 10% for 1976. It is thus
likely that during the twelve months of 1971 a backlog of marriages
which existed only in name were finally legally dissolved.

In the present survey there were, however, no notable differences
between petitioners divorcing within each of the three chosen time
segments, neither in terms of the *de facto* and *de jure* duration of
their marriages, nor in relation to other survey variables which
were examined as possible discriminators (these were pre-marital
pregnancy, social class, age at marriage and sexual difficulties
during marriage). This absence of any significant differences in the
present survey between those divorcing in the first eight months of
the working of the new Act and those divorcing in the following six
months seems largely accounted for by the build up of petitions
awaiting hearing. Furthermore, the distinction between pre- and
post-Act divorcees, as originally defined in this study, turned out
not to apply, since although all the petitions presented in 1971
were *heard* under the rules of the new Act, in practice a great many
of them were first *presented* to the courts in 1970, under the old
law. Hence, many of the newly eligible 1971 categories of
petitioners who would previously have been unable, or
unwilling, to show evidence of any matrimonial offence would
be appearing in the courts much later into 1971.   Accordingly,
it was decided to treat pre- and post-1971 divorce petitioners
as a single group, homogeneous in the important sense that they had
all experienced divorce.

The sample of people still in their primary marriage was selected
from those electoral wards covering a twenty mile radius of the
county court which heard the divorce petitions (the vast majority
of divorce petitioners lived within this area). Details of the
sampling procedures and of the samples of the divorced and the
continuing married are given in Appendix I. It should be noted that
the sampling frame for the. divorced had to be limited to the
petitioners in the divorce cases. Respondents (i.e. prior to 1971
the guilty party) could not be included in this sampling frame since

their names and addresses were not always reported in the newspaper.
This is a methodological limitation and it must therefore constantly
be borne in mind that statements about the characteristics of survey
divorcees refer largely to only one party to the divorce, namely to
the petitioner. It was possible to obtain certain information about
the spouses of informants (both divorced and continuing married), but
the source was (with the exception of the Eysenck P Q* personality
inventory) always the informant and hence it must be considered less
reliable than if the spouses were answering for themselves.

In the survey female informants were generally interviewed by
female interviewers, and the male informants by male interviewers.
Initially it was felt that the questions about sex might cause
difficulties if asked by interviewers of the opposite sex. Towards
the end of the fieldwork, however, some male informants were interviewed by female interviewers because the duration of the fieldwork
among the male sample had considerably exceeded original estimates.
It had often taken some time to establish initial contact with men,
especially divorced men. Three of the female interviewers, who had
time available, were therefore asked to interview some men. Reports
from the field indicated that this arrangement worked satisfactorily,
and a subsequent analysis of the survey sex questions and the items
on the Eysenck P Q form showed no differences in the informant
responses which could be attributed to the sex of the interviewer.

The overall response rate was 67%, with 70% for those still in a
primary marriage, and 63% for those whose primary marriage had been
terminated by divorce. The response rate varied as Table 2 shows.

TABLE 2   Response rates for men and women informants

	Divorced				Continuing Married				Total			
	M No.	%	W No.	%	M No.	%	W No.	%	M No.	%	W No.	%
Completed	184	55	336	68	199	72	371	69	383	63	707	69
Refusals	87	25	97	20	58	21	139	26	145	24	236	23
Untraceable	59	18	57	11	18	7	24	4	77	13	81	8
Death	7	2	5	1	–	–	–	–	–	–	–	–

The response rate was in line with that for other comparable social
surveys; for instance, Gorer (1971) obtained a response rate of 66%
and Young and Willmott (1973) one of 64%.

*   This was a personality inventory which provided scores for
    extroversion, psychoticism, neuroticism and also a lie score
    (see Appendix VI).

THE INTERVIEWS

Two data-collection instruments were used in each survey interview.
The first was the main structured interview schedule, consisting
largely of precoded questions, with some open-ended questions where
appropriate, which took between one and two hours to complete. The
second, the Eysenck P Q form, was self-completed by informants (and
their spouses wherever possible) and usually took about five
minutes. Fieldwork took place between September 1972 and January
1973. Interviews were deliberately arranged to ensure that
informants were interviewed alone and in all but a few cases this
was possible; where it was not, these informants were counted as
refusals.

THE CONTENT OF THE INTERVIEW SCHEDULE

The majority of the items included in the interview schedule were
of the kind which have a high likelihood of truth in a large-scale
social survey type of interview, in the sense that they are relatively
unlikely to cause informants either to withhold information or to
give only what they considered would be an acceptable response. Such
items covered questions about age at marriage, year of marriage,
engagement, place of marriage, honeymoon, family of origin and family.
of marriage size and structure, accommodation history, pattern of
formal schooling, work pattern, and aspects of their health histories
in childhood and adolescence. The data required on these items were
relatively superficial and straightforward and a structured interview, administered by a skilled interviewer, is generally considered
to be a suitable vehicle for obtaining such information.
   Whilst the previous items, as obtained by the survey method,
provided a skeleton of the characteristics of informants and their
marriages, there were many other important features which it was felt
could only have been elicited through the exploration of areas which
may either have caused the informant embarrassment, or which would
have necessitated an interview in considerable depth regarding the
expectations, attitudes and beliefs of the individuals concerned.
Accordingly, because of the constraints of the questionnaire method,
many items which might have considerable bearing upon divorce could
not be included in the questionnaire. However, at the pilot stage
of this research it seemed that exploratory questions, albeit
restricted in scope, could be asked in certain of these sensitive
areas and were therefore included in the main stage. For instance,
it proved possible to ask questions about sexual satisfaction, and
pre-marital and extra-marital affairs, but these were deliberately
located at the very end of the interview when trust and rapport
would have been well established. Additionally, information
about pre-marital problems, post-puerperal depression, parental
marital status, parental preference, and religious adherence
and practice, were also collected. Informants were also asked to
rate their spouses on a battery of items which covered aspects of
the latter's behaviour and temperament, and the continuing married
were asked to rate their own marital happiness; these latter two
sections of the data obviously required particularly cautious
interpretation.

Divorced informants were not asked directly to describe what they considered were the causes of their marital breakdown, because the pilot work had shown that the agreement, by informants who had recently divorced, to be interviewed as part of a survey of marriage and family life, was frequently conditional on there being no questions specifically about their divorce. Nor was it thought possible to approach this subject in a more oblique manner during the interview, since the interviewers in the survey had been chosen for their ability to operate a highly structured questionnaire and their skills, in general, would not have enabled an easy departure from this procedure. However, some clues as to the circumstances which petitioners perceived as having led to the divorce, were apparent from replies to some of the open-ended questions, and reference is made to these in the discussions.

THE IDEAS WHICH UNDERLIE THIS STUDY

There were three principal sources from which the notions implicit in this study originated. The first and major source derived from the clinical field where the context was essentially psychiatric. The second source was the field of marriage counselling, and the third was the corpus of survey and demographic work (mostly American) on divorce. The latter has obvious relevance to a study of who divorces, but there are certain difficulties in using both the clinical and the marriage counselling findings in research about marital dissolution. First, the field of marital therapy and marriage counselling is largely concerned with those who are unhappily married and not with those who divorce. This present study of divorce behaviour compares those who divorce with those who are continuing with their primary marriages, and it is possible that factors which are part of the underlying mechanisms of marital unhappiness may not be powerful discriminators between the survey divorced and continuing married, if the latter includes unhappily married informants. Although the vast majority of continuing married informants, when asked, rated their marriages as extremely happy, a survey interview is too crude a tool to assess such a methodologically and theoretically problematic area as marital happiness.

The second difficulty connected with findings originating from marital therapy and counselling, is that the underlying mechanisms of marital unhappiness and severe marital problems among such groups tend to generate a concept of marital breakdown as a pathological condition in which at least one partner appears to have had unsatisfactory emotional experiences in his family of origin (Dominian, 1968). In a more representative population of unhappy marriages, this may not be applicable. The idea that the problems associated with divorce, both for the individual and for society, may have their origins in the intrinsic historical structure of marriage, is one which has recently been gaining credence. Those who emphasise the pathological nature of marriage have recently moved a considerable way along a continuum which ranges from a somewhat mild assessment of dysfunction- alism to an analysis of the family system itself as largely pathogenic. Whereas the earlier structuralists were concerned simply that the nuclear family should not become too inward looking, more recent and more radical critics such as Laing and Esterson (1970) and particularly Cooper (1972) have regarded the family itself as being capable of exerting a distorting influence upon its members. Another dimension of critical opinion of modern marriage is found in the writings of the feminist movement. Here too, the range of criticism is vast and includes those who wish simply to record the need for equality of the sexes in marriage, as well as the more revolutionary perspective which looks for not only the abolition of gender roles but the restructuring of society.

This present study is about who divorces, and there exists no neat psycho-sociological framework, originating from a comprehensive body of theory which might underpin such an investigation. Instead, therefore, an attempt was made to construct a model of divorce from these three sources of available data, to which the study could be committed. This model of divorce, to some extent a heuristic device, had incorporated into it, as basic elements, the notions on the one hand of personal vulnerability and, on the other, of environing disadvantage, which could be singly or jointly present. It was the intention to test the commonly accepted clinical view that the divorced would reveal a higher degree of personal vulnerability than the continuing married which, for example, might have led them perhaps to escape into marriage at an earlier age, with its attendant risks, or might have rendered them unable to cope with an unfavourable environment at a later stage in the marriage. This first basic element of personal, historical vulnerability was considered to have both physical and psychological components and encompassed such variables as psychological stresses during childhood and adolescence, hospitalisation and family structure. These variables reflected the commitment in the study to a viewpoint largely shaped by clinical workers in the field of marital breakdown. The second key element in the model, that of environing disadvantage, was conceived as largely spanning in time the years of the courtship and marriage itself (in the case of the divorced, those prior to the final separation), and covered for example such areas as ritual preparation for marriage, housing during marriage and the work record of the spouses, as well as looking at their sexual relationship and the timing of any children of the marriage.

The extent to which those who divorce may be considered as more vulnerable or more disadvantaged than those who continue with their marriages could not be explored in great depth in this survey. This was because, as has already been mentioned, the exploration of many of the subtle or socially sensitive factors felt to be contributing elements in a model of who divorces, could not be satisfactorily achieved in a social survey interview. Nevertheless, sufficient items have been included which do permit some assessment of the model, and which will, it is hoped, contribute to the understanding of the processes associated with divorce.

Chapter 2

EARLY BACKGROUND INFLUENCES:
Family Structure; Health

FAMILY BACKGROUND

It has been said that divorce begins before the first quarrel, or
indeed before the couple even meet, and that it is largely an
individual's early experiences, of his parents and his siblings,
which determine both his capacity to cope with the stresses endemic
in a marital relationship and also his repertoire of mechanisms to
deal with such stresses. The subtleties of the relationships between
the parents themselves, between the parents and their children and
between the siblings themselves could, obviously, not be explored
in this study and the present enquiry was therefore restricted to
three aspects of the families of origin of informants and their
spouses. First, the extent to which broken or unhappy parental
marriages may be considered to 'cause' broken or unhappy offspring
marriages; second, the extent to which having a particular preference
for one parent whilst growing up may affect an individual's own
subsequent marital outcome; and third, the ways in which an individual's position in the actual sibling structure may influence the
stability of his own marriage. Wherever possible, the discussion
includes the spouse's background and comparisons are made between
the backgrounds of the two partners. The information about the
spouse's family background was obtained entirely from the survey
informants and in some cases, particularly amongst D, little or
nothing was apparently known about this. Hence, many of the intended
comparisons regarding the family structure of both marriage partners,
could not be made for all informants.

PARENTAL MARRIAGES

The relationship between the outcome of parental marriages and those
of their offspring is a complex one to explore. For example, there
is the question of whether, and if so to what extent, the ways in
which the parents relate to one another may both shape and affect the
marital relationships of their own children. Parents may serve as
the principal models for their offspring's marital relationship not
only in terms of gender related roles, but also through the importance

they placed upon the maintenance of the marriage bond. Second,
there is the question of the effect that any disharmony between the
parents may have upon the emotional development of their offspring,
in terms of its influence upon the child's progress from emotional
dependency to some degree of psychological maturity, with the
corresponding ability to engage in and sustain close human relationships. It is particularly important also to consider whether, and to
what extent, the breaking of the parental marriage bonds *per se*
(whether through death or marital breakdown), has upon the offsprings'
emotional development and upon their subsequent ability to maintain
close marital bonds themselves. Table 3 shows the relationship
between parental marital status, as described by informants, and the
marital status of informants themselves.

TABLE 3   The outcome of the parental marriages of survey informants
(before informant was 16)

Parental marriage	D n=520 %	CM n=570 %
Intact and happy	72	76
Intact but unhappy	12	7
Divorce	2	1
Separation	3	3
Maternal death	4	5
Paternal death	7	7
Both parents died	$\emptyset$	1

The data in Table 3 form the basis for the examination of three
aspects of the relationship between the outcomes of parental and
offspring marriages; first, the extent to which there is an association between parental divorce and offspring divorce; second, the
extent to which there is an association between parental marital bond
breaking (whether through marital breakdown or death) and offspring
marital bond breaking (divorce or separation), and third, the extent
to which there is an association between parental marital unhappiness
and offspring marital unhappiness. The data about spouse parental
marriages, since it is incomplete, is examined separately later in
this chapter.

Parental divorce and offspring divorce

An association between parental marriages which end in divorce, and
divorce in the offspring of such marriages, has been demonstrated by
Gurin *et al.* (1960), Landis (1962), Bumpass and Sweet (1972) for the
USA. These studies have shown that the children of divorced parents
were themselves more likely to divorce than were the children of
non-divorced parents. It should be noted, however, that this
apparent predisposition to divorce in the offspring of divorced
parents (which is known as the transmission hypothesis), is not
particularly strong. Causal explanations of the association are

bound to be problematic. One explanation which has been developed
in the literature is that of the role model rationale, in which it
is proposed that to be a successful marriage partner, a child must
learn culturally appropriate sex and marital roles, and that this
is most effectively achieved when two loving and competent partners
serve as models for the child. The 'transmission' of marital
instability is said to occur either because the continuity of parental
role models is destroyed by the parents' breaking up, or because the
so-called 'divorce-bound' parents do not successfully socialise their
children with regard to appropriate sex and marital role models.

This explanation of the transmission process has been criticised
by Heiss (1972) and Pope and Mueller (1976), whose own data analyses
indicated numerous inconsistencies within the role-model rationale.
According to Mueller and Pope (1977) (in a survey amongst women),
the transmission of marital instability can, in part, be accounted
for by what they describe as mate-selection rationale, in which it
appears that the circumstances of parental marital instability lead
to high risk mate selection outcomes for the children, which in turn
results in their greater risk of divorce. Levinger and Moles (1976),
however, whilst accepting that the Pope and Mueller findings show
one way in which social context can affect marital stability,
nevertheless believe that the chain of events implied by this kind
of cross-sectional data seem too complex to be summarised by any
one explanation of the transmission of marital instability.

From a psychological standpoint, it has been argued that the
children from broken homes are so emotionally affected by the break-
up of their parents' marriages, that they find it difficult to
sustain close human relationships and hence are predisposed to
divorce. If it is the parental marital break-up *per se* and not the
climate in the parental home prior to the divorce which is the cause
of any emotional damage to the children, then one would perhaps
expect that the children from broken homes would have more emotional
problems than the children from intact but unhappy homes. On the
evidence available so far this does not appear to be the case.
According to Despert (1953), the determining factor in a child's
adjustment is the emotional climate in the home and not the divorce
itself. Goode (1956) has noted that the research evidence points
to the effect of continued home conflict as having more serious
implications for the child's adjustment than the divorce itself.
Certainly, it is a clinical impression that the occurrence of
offspring marital instability results as much from parental unhappiness as from parental marital instability. Landis (1962) found
few differences between the children from divorced homes and those
from intact homes, on most of the variables he tested, which included
relationships with parents, self-evaluations and dating histories.
Finally, in a review of the literature on the associations between
broken homes and offspring behaviour, Rutter (1977) concluded that,
having due regard to genetic contribution, marital discord can lead
to antisocial behaviour, but it is the ongoing disturbance in family
relationships rather than family break-up as such, which apparently
does most of the damage to the children of the marriage.

Another possible explanation of the association found in the USA
between parental and offspring divorce is that the resort to divorce
in the event of severe marital discord may be a course of action more

easily considered by people whose own parents have divorced, since divorce is less likely to challenge or threaten their existing values. Close kinship stigma would be absent in such instances, and indeed support during the divorce process may be offered, so that there is even likely to exist what Hart (1976) terms a 'positive sanction for divorce'. The same may not necessarily hold for individuals who may be unhappily married but for whom there is no kinship precedent for divorce, and for whom normative prescriptions may include the expectation that marital unhappiness should be contained within a socially intact marriage. It can be seen from Table 3 that the incidence of parental divorce in the present sample was very low and, although higher for D (2% D : 1% CM), there are insufficient cases for any association between parental and offspring divorce to be concluded. Although Hart (1976) did note a propensity to divorce amongst the offspring of divorced parents, the present data suggest that, since divorce on any notable scale is relatively recent, it will be some time before any association between divorce in successive generations can be assessed for the UK.

Whilst the inter-generational transmission of divorce has received some attention in the literature, little is known about the effects which sibling divorce may have upon either the other unmarried or still married siblings. The data from this study showed that the survey D were slightly more likely than the CM to have a divorced sibling (16% : 12%). Although it is possible that this may be connected with inter-generational transmission, it could equally well be reflecting the influence of sibling divorce *per se* on other siblings.

Marital bond breaking in parental and offspring marriages

Parental marriages broken by death were more common in the survey than were those dissolved by divorce or separation. There appeared to be no general link between parental marital bond breaking *per se* and offspring marital bond breaking, since although the survey findings indicated a slight association amongst D families of origin, the opposite was so for CM, as Table 4 shows.

TABLE 4   The relationship between marital bond breaking in two generations (parental bond breaking includes marriages broken by divorce, separation or death)

	D		CM	
	Parental bond broken	Parental bond intact	Parental bond broken	Parental bond intact
	n = 84	n = 436	n = 91	n = 479
	%	%	%	%
Sibling divorce/ separation	19	15	8	12
No sibling divorce/ separation	81	85	92	88
Mean number of offspring bond breaking	0.226	0.171	0.088	0.137

Whilst it is so that the survey data did not indicate any general link between parental bond breaking *per se* and offspring marital breakdown, it was none the less felt that some of the circumstances of the parental bond breaking should be examined. Three aspects were considered: first, the age of the informant when the bond breaking occurred; second, the guardianship of the child following the bond breaking; and third, the extent of parental remarriage.

The number of informants affected by parental loss is too small to permit analysis by the particular types of loss. However, the survey data showed that D who experienced parental 'loss', were more likely than CM to have been under 5 years of age when their parents' marriage bond was broken (39% : 31%). It seems probable that bond breaking within marriages containing children under 5 years of age is, for a variety of reasons, more likely to result in the risk of psychosocial disadvantage for such offspring than if the bond breaking were to occur within marriages containing school age or older offspring. First, this might be because the financial disadvantage experienced by single parent families is generally likely to be the greatest for those with pre-school children, since the remaining parent may either be unable to become a wage earner, or be obliged to pay for substitute parenting. Second, the stresses upon a single parent resulting from the absence of the emotional, social and material support usually provided by a spouse, are likely to be increased by the stress resulting from the needs of a pre-school age child, making the satisfaction of those needs less likely. Third, the absence of one parent during what is regarded by some psychiatrists as a particularly critical period in the development of gender identity, may lead to later emotional disturbances and to difficulties in bonding in adulthood. On this latter point, there is tentative evidence from the survey to suggest that D whose parents' marital bond was broken may have had less experience of a parent of the same sex whilst growing up (although not necessarily whilst under 5 years), than their CM counterparts, since, after the parental loss, DW were less likely than CMW to have been looked after by their mother. This can be seen in Table 5.

TABLE 5 Main guardianship arrangements for survey informants whose parents' marriage was broken by divorce, separation or death

	D n=84 %	DW n=53 %	DM n=31 %	CM n=91 %	CMW n=57 %	CMM n=34 %
Mother	77	76	81	78	81	74
Father	5	6	3	4	4	6
Relatives	12	12	13	11	11	12
Other	5	6	3	5	5	6

According to Rutter (1977), it remains uncertain how far parental re-marriage helps or hinders the child's psychological development. There is, however, some evidence to suggest that the arrival of a step-parent may be stressful (Heilpern, 1943; Podolsky, 1955) and there can be an increased risk of a psychiatric disorder developing

(Langer and Michael, 1963). The effect of re-marriage upon a child
is likely to depend upon a variety of factors, only some of which
were explored in this study. The relationships between the child
and the parent with whom he lives, between the child and the 'lost'
parent, as well as with the new step-parent, must all be factors of
critical importance in determining the impact of parental re-marriage
upon the child.

In this study it was not possible to explore the subtleties of
those relationships and the enquiry was confined to establishing
whether or not re-marriage had occurred and the age of the informant
when any re-marriage took place. The survey findings demonstrated
that D were more likely than CM to have lived with a step-parent,
and particularly a step-father, before they were 16 years old.
This can be seen in Table 6.

TABLE 6   Parental 'loss' and re-marriage amongst D and CM

	All D who 'lost' a parent through divorce or death	All CM who 'lost' a parent through divorce or death
	n=69	n=79
	%	%
Re-marriage by mother	32	20
Re-marriage by father	23	20
No re-marriage	46	61
Don't know	6	3

Note: The percentages total more than 100 because of re-marriage by
       both divorced partners.

In view of the economic hardships experienced by many single
parents, which may have implications for environmental disadvantage
for the offspring of such families, more parental re-marriage might
therefore have been expected amongst CM rather than D. Whilst the
numbers of informants who experienced parental re-marriage are few,
and any interpretation correspondingly difficult, the survey data
suggest that parental re-marriage may, perhaps, be more of a stress
factor for children than the actual 'loss' of a parent. There was
little difference between D and CM with regard to the age of the
informants when any re-marriage took place.

Parental marital unhappiness and offspring marital unhappiness

It will be recalled from Table 3 that D and CM informants were more
or less equally likely to have experienced parental marital bond
breaking, whether through separation, divorce or death (16% : 17%).
However, when the relationship between discord in parental marriages
and discord in the marriages of their offspring in general was
examined, a slight association between the two was apparent for both
D and CM, indicating a tendency for marital unhappiness in one
generation also to be manifest in or 'transmitted' to the next

generation. Table 7 shows the results of the survey analysis of
the relationship between parental and offspring marital discord.
Parental and offspring marriages (including the marriages of
informants and their siblings) which either ended in divorce or
separation, or were judged as unhappy by informants, were considered
as discordant.

TABLE 7   The relationship between marital discord in two generations

	D		CM	
	Parents happy	Parental discord	Parents happy	Parental discord
	n=376	n=88	n=434	n=63
	%	%	%	%
No offspring marital discord	80	73	86	78
Offspring marital discord	20	27	14	22
Mean number of 'discordant' offspring marriages	0.23	0.36	0.15	0.32

In the survey, however, the majority of D (72%) said that they
grew up in stable homes with happily married parents, so that their
own marital unhappiness cannot therefore be regarded as a consequence
of their own parents' marital conflict. This is surprising, since it
is widely accepted that the children of happily married parents are
themselves likely to form stable, happy marriages. If informants
had accurately perceived and reported the quality of their parents'
marriages, then the relationship between the parents would appear to
have little effect upon the success of offspring marital relationships, and other aspects of an individual's family of origin may be
more influential in determining marital happiness or stability.
For example, it has to be borne in mind that, whilst the relationship
between the parents may well determine the prevailing atmosphere in
the home, the relationship between the parents and their children,
although taking place against the backcloth of the marital relationship and inevitably affected by it, is a separate issue. The value
that an adult has learned to place upon himself, in terms of a sense
of his own identity and intrinsic worth, is probably closely related
to the personal experiences of his childhood, not simply as a
passenger within the marital relationship, but as a person who has
a particular meaning for his individual parents. Whether or not a
child successfully negotiates the stages towards psychological
maturity will depend upon the opportunity he is given to do so.
Whilst there is a probable causal connection between a childhood in
which psychological development was inhibited and subsequent adult
difficulties in forming or sustaining close relationships, it does
not necessarily follow that 'happily' married parents are able to
provide a satisfactory environment for the emotional development of
their offspring. Although parents who are themselves psychologically
mature will relate effectively both to each other and to their
children, thus facilitating the latters' own emotional development,

all that is known from the present survey about happily married
parents is that they had a stable marriage and a relationship which
their child believed was mutually satisfying. In many cases, th
is no reason to equate parental happiness with parental emotiona
maturity.

Given that the outcome of parental marriages seems to have poor
predictive value for offspring marriages, the quality of the parent-
child relationship is therefore perhaps a more useful area to
explore. Clinically, it does seem that individuals with severe
marital problems also have difficulties in their relationships with
at least one parent. Such clinical data regarding parent-child
difficulties would be, of course, elicited after many hours of
discussion with individuals, in many cases after any earlier, more
rosy, pictures which clients had painted of their own relationship
with their parents would have been discarded. Such a delicate area
of enquiry as the relationship between informants and their parents
could not possibly be explored during a large scale social survey
type of interview, and accordingly, questions about the parent who
was preferred during childhood were included as indicators of one
aspect of the relationship between informants and their parents.
Informants were asked: 'Children sometimes feel closer to one of
their parents rather than the other. When you were younger, that is
before you were 16 years old, did you prefer one of your parents to
the other?' Those who expressed a preference were asked, 'Why do
you think that you preferred your _mother/father_?'

A preference for one parent

Whether or not a child preferred one parent to another was of
interest for two main reasons. First, a preference for one parent
may be regarded as an indication of closeness with one sex rather
than with another, and this could have implications for the development of stereotypes relating to mate selection. Second, the reasons
for the parental preference could perhaps give clues both about the
relationship with the parent who was not preferred, and about the
overall picture of the parent-child relationship. When an informant
did not express a preference for either parent whilst growing up, it
could, of course, mean either that the parents were equally liked or
disliked, or that they were equally regarded with indifference, but
the reasons for the absence of any parental preference were not
explored in the survey.

Informants who were only daughters were more likely to have
preferred their fathers whilst growing up, and this was especially
so for D. Also, D informants who were only sons were marginally
more likely to express a preference for their mothers, but there was
little difference in this respect among CM. This can be seen in
Table 8.

There were also overall differences between D and CM women
regarding the preferred parent, for DW were more likely than CMW to
prefer their father and significantly less likely to prefer their
mother. This can be seen in Table 9.

TABLE 8   The relationship between being an only daughter or an only son and the choice of preferred parent whilst growing up

	D			CM		
	Mother preferred n=139 %	Father preferred n=98 %	No preference n=227 %	Mother preferred n=181 %	Father preferred n=81 %	No preference n=261 %
Only daughter	17	39	20	25	31	20
Only son	14	3	10	9	9	11
Other	69	58	70	66	60	69

TABLE 9 Parental preference of informants during their childhood and adolescence

	DW n=336 %	CMW n=371 %	DM n=184 %	CMM n=199 %
Adequate parental recall	91	93	86	89
Inadequate parental recall	9	7	14	11
Those able to recall both parents well	n=306	n=345	n=158	n=178
Preferred mother	26	35	36	34
Preferred father	28	18	8	10
No preference	45	47	56	56

A social class analysis of parental preference in relation to DW and CMW demonstrated that the differences between them were largely due to the differences between women with manual worker backgrounds. CMW from working class backgrounds were much more likely to express a preference for their mothers than were DW from similar backgrounds (36% CMW : 26% DW), and they were correspondingly less likely to prefer their fathers (18% CMW : 28% DW). In view of the working-class tradition of relatively close mother-daughter ties which persist into marriage and which may form an important support system for working-class brides, the data suggest that this D sub-group may have been more at risk to stress within marriage, because they may have been less able to take advantage of the maternal support system more typical of their social class. Teenage brides may also be considered as a group relatively more than other groups, in need of a support system following marriage and, in this respect, there may have been differences in the experiences of teenage D and CM brides. D teenage brides were less likely than CM teenage brides to have preferred their mothers (27% D : 34% CM) and this relative lack of 'closeness' to their mothers may have meant correspondingly less maternal support following marriage.

Although some 30% of men expressed a maternal preference, since DM and CMM were more or less equally likely to have preferred their mothers, a male preference for a parent of the opposite sex therefore seems unlikely to have implications for divorce. However, it is possible that the difference between DW and CMW with regard to paternal preference (28%; 18%), may be indicative of a stress factor within D marriages relative to those of CM. How such a stress factor may operate within marriage is uncertain, but clinical work amongst unhappily married couples does suggest the existence of a category of women who have idealised their fathers to the extent that the development of their own marital relationship is hindered by their need to find in their husbands the qualities they believed were present in their fathers, and the inevitable disappointment which arises when the husband is unable to meet such a need can thus potentially be a source of serious marital difficulties.

In view of the relatively high percentages of all groups who expressed no particular preference for either parent, it was perhaps

to be expected that those who did prefer one parent would have
fairly strong reasons for doing so. However, this was not always
the case, for this preference was couched in various ways. Most
usually, especially among CM, the parents were directly compared
with each other, with one emerging more favourably. At other times,
particularly for DW, one parent only was referred to, and in very
positive terms, as if that parent alone had made an impact: 'father
was such a gentle and lovable person' (preferred father). Occasion-
ally there was only a negative mention of the *non*-preferred parent
'father was strict and remote' (preferred mother), and this negative
emphasis was more frequently the case for D than CM.

However, despite this disparity (and resultant coding problems)
in the answers to the questions about the preferred parent, overall
certain trends emerged. The reason most frequently given by all
groups lay along the positive dimension of the preferred parent being
more loving/patient/understanding/having more time for informant':
30% DW; 31% CMW; 31% DM; 25% CMM, exemplified in such replies as:

(Mother preferred): 'She was so patient, she never lost her
temper and was always there when I needed her.' CMW

(Father preferred): 'My father was more sympathetic and understanding.' CMW

(Father preferred): 'He showed more love to me than my mother
did.' DW

It is interesting that the second most frequently mentioned reason
given by all informants except CMM (20% DW; 20% CMW; 23% DM; 15% CMM),
although being positively expressed for the preferred parent,
additionally had a strong negative loading on the non-preferred
parent. This reason was along a dimension of strictness and quick-
temperedness: *preferred parent was not so strict/other parent very
difficult, quick-tempered*'. This can be illustrated by such answers
as:

(Mother preferred): 'My dad was always quick-tempered and you
always go to the one you think you'll get more sympathy from.
But I liked me dad.' CMW

(Mother preferred): 'My father was very strict in all ways - a
no-nonsense father - one word out of place and that was it - and
he was very insistent on Sunday school and chapel and the time
you came in at.' DM

(Mother preferred): 'Father was stern, abrupt, uncouth and no
patience.' DM

Another frequently mentioned reason for preferring one parent was
the relative absence of the other parent (usually, but not invariably,
the father), which could have been due to war service for older
informants, or because of the demands of the father's job. Absence
which was given as being due to war service can be considered as a
separate category, since its impact would be very different from the

absences due to irregular working hours. It is interesting that
DM were the sub-group who most frequently mentioned 'Father away
in the war' (2% DW; 4% CMW; 9% DM; 5% CMM), which may be of some
importance in that their fathers may have been absent from home a
large part of the time during their formative years. However, when
we examined the reasons given by informants who preferred their
mother because they saw so little of their father due to their
father's job, or particular life-style, we found that it was most
frequently mentioned by CMM and least by DW (8% DW; 13% CMW; 16% DM;
20% CMM).

The range of jobs which, in one way or another, could have
prevented the father from being experienced as a well known and
significant parent, was wide, as can be seen from the following:

'My dad was on shift-work and he spent a lot of time in bed at
odd hours, so we didn't really see a lot of him.' (CMW whose
father was a night-foreman at a mill.)

'My father was in business, out all the time except Sunday so we
didn't see much of him.' (DW whose father ran his own ladies'
hairdressing business.)

Sometimes the absences were more prolonged, due to a job which
involved travel, as seen in references to 'away a lot on business
trips' (father a sales-director of a textile firm) or 'away a lot
working' (father a long-distance lorry driver).

Although the absence of the father must, in some instances, have
shaped the informant's own expectation of married life, the effect of
such absence must largely depend upon the quality of the parental
marriage, the quality of the relationship with the child, and how the
absent father was presented to the informant by the mother. Absence
itself did not preclude parental preference, since in a few cases
absence could produce rarity value, for as one CMW said of her naval
father who was her preferred parent:

'I think it's because they are not there quite so much - you are
thrilled when they come home. He was in the Navy and knew so
much about everything, I thought he was wonderful.'

One group of answers which highlighted a difference between sub-
groups sprang from the concept of 'being spoiled/able to "manipulate"
the preferred parent'. This was most frequently found in DW: (12% DW;
5% CMW : 4% all men). Almost invariably, the DW referred to their
ability to get their own way with their father.

'I could twist him round my little finger.'

'I could always seem to get more off him, get my own way.'

'I only had to ask for something and I'd get it.'

'I could get round father, being the youngest he tended to spoil
me a bit.'

The emerging picture of some DW as being able to 'get round' their
fathers is to a lesser extent mirrored in DM in such comments as:

'She always seemed to give in to me more easily - there's a certain
competition between father and son.'

It seems possible that such a specific learned pattern of interaction
with the preferred parent might, if well embedded, make for difficulties in a marital relationship.

One group of reasons given for preferring one parent was connected
with the relationship being better, either because the informant felt
more affinity with the parent of the same sex, or conversely, an
attraction to the parent of the opposite sex. Interestingly, the
mother seemed to be the preferred parent for more of both CMW and
CMM, so that 5% of the CMW said such things as:

'Mothers are more understanding towards their daughters - cover
up if you come in late and that sort of thing.'

'I was close to her - could talk to her about my periods and other
problems. You couldn't talk to a man about that sort of thing.'

'Just a natural instinct - she's more like a sister to me.'

This may well indicate some form of gender identification which may
have implications for the offspring's marriage.

Another interesting group of preferences was related to the
perceived affinity between the informant and parent attributed to
temperamental similarity, irrespective of gender of the parent, shown
in such ways as strongly shared interests. This was mentioned most
frequently by CMW and DM (5% DW; 11% CMW; 10% DM; 2% CMM). A further,
albeit small, cluster of reasons for parental preference was derived
from a negative view of the non-preferred parent as being cruel to,
or arousing fear in the informant, particularly female informants
(5% DW; 4% CMW : 1% DM):

(Father preferred): 'He never hit us or swore at us as my mother
did.' DW

(Mother preferred): 'I was frightened of father, he was very
violent and used to hit me around.' DW

Associated with this, were reasons where the non-preferred parent was
described as having been cruel to the preferred parent: 4% all women,
1% all men.

A further negative view of the non-preferred parent perceived him/
her as disliking the informant, and this was slightly more evident
for female informants: 4% all women, 1% all men.

PARENTAL MARRIAGES OF INFORMANTS' SPOUSES

Table 10 shows the outcome of parental marriages of the spouses of
survey informants.

TABLE 10

Spouse parental marriage	D n=520 %	CM n=570 %
Intact and happy	54	73
Intact but unhappy	13	2
Intact but quality unknown	17	8
Divorce	3	1
Separation	4	2
Maternal death	3	5
Paternal death	6	8
Both parents died	Ø	1
Don't know	Ø	Ø

It can be seen from Table 10 that D were far more likely than CM to believe that their partners' parents were unhappily married. It will be recalled from Table 3 that 12% D, 7% CM, claimed that their own parents were unhappily married.

Although the extent of ignorance about the quality of intact parental marriages makes it impossible for full comparisons between D and CM to be made, the prevalences of broken parental marriage bonds (whether through marital breakdown or death), could be compared for the four survey sub-samples, and this data indicated that D marriages were slightly less likely than CM marriages to have been composed of offspring from an intact parental marriage (65% D partners, 69% CM partners came from intact parental homes).

THE FAMILY CONSTELLATION

The term family constellation was coined by Toman (1961) to describe the sibling structure of an individual's family of origin. It is Toman's contention that marital success or happiness are, to a large extent, predetermined by the marriage partners' ordinal positions in their own family constellation; marital compatibility will be best achieved when the sibling constellations of the spouses are identical, so that the roles learned by each marriage partner relative to their other siblings, complement rather than clash with one another. According to Toman (who bases his suggestion on his own clinical research into this area), marriages which are most likely to succeed are those between, for example, the older brother of a sister and the younger sister of a brother – the so-called completely complemen- tary sibling roles. When counterparts marry, for example when an older brother of brothers marries an older sister of sisters, divorce may be more likely because their sibling constellations are totally different and the sibling roles learned by the marriage partners are likely to clash. Although Birtchnell (1974) found, within his survey, that birth order had little effect upon the likelihood of being divorced, it was considered worth examining Toman's theory at the analysis stage of the present survey.

Only children

Since only children have, according to Toman, 'no brother or sister
relationship upon which to base their marital relationship' they
might thus be expected to be more prevalent amongst D. This was not
the case in our survey, for 14% D and 15% CM informants were only
children. However, if the absence of siblings really does have
implications for marital adjustment in the way that Toman suggests,
it might be expected that the marriages of only children would be
in difficulty earlier, if they are D, and, if they are CM, they would
be more likely to have had serious marital problems. Whilst the
evidence from the survey data is slight, it can be seen in Table 11
that in marriages in which it is the wife who is the only child, then
those marriages are in difficulties relatively earlier. Similarly,
with regard to CM marriages, it can be seen in Table 12 that serious
marital difficulties were more typical of those CM marriages in which
the wife was an only child. In view of the additional adjustment
which it appears that a wife must make to marriage, it may be that
only daughters are less equipped to cope with stress than are women
who have grown up with siblings.

TABLE 11   Only children and the start of serious marital difficulties
amongst D

	Difficulties in 1st year	Difficulties after 1st year
	n=192	n=328
	%	%
Wife an only child	16	13
Husband an only child	14	15
Both partners only children	2	2
Neither partner an only child	68	70

TABLE 12   Only children and serious marital difficulties amongst CM

	Serious difficulties	No serious difficulties
	n=78	n=492
	%	%
Wife an only child	18	13
Husband an only child	9	12
Both partners only children	1	2
Neither partner an only child	68	73
Insufficient data for comparison	4	-

It is also evident from the survey data that the marriages of
teenage brides, but particularly those of D teenage brides, were less
likely than those of older brides to include a partner who was an
only child. In families consisting of more than one child it is
likely that parental interest, concern or ambition will be divided

amongst siblings rather than being concentrated on any one child,
and, therefore, early marriage seems more likely among such larger
families; first, there is some evidence to suggest that only children
may be relatively higher academic achievers (Douglas, 1964); it is
therefore possible that they may marry later because they have the
option of higher education or of pursuing some kind of career.
Second, in many instances the impact upon the parents of the offspring's departure from the parental home at a relatively early age
may be cushioned by the presence of other siblings. Third, some
home situations such as those in which there are several siblings
perhaps in overcrowded conditions, might act as a spur for offspring
to enter marriage at an early age, either as a means of escaping
from home, or even because parents may encourage them to do so.

The number of siblings in the family of origin

On average, D had slightly more siblings than CM; the mean family
size of D (i.e. informant plus siblings) was 3.96, with 3.80 for CM.
Table 13 shows the distribution of the number of children in
informants' families of origin.

TABLE 13   The number of children in the families of origin of the
marriage partners

| | D n=520 % | | CM n=570 % | |
Number of children	Informant's family	Spouse's family	Informant's family	Spouse's family
1	14	15	15	11
2	22	18	21	22
3	18	22	19	19
4	13	11	16	16
5 or more	33	32	29	32
Don't know	–	2	–	–

It can be seen that the differences between D and CM in relation to
the size of both partners' families of origin are slight; furthermore
comparisons between D and CM within equivalent marriage cohorts,
social classes and age of the bride at marriage showed patterns of
broad similarity to that of D and CM generally.

Growing up with siblings of the same sex or of the opposite sex

It seems plausible that marital adjustment will be easier for
partners who have grown up with siblings of the opposite sex, and
this was to some extent substantiated in the survey as can be seen
in Table 14.

TABLE 14   Marriages between individuals from same sex or different
sex families of origin

	DW n=336 %	DM n=184 %	CMW n=371 %	CMM n=199 %
Husband of the marriage having no sisters, and wife having no brothers	11	11	10	11
Both husband and wife having brothers and sisters	47	42	49	48
Husband of the marriage having no sisters but wife having brothers	25	26	19	20
Wife of the marriage having no brothers but husband having sisters	16	21	23	21

The data in Table 14 does not support Toman's general findings that
marriages in which neither partner grew up with a sibling of the
opposite sex are highly divorce prone, since their incidences are
virtually identical for D and CM. It can be seen, however, that the
husbands in divorced survey marriages (i.e. DM and husbands of DW),
are slightly more likely than husbands in continuing marriages
(i.e. CMM and husbands of CMW), to have grown up without a sister.
It can also be seen that wives who petition for divorce (i.e. DW
but *not* wives of DM) were the least likely to have grown up *without
a brother*. This suggests that the experience of growing up with a
sibling of the opposite sex may, in general, be more important for
men than for women, since men who lacked this experience were
slightly more prone to divorce than were men who grew up with a
sister.

Interestingly enough, the partners in 'teenage' or 'pre-maritally
pregnant' marriages, whether D or CM, were generally more likely
than the partners in 'older' or 'non Pmp' marriages to have grown up
with siblings of the opposite sex. This experience may perhaps have
generated an ease with the opposite sex generally, which may have
facilitated earlier and more intimate associations.

Growing up with older and younger siblings

The incidence of an older brother or sister was virtually identical
for the two main survey samples generally, but there were some
sub-group differences, notably that teenage brides were slightly
less likely than older brides to have grown up with an older sister.
Since they were also more likely to be the elder sister themselves,
it seems possible that they would have had responsibilities for
younger siblings from which marriage might, for some of them, have
been a means of escape.

The sibling constellation of the partners

Comparison of the sibling constellations of all informants proved
impossible because the number of combinations exceeded the capacity
of the computer programme being used. Therefore, families of origin
(either informant or spouse) consisting of 4 or fewer siblings were
taken as the basis for examining Toman's belief that the marriages
of couples whose sibling constellations either clashed or were
imperfectly balanced, would be more prone to divorce. Some 79% of
D couples and 84% of CM could be compared in terms of the sibling
constellation of their families of origin. However, the data
obtained provided no support for Toman's theory; in fact CM were
slightly more likely than D to have had clashing sibling constellations, as Table 15 shows.

TABLE 15

	Marriages of informants	
	D n=413 %	CM n=480 %
Partners with 'perfect' complementary sibling constellations	21	20
Partners with 'imperfect' sibling constellations	57	53
Partners with clashing sibling constellations	22	27

ASPECTS OF CHILDHOOD AND ADOLESCENT HEALTH

A range of items was included in the survey which related to the
childhood and adolescent health of informants (see Appendix III).
The decision to include such items was principally rooted in
Dominian's clinical experience. His early work in the field of
marital therapy had had a psychiatric orientation, in that individuals
seeking help with their marital problems were likely either to have
been referred for marital therapy by their GPs, or were most likely
to be already receiving psychiatric help for emotional difficulties
of varying severity. It was frequently the case that these clients
had either a history of poor physical health, particularly in childhood, or had presented with probable psychosomatic conditions.
A frequent co-existence of physical and psychiatric disorders is not
uncommon, for 'In susceptible people, physical and psychiatric
disturbances may occur together at times when life experiences are
stressful' (Lloyd, 1977).
    A further feature of those receiving marital therapy in a clini-
cal context, was the apparently unsatisfactory nature of their
relationships with their parents, and there was a constantly
recurring clinical impression of a causal connection between inadequate parent-child interaction and certain psychosomatic conditions.

Additionally, there was a further clinical impression, that amongst individuals whose physical health had been poor during their childhood and adolescence, or who had experienced extensive or recurring hospitalisation whilst growing up, there was also either associated or causal stress within the parent-child relationship. This stress in many ways appeared to have been related to inappropriate parental management of problems arising either from the physical illness or from the separation in hospital. There is currently an awareness of the psychological consequences or *sequelae* to physical illness, demonstrated by Lloyd, who notes the wide variety of patterns of psychological response and processes of coping with physical illness in a patient of any age. Childhood illness under any circumstances is certain to evoke parental worry and anxiety, but this anxiety may in some instances be extreme, which can result in over-protective and constraining responses towards the child, or, alternatively, the parents may fail to meet the child's physical or emotional needs during these periods, and even, in some instances, may seek to deny the existence of illness. Additionally, poor physical health may in itself interfere with emotional development by imposing restrictions which may exclude a child from the normal society of his peers at critical points in his life, which thus may promote undue attachment to the parents. In these ways, psychosocial development may be seriously affected by prolonged or severe physical illness, or hospitalisation, unless appropriate and adequate responses for support and personal development are given to the child at such times. Nor must the possible transactional effects of illness and injury be overlooked, for the sick child himself has a role in shaping parental behaviour and may influence his familial environment in such a way as to augment the disadvantages already incurred by the illness itself.

The prevalences of certain of the clinically observed features of child and adolescent health were established for the survey D and CM in order to see their extent, first, in a non-clinical group of individuals with past experience of serious marital problems (evidenced by divorce, i.e. the survey D), and second, amongst a group with apparently no such experience (evidenced by an intact marriage, the survey CM). However, whereas the clinical interview is a suitable instrument for obtaining extensive background data so as to provide a context for relating the health histories to the parent-child relationships of clients, the survey interview is not. In the absence, therefore, of such detailed data, the presence of the selected features amongst survey informants can be considered only as indication of a possible increased risk of impeded emotional development during childhood and adolescence, and not as direct evidence of unsatisfactory relationships between them and their parents.

The prevalence in the survey of any one of the severe or the chronic illnesses which in Dominian's work had had a clinical significance was low, and D were no more prone than were CM. Similarly, the prevalence of certain conditions which were believed to have a probable psychosomatic origin was also low, and there was no evidence that D, as a group, were more prone than were CM. Therefore, it seems likely that the contribution of severe, chronic or psychosomatically based conditions to the underlying mechanisms

of marital breakdown in a more general population of divorce is
minimal.

Hospitalisation

Comparison of the childhood hospitalisation patterns of D and CM
was of interest for two main reasons. First, because hospitalisation is a separation experience which, *per se*, may have implications
for emotional development and second, because the need for hospital
admission may be reflecting underlying stress factors within the
child's background resulting from certain kinds of environing
disadvantage.
     According to Bowlby (1973) many young children show acute symptoms
of distress when admitted to hospital and this stress reaction may
persist, resulting in disturbed behaviour lasting many months.
However, most separation experiences appear not, in themselves, to
be associated with persistent long-term problems (Bowlby *et al.*,
1956; Morgan and Ricciuti, 1969; Andry, 1960; Douglas *et al.*, 1968),
although children who have experienced separation in early childhood
also appear to have a slightly increased risk of developing later
psychological disturbance (Ainsworth, 1962).
     Whilst the child's separation from his mother may, in part,
account for a stress reaction, several findings have suggested that
this may not be the major factor. For instance, the risk of
emotional disturbance following hospitalisation is apparently
increased if there is a poor relationship between the child and his
parents, or if he comes from an unhappy or unstable home (Fagin,
1966; Quinton and Rutter, 1976). Wolff (1973) has noted that the
quality of the hospital environment can reduce the extent of distress during hospitalisation, as can high quality parental care
during the separation experience (Robertson and Robertson, 1971).
In a review of the findings from studies on separation experiences,
Rutter and Madge (1976) have concluded that whilst separation may
be regarded as constituting a genuine stress for the child,
associated unpleasant experiences and poor quality parental care may
be more important factors.
     Whilst single hospital admissions lasting less than one week
appear to have no long-term implications for emotional development,
recurrent admissions, in particular when at least one has occurred
when the child was under 5 years, are associated with increased risk
of both psychiatric disorder and delinquency (Douglas, 1975; Quinton
and Rutter, 1976). The evidence to date suggests that repeated
hospital admissions tend to be typical of children from disadvantaged
homes and their disturbed behaviour in adolescence may result rather
more from their adverse home circumstances than from their repeated
experiences of separation through hospitalisation.

Survey findings on hospitalisation

D informants were slightly more likely than CM to have been at risk
to either the short-term stresses or the long-term effects of
separation in hospital, since 43% D : 37% CM had been hospitalised

before they were 16 years of age. However, the differences between
D and CM were almost entirely due to the hospitalisation patterns
of DW since there were few differences between DM and CMM. Table 16
shows the prevalence of hospitalisation during childhood or adolescence for survey informants.

TABLE 16   The proportion of informants who were ever hospitalised
before 16 years of age

	D	CM	DW	CMW	DM	CMM
	n=520	n=570	n=336	n=371	n=184	n=199
	%	%	%	%	%	%
Hospitalised	43	37	47	34	36	38
Never hospitalised	57	63	53	66	64	62

As well as being the most likely to have been hospitalised, DW were
also hospitalised the most frequently, for 14% of those who had ever
been in hospital had had three or more stays; this compares with 6%
for CMW, 11% for DM and 5% for CMM. Furthermore, DW were the most
likely to have been under school age when first hospitalised: 29%
of DW who had ever been hospitalised were under 5 years when first
admitted, compared to 19% CMW, 22% DM, 25% CMM. Finally, DW thus
affected had had relatively longer periods of hospitalisation; in
particular their first hospitalisation was the most likely to have
lasted longer than 4 weeks (24% DW; 21% CMW; 17% DM; 19% CMM).

INDICATIONS OF STRESS DURING ADOLESCENCE

The interview schedule included a battery of 5-point bipolar scales,
which were shown to informants who were asked to indicate, with a
tick or a cross, their own experience on the dimensions listed,
during the years when they were aged 12-16 years. Each scale was
the continuum of a fear or difficulty, one end of the scale being
the extreme presence of a fear or difficulty, the other end being
the total absence of that fear or difficulty. The items which
constituted the extreme negative end of the continuum were as
follows:
1   Disliked school
2   Could not concentrate in school
3   Worried about my personal appearance
4   Shy with opposite sex
5   Suffered with my nerves
6   Wet the bed
7   Quick temper
8   Lacked confidence
9   Found it difficult to make friends
10 Got miserable and depressed

The items used in the schedule were derived from the Slater and
Roth (1969) battery of neurotic symptoms in childhood which forms
a standard part of case-history data collection for adults with

psychiatric disorders. Although recent research evidence does not
support, in any general way, the belief (implicit in much clinical
work) that there is temperamental stability over time of neurotic
conditions first present in childhood, it does appear that there is
some link between child neurosis and adult neurosis in a minority
of cases (Rutter, 1972a; Hersov, 1977).

It was not, however, our intention to use childhood 'neurotic
symptoms' as indicators of adult neurosis. The term 'neurotic trait'
is used, in the context of this research, to describe a fear or
difficulty during adolescence, the presence of which may indicate
underlying stress. It is arguable whether or not these so-called
'neurotic traits' are in fact valid indications of emotional
disorder, for epidemiological studies have shown that essentially
normal children can exhibit these phenomena, together with 'fears
and worries', so that it has been asserted in an American study that
'a large number of fears and worries is exceedingly widespread among
children... (and) ...we do not know if the fears and worries are
indicative of maladjustment, personality deviation or emotional
disturbance or if they are a concomitant of the wide range of developmental phenomena in essentially normal children' (Lapouse and Monk,
1959). In this country, Shepherd, in the Buckinghamshire Child
Survey demonstrated that 'a supposedly normal population can include
children with behaviour disturbances comparable to those of patients
at a child-guidance clinic', and concluded 'on the basis of this
study, then, we would suggest that many so-called disturbances of
behaviour are no more than temporary exaggerations of widely
distributed reaction-patterns' (Shepherd et al., 1966).

Notwithstanding any clinical validity the items included in the
schedule may have, the data collected in this present survey could
clearly not be regarded as diagnostic evidence of emotional disorder
in adolescence. An additional note of caution must also be added,
since it is not possible to assess the data in terms of historical
accuracy, so that the findings can only be regarded as possible
indicators of stress during adolescence and the most useful
interpretations of them must therefore be based upon any broad
differences apparent between the two survey groups of D and CM.
Table 17 shows the commonness of the *extreme* presence of the items
which were felt to be relevant to adolescent stress.

TABLE 17 The proportion of female/male informants who experienced
certain fears of difficulties to an extreme degree during their
adolescence

		DW n=336 %	CMW n=371 %	DM n=184 %	CMM n=199 %
1	Shy with opposite sex	35	20	21	23
2	Worries about appearance	33	21	18	18
3	Quick temper	24	19	16	18
4	Dislike of school	23	16	9	13
5	Lacked confidence	23	16	6	8
6	Unable to concentrate in school	14	10	8	8
7	Nerves	11	5	4	2
8	Depression	10	4	1	2
9	Difficulties in making friends	9	3	2	3
10	Wet the bed	3	2	1	-

It is evident from Table 17 that although the rank order of commonness of the items was very similar for men and women, women generally
were more prone to such experiences than were men, and DW appeared to
have been the most prone. When the scores for fears and difficulties
during adolescence were considered overall, it was again evident that
DW were slightly more likely to have been at risk to stress during
their childhoods and adolescence, since they scored 24 out of a
possible 50 (50 being the maximum score possible if each fear and
difficulty had been experienced to an extreme degree); CMW scored
22; DM scored 21 and CMM scored 22.

SUMMARY

Family background

The data from this survey suggested a slight association between
parental marital unhappiness and offspring marital unhappiness but,
contrary to the findings from American studies, there was no evidence
to indicate that parental divorce is a predictor of offspring
divorce. Neither did broken parental marriage bonds (whether broken
through divorce, separation or death) appear in this study to be
associated with subsequent offspring marital breakdown (whether
divorce or separation). However, certain circumstances of parental
marriage bond breaking may have implications for the durability of
offspring marriages; for example, children who were under 5 years
when their parents' marriage broke down, or who afterwards lived
with a step-parent, seemed more likely to divorce.
    The sex of the parent whom daughters preferred whilst growing up
may have some relevance to marital durability; having a preference
for the father seemed, for women in this study, to be a marginal
predictor of divorce, whilst a maternal preference appeared to be
associated with marital stability, especially for working-class
women.
    The findings about family structure from this study suggested
that, in general, neither the sibling structures of the marriage
partners nor the inter-relationship between each spouse's ordinal
position in his or her sibling constellation has much influence
upon marital outcome. However, two possible pointers to divorce
were apparent; first, that marriages in which the wives are only
children may be relatively divorce prone and, second, husbands who
have grown up without a sister may also be more likely to divorce.

Aspects of childhood and adolescent health

Certain chronic or severe physical ailments which had appeared,
clinically, to have relevance to marital durability did not correlate with divorce in this present study. Additionally there seemed
to be no link between divorce and certain conditions which, clinically, appeared to have a psychosomatic origin. However, having
been at risk to certain other stresses connected with health whilst
growing up may affect marital durability; for example, certain
patterns of hospitalisation appeared to correlate with divorce.

Chapter 3

SHAPING INFLUENCES:
SocialClass, Education, Religion

Social class, education and religion are generally considered to be
important shaping influences upon an individual's personal and social
expectations, attitudes and behaviour. It is, therefore, not
altogether surprising that American research workers have found that
certain features within each of these broad categories of experience
appear to be systematically linked with divorce rates. The explanations postulated by social scientists for these variations have
tended to be functionalist in origin, since they have been viewed
largely as resulting from the different barriers and sanctions to
divorce operative within the various groups or affiliations (Scanzoni,
1965; Goode, 1966; Hart, 1976). These barriers and sanctions are
complex, since the normative frames of reference they sustain reflect
a range of social, as well as moral influences, and the economic
viability of divorce may also be an important contributing factor.
However, despite the recognition of the wide range of elements which
combine together to compose these group influences upon divorce
behaviour, there so far appears to have been little attention given
to one aspect, namely that marital stress itself may vary in both
form and extent according to social class, education or religion.
   In this chapter divorce behaviour is explored in relation to the
variables of social class, education and religion, not only in terms
of the possible barriers to divorce and the sanctions which may ensue
from it, but also in relation to the extent to which individuals of
differing social classes, educational levels or religious backgrounds
may have been more at risk to certain stresses, both prior to and
during their marriages. Social class, education and religion are
considered here as three separate, although inevitably overlapping
influences. The allocation of informants to their particular social
class was carried out in accordance with the Registrar General's
classification of occupations (1970) (see Glossary).

SOCIAL CLASS

An interest in social class as a factor in divorce stemmed originally
from US Census Reports, which have consistently shown an inverse
relationship between divorce and social class; in other words, it

appears that, within the USA, the lower the social class to which an individual belongs, then the greater the risk of divorce. This progressive increase in the probability of divorce has been explained by some in terms of variations in the life styles of the different social classes, which accordingly may make divorce more likely for individuals in progressively lower social strata, a point of view held by Goode (1966) who postulated that 'the objective complexities and difficulties ensuing from divorce are greater for upper strata marriages, so that they are more likely to stay together.'

.This inverse relationship between divorce and social class observed for the USA does not, however, appear to be the case within the UK. For instance, Rowntree and Carrier (1958) found that, within both a divorced and a continuing married population, there was an equal distribution of manual worker marriages. And, more recently, Gibson (1974) showed that not only was there no direct association between high divorce rates and low social class but conversely, even a slightly greater tendency for non-manual workers to divorce. However, what he did note was that, of all social classes, social class V had the greatest propensity to divorce, followed by social class III non-manual. Table 18 shows the divorce rates calculated by Gibson for the Registrar General's six social classes.

TABLE 18   Social class variations in the divorce rate (England and Wales 1961)

RG social class	Divorce rate per 10,000 married women under 55 yrs
I	22
II	25
IIIn-m	43
IIIm	29
IV	25
V	51

It is worth noting, however, that although social classes V and IIIn-m have, relative to other social classes, the highest divorce rates, on the statistics available so far,* they still cannot, as a group, be said to be markedly divorce prone, since only 5 marriages in every 1,000 marriages for V, and 4 marriages in every 1,000 IIIn-m marriages appear to end in divorce.

It is apparent from Table 18 that the underlying causes of the particular social class pattern of divorce which has so far emerged for the UK cannot be accounted for in terms similar to those which are acceptable when a simple inverse relationship between social class and divorce exists, as appears to be the case for the USA. Neither does the search for patterns of any similarity between social classes IIIn-m and V immediately prove useful, since these two groups appear

*   The production of data relating to social class variations in the divorce rate based upon 1970 census figures are currently in hand at the Office of Population Censuses and Surveys and will shortly be published.

to have little in common, either with regard to any social, financial, moral or religious barriers to divorce, or as far as any economic, moral or social sanctions which might result from divorce are concerned. These two relatively divorce-prone social classes, do, however, appear similar in one particular respect, namely that of 'hierarchical position', since they both occupy the bottom layer of their own broad occupational groups; social class IIIn-m is the lowest rung of the non-manual classification and social class V is similarly placed within the manual-worker group.

The actual significance of this similarity in rank of social classes IIIn-m and V within the non-manual and manual worker hierarchies is uncertain, but it is postulated by us that each of these social classes may be more likely than the others higher up in their respective hierarchies to be at risk to environing stress, although not necessarily for the same reasons. This possibility, that the similar and relatively high divorce rates of informants in social classes IIIn-m and V may in part be explained in terms of their greater personal vulnerability and greater risks of environing stress, resulted from a wide-ranging social class analysis of the survey data. From these particular analyses D informants with social class V backgrounds appeared to have been the most at risk, both prior to and during their marriages, with D IIIn-m informants also emerging as a social class group relatively more at risk to stress, although their pattern of risk was markedly different from that which emerged for D V.

In the following two sections the survey findings for social classes V and IIIn-m are described largely without percentages, in order to simplify the presentation of the material; the full tabulations which relate to the findings noted are contained in Appendix III. Neither does this section include any detailed discussion of the assumptions underlying each survey item regarded as relating to stress and vulnerability, since these are referred to in other chapters; the main object of these sections on social classes V and IIIn-m is to demonstrate their overall patterns of the risk which emerged from the survey data.

Barriers to divorce

It might be expected that where there was a relatively low divorce rate one would also find stronger barriers to divorce; for instance, there has been formal religious opposition to divorce in the traditional teaching of the Roman Catholic Church. Also, low divorce rates might be expected among groups with a great deal of financial investment in marital property and possessions, and for whom divorce would entail severe curtailment of an affluent life style; such groups may, therefore, be considered as having an economic barrier to divorce. A third major barrier to divorce may be termed a normative barrier, when the overall received social class group values do not favour divorce. The presence and influence of one or more of such barriers to divorce may act as a deterrent to divorce, and correspondingly the absence or disregard of such barriers may result in higher divorce rates.

Social class V

The finding by Gibson that social class V, the unskilled manual
group, is the most divorce prone, is in line with American findings
on divorce rates and social class, and a functionalist explanation in
terms of weaker barriers and sanctions to divorce seems adequately to
explain such divorce behaviour. In this section, the barriers and
sanctions to divorce which may affect social class V are commented
upon, but the major part of the discussion centres upon the extent to
which the paucity of resources usually found amongst this social class
may also be interpreted as evidence of environing disadvantage, which
accordingly increases the risk of stress developing within such
marriages.
   One of the strongest barriers to divorce is likely to be an
economic one, since a drop in living standards is likely to result
if the pre-divorce marital income has, after divorce, to be divided
between two households instead of one. It has, however, been
suggested by Goode (1966) that marriages from lower strata may be
less constrained by economic barriers than would marriages from upper
strata, for two main reasons. First, he considers that more of the
income in upper strata marriages is set aside for long-term investment
in houses, insurance schemes and the like, whereas relatively more
income in lower strata marriages is spent on consumer goods;
consequently, it is far less easy for the husband in the upper strata
to abandon such obligations. Second, the potential financial loss
for the upper strata wife is perhaps greater than that for wives in
lower strata, since in the event of her having to work and support
herself after the divorce, the difference between the potential
earnings of the lower class wife and her husband may well be smaller
than between those of the wife and husband in the upper strata.
Notwithstanding the financial disadvantage or hardships which may
result from divorce, and which, for many, may constitute an economic
barrier, it seems reasonable to suppose that in marriages in which
the husband fails to provide adequately for his family, there may
even be a financial incentive for the wife to sue for divorce, since
after divorce she is likely to have a more constant income, either
from her own earnings or from social security payments. The present
survey data suggest that such a possibility would be the most likely
to apply to D V marriages, and there is some supporting evidence for
this from Hart (1976) which points to positive economic benefits of
divorce for some women, in particular those in the lower strata.
   With regard to any normative barrier to divorce, the attitudes
of CM V regarding divorce were taken as representing the 'norm' for
social class V. CM informants were asked whether or not they believed
that divorce was a right course of action for couples who were
unhappily married, both for couples without children and for those
who had them. If divorce were more normatively available for social
class V, in the sense that divorce would be relatively less likely to
be disapproved of by other members, then CM V might be expected to be
more in favour of the use of divorce to end an unhappy marriage than
would other CM social classes. However, in the present survey, there
appeared to be no evidence of a weak normative barrier to divorce
for social class V, since CM V were the most likely of all CM social
classes to disapprove of divorce for childless couples and were

similar to other groups in their general disapproval of divorce for
couples with children. A further barrier to divorce has traditionally
been a religious one and the survey data suggest in this respect that
social class V may also be regarded as experiencing a relatively weak
barrier to divorce, since survey informants in this social class (both
D and CM) were among the least likely to claim any religious affiliation or practice either prior to or during their marriages.

Environing disadvantage and the divorce proneness of social class V

The functionalist explanations of the variations in divorce rates, in
terms of the benefits and disadvantages ensuing from divorce, make
little reference to variations in stress within the marriages of
different social classes. The possibility that, regardless of the
ways in which marital conflict may be managed (whether by divorce or
in other ways), there may actually be more marital stresses or
tensions in some social classes rather than in others, was felt to
merit exploration and D V did emerge as being relatively more at risk
to marital stress resulting from environing disadvantage than did all
other groups.
     The economic position of social class V relative to other social
classes, may be regarded as generally disadvantaged, and whilst such
disadvantage has immediate relevance to the instrumental side of
marriage, in that marital tensions over fundamentals such as money
and housing seem more likely to arise, the affective side of marriage
seems also less likely to develop smoothly, because of this increased
risk of instrumental problems arising.
     It was evident from the survey that informants with social class V
backgrounds experienced more environing disadvantage than did
informants from other social classes. First, the environment in which
social class V informants grew up was more likely to have been overcrowded, since they came from relatively large families of origin.
Second, their job opportunities would have been fewer and less
financially rewarding, since they were the least likely to have had a
selective education or to have had any further education.
     The marital environment of survey social class V informants may
also be regarded as potentially more economically disadvantaged than
that of other social classes. First, because social class V informants married at the youngest ages, they would, therefore, have had
the least likelihood of accumulating any savings; and second, their
early age at marriage also has implications with regard to their
economic position, which was likely to remain low, since their
marital responsibilities probably neither encouraged nor permitted
any participation in job-training schemes which might have led to
improvements in their long-term economic position. Third, unemployment was more likely to have been experienced by social class V
husbands than by those of any other social class.
     Social class V marriages may also be regarded as relatively dis-
advantaged and hence more at risk to stress, when any formal preparation for married life is considered, since these marriages were the
least likely to have been marked by social ritual, both during the
courtship and also with regard to any ritual associated with the
wedding. This may mean that adjustment to marriage and to marital

roles may accordingly have been less easy for them. Additionally, stresses stemming from the quality of the marital housing seem more likely to have arisen for social class V, since, notwithstanding their known over-representation in sub-standard housing, they were the most likely survey social class to have shared their marital accommodation.

It was evident that survey D V appeared to be the most likely of any D social class to have been at risk to stress arising out of environing disadvantage, and CM V emerged similarly so amongst CM social classes. However, the disadvantage of D V was invariably more pronounced than was the case for CM V. For example, whereas both D V and CM V came from the largest families of origin, D V grew up in larger families than did CM V. Similarly, with regard to age at marriage, although both D V and CM V married relatively younger than informants in other social classes, D V generally married younger than did CM V.

Notwithstanding that divorced informants from social class V showed the greatest evidence of the type of environing disadvantage which seems most typical of social class V, they also appeared the most disadvantaged of any D or CM social class on other items in the survey which one would not immediately expect to have a class bias. For instance, D V informants were the most likely to have been hospitalised whilst growing up, to have had relatively more stays in hospital and to have been relatively younger when first hospitalised; hence they may perhaps be regarded as having been the most at risk to stresses arising out of separation from parents and siblings.

The courtships of D V informants also showed more indications of stress, relative to those of any other social class, whether D or CM; first, serious pre-marital difficulties were among the most evident and second, parental opposition was the most marked. Neither of these two problems during courtship appears to be class related, but rather generally more typical of D than CM and the most applicable to D V. Finally, the marriages of D V informants also seemed the most marked by an experience which may be regarded as more typical of D rather than CM and which seems likely to increase the risk of marital stress, namely that frequent job changing in the early years of marriage was the most noticeable amongst D V husbands.

It is apparent from the previous discussion of survey items that D V informants may be regarded as the most vulnerable of any D or CM social class group, partly because of their greater experience of the disadvantages usually associated with their social class of origin, but also because they appeared to have been more at risk to certain other stresses which are not necessarily class related, but which appear to have implications for marital stability.

The reasons for the high loading of D V upon survey items which may be regarded as increasing the risk of stress both prior to and during marriage are not clear, but certain marked differences were apparent between D V and CM V which, perhaps, point to factors which may protect CM V against the environing disadvantage evident among social class V. First, the family backgrounds of CM V, whilst similar in some respects to D V, differed with regard to the birth rank of informants, for CM V were less likely to have been an elder sibling and, in families with many children, this may well have implications for early marriage. It was evident from the survey data that although informants in social class V married at the youngest age, D V married by far the younger and this may be related to their experience in their families of origin, where they may have received relatively less attention, and have had undue responsibilities which may accordingly have made them more anxious to leave home.

Another difference between D V and CM V which may have implications for marital stress, was the contrast in their choice of the parent they preferred whilst growing up. CM V expressed a marked preference for their mothers, but whilst D V were far less likely to express a parental preference at all, they were more than twice as likely as CM V to have preferred their fathers whilst growing up. It is tentatively suggested that CM V women may have been closer to their mothers than were D V women, and that this closeness may have implications both for role adaptation during marriage and also for maternal support following marriage, both of which could be regarded as factors facilitating marital adjustment amongst social class V.

Finally, there were aspects of the reproductive side of the marriages of D V which were markedly different from those of CM V and which may also have implications for marital stability amongst social class V. The first is that D V were far more likely than CM V to be childless, although it is not known whether this was a result of infecundity (inability to have a child), or infertility (a marriage without children). One possible cause of this relative childlessness may be the shorter period of cohabitation apparent amongst D V which accordingly reduces the chances of such marriages being fertile. However, shorter *de facto* durations of marriage were evident for all D social classes, relative to their CM counterparts, and D V did not show the most marked differences, which suggests that unequal opportunities to conceive may not be the only factor associated with their childlessness. Whilst the reasons for infertility and its implications for social class V marriages are not known, nevertheless, in the light of their relatively higher reproduction rates generally, childlessness may be considered unusual and may perhaps constitute a stress upon such marriages, either because it may cause the partners to doubt their own sexual virility and identity, or as Ineichen (1977) suggests, because of stresses arising out of the pressure of the expectations and attitudes of others.

A further difference between CM V and D V related to the sexual dimension of their marriages in that there was a greater prevalence of an extra-marital affair evident amongst D V. How this difference may be interpreted is problematic, but assuming that the reports of CM V and D V were genuine, possible explanations of the data could be either, that it might be reflecting the greater sexual needs of D V which might lead to marital tensions and instability, or alternatively, extra-marital affairs may, in themselves, be a reflection of D V's need for emotional closeness and confirmation of their identity, and as such may perhaps be regarded as providing further evidence of their vulnerability.

Social class III non-manual

Social class IIIn-m has emerged as the social class with the second highest divorce rate, being similar to social class V and very

different from all other social classes in its proneness to divorce
(Gibson, 1974). The reasons for the relatively high divorce rate of
social class IIIn-m are, however, more difficult to discern since,
as we shall show, neither a functionalist interpretation based upon
the presence of weak barriers and sanctions to divorce, nor the kind
of explanation suggested by widespread environing disadvantage,
appeared to apply in any general sense to this social class. Within
the literature, this social class has been presented by Lockwood
(1958) as ambiguous, in that historically it has been 'precariously
poised between the middle and working classes proper', and the
black-coated worker whom he studied, who could be said to epitomise
this class, was described by him as a 'marginal man'. This description of marginality and ambiguity of social position, seems likely
to have become more marked in recent decades, as a result of social
changes such as the spread of literacy and the increased emphasis
laid on productive contributions to society, all of which have
combined to blur the status distinction of the members of this group,
and in some ways to lower their social prestige. This loss of
certain distinguishing features, and the attempt to sustain a
position within a field of status indeterminacy, suggest that
marriages within this social class may well be almost bound to
reflect some of the stresses which may presently reside in the member-
ship of the class itself.

Lockwood has defined the parameters of this group in generalities
such as later marriage, smaller family size, and educational aspirations for their children, together with careful husbanding and
planning of resources to enable adequate living arrangements. The
profile which he portrays is of a group aspiring to what are regarded
as middle-class values. There is evidence in these respects from the
survey data that the marriages of D IIIn-m may have been disadvantaged
from the start. From social class analyses of the present survey data
social class IIIn-m emerged, as did social class V, as a group with
special characteristics and it is this distinguishing pattern which
largely forms the basis of the tentative explanation offered for the
relatively high divorce rate of social class IIIn-m. The barriers
and sanctions to divorce, the extent of any environing disadvantage
and the distinguishing features of social class D IIIn-m are each
discussed in turn.

Barriers to divorce for social class IIIn-m

A functionalist explanation of the relatively high divorce rate of
social class IIIn-m is not sustained by the survey findings. First,
it was evident from the survey data that social class IIIn-m in
general, as typified by the survey CM IIIn-m, would be unlikely to
have weak economic barriers to divorce; indeed, it seemed probable
that they would be substantially disadvantaged financially after
divorce. This is because during their marriages CM IIIn-m appeared
to have accumulated certain assets; first, they were among the most
likely to have occupied independent accommodation during marriage;
second, CM IIIn-m wives were the most likely to have worked during
their marriages and were the least likely to have had children in
the first two years of marriage. Both of these features seemed

likely to lead to a degree of material investment which could be
seriously disrupted by divorce. Although, overall, social class
IIIn-m may be said to have less to lose from divorce than other
non-manual social classes, after divorce they seem likely to be
more materially disadvantaged than would manual workers, so that a
weak economic barrier to divorce seems unlikely in itself adequately
to account for the relatively high divorce rate of social class
IIIn-m.

Second, relative to other social classes, CM IIIn-m (again for the
purposes of this survey CM IIIn-m are considered as representing the
attitudes of social class IIIn-m) did not appear, overall, to have a
weak normative barrier to divorce. The survey findings regarding
general attitudes towards divorce demonstrated that CM IIIn-m had
a more mixed attitude towards it than did any other CM social class,
for they were the most likely to favour divorce for childless
couples but the least likely to approve of it for those who had
children. Therefore, in practice, it seems probable that, overall,
there would exist for social class IIIn-m a relatively strong
normative barrier to divorce.

Third, the divorce proneness of social class IIIn-m does not
appear to be due to relatively low levels of religious allegiance
and practice, since CM IIIn-m were the most likely CM social class
to claim religious affiliation during marriage and were also the
most likely to be churchgoers during their marriages.

Environing disadvantage and the divorce proneness of social class
IIIn-m

Whereas environing disadvantage, which seemed likely to increase the
risk of marital stress and breakdown, was evident from the survey
findings on social class V, it was equally clear from the general
survey analyses on social class, that the marriages of social class
IIIn-m (again as typified by the survey CM IIIn-m) appeared, if
anything, to be set for relatively high stability, rather than for
the reverse: first, theirs, of all social class groups, were the
most marked by the rituals of engagement, church wedding and honeymoon; second, they were the least likely to have had pre-marital
difficulties; third, they showed considerable evidence of foresight
and planning in regard to their housing history and the timing of
children; finally, neither the work record of CM IIIn-m husbands,
nor that of their wives, seemed likely in any obvious sense to
create any disruptive stresses of an instrumental nature within
their marriages.

It was, therefore, apparent from the survey data that the
relatively high divorce rate of social class IIIn-m could not
readily be explained in terms of increased risk arising out of
relatively widespread environing disadvantage.

The characteristics of D IIIn-m

Since the divorce proneness of social class IIIn-m does not appear
to be facilitated either by weak barriers to divorce, by weak

economic sanctions after divorce, or by environing disadvantage, the possibility that the members of this social class may actually experience relatively more marital stress because of some feature or features of their life styles was explored.

The impression of D IIIn-m which emerged from the survey data was interesting. In certain ways D IIIn-m appeared similar to CM IIIn-m and the notions of social and material advancement found in the latter at first seemed applicable in a general, although lesser, way to D IIIn-m. However, when the six D social classes were compared with their CM counterparts, D IIIn-m informants emerged as relatively atypical of their social class of origin (CM IIIn-m being considered to represent social class IIIn-m) over and above those differences which were a consistent feature of almost all D - CM survey data comparisons.

This pattern of relative atypicality of their social class of origin spread across many aspects of the backgrounds and marriages of informants in social class IIIn-m. For instance, D IIIn-m were far less likely than CM IIIn-m to have had either a selective education or any further education. Nor did D IIIn-m show the same high levels of religious affiliation and practice as CM IIIn-m either prior to or during marriage. Additionally, the overall pattern of foresight and planning which seemingly characterised CM IIIn-m with regard to their courtship, wedding, child spacing, housing and employment was strikingly different for D IIIn-m. There was also a slight indication that D IIIn-m may have been more at risk to certain stresses whilst growing up, for they appeared as the social class group the most prone to stammering, a condition likely to be associated with social embarrassment and which may have implications regarding emotional development.

Another interesting finding which emerged from the survey and which illustrates further the relative atypicality of D IIIn-m, was the contrast between D IIIn-m and CM IIIn-m in terms of pre-marital difficulties between the partners. D IIIn-m experienced far more pre-marital difficulties than did CM IIIn-m and this contrast is all the more interesting when considered in the context of the courtships of D IIIn-m and CM IIIn-m. Both courtships were, relative to other D and CM social classes, similarly characterised by parental approval and ritual preparation for the marriage, which together may perhaps be considered as setting the seal of public approval upon the marriage; consequently, in the face of such public declarations of intent, the pre-marital conflicts of D IIIn-m couples would, perhaps, be relatively less likely to result in an abandonment of wedding plans.

The possibility of a social 'malaise' within social class IIIn-m has been referred to earlier in this chapter, and the strains which might arise in a class which has middle-class goals, but a legacy of behavioural socialisation which may well stem from more working-class origins, would make the divorce-proneness of this group perhaps not so surprising after all. It seems possible that the CM IIIn-m represent those able to make a reasonably successful adaptation to the demands of the group, so that they are socially more integrated. The members of the D IIIn-m however, may have been less well able to fit into this required pattern of living, either through their early backgrounds or through insufficient ability to

manage their resources. It also seemed possible that the aspirations
of social class IIIn-m towards social and material advancement might
create tensions within this social class which could be counter-
productive, for two main reasons: first, such aspirations might cause
an intellectual and social gulf between parents and their children,
of a kind more marked than any generational gap which might arise,
either amongst traditional working classes or within the more
established professional classes. Second, individuals whose life
style is geared towards social and material advancement, and who
aspire to the ideals and values of another social group, seem
relatively more likely to be at risk to emotional stress, since the
feedback they receive from the values of their own social group
concerning their individual personal worth would not, because of its
emphasis upon achievement rather than upon the acceptance of an
individual, be very helpful for identity development.

These two strands of stress which might arise more within social
class IIIn-m, namely that of unsatisfactory parent-child relationships and of insecurity of identity amongst members, have implications both for marital unhappiness and for marital stability. First,
the striving for material and social betterment may mean that the
emphasis in the marriage will tend to be placed upon the proper
performance of expected marital roles, and conflict will result when
there are failures in this area; the relative atypicality of D IIIn-m
in their housing, fertility and work patterns, suggested a degree
of inability to achieve class goals. Second, whilst it appears that
the divorce proneness of social class IIIn-m is not readily explicable in terms of weak economic, moral or normative barriers to
divorce, it may be that there are relatively weak emotional barriers
to divorce amongst this social class, in the sense that the insecurity of identity which could apply to individuals in social
class IIIn-m means that they may be perhaps less likely themselves
to form strong affectional bonds. Therefore, their marital bonds
may be relatively weaker, and divorce as a means of dealing with
marital conflict may be more easily resorted to by individuals in
this social class.

HOMOGAMY OF SOCIAL CLASS AND DIVORCE

Homogamy of social class of origin

All the research studies so far carried out on mate selection have
shown that homogamy (choosing a partner with similar characteristics
to oneself) is the norm, particularly when marriages are examined
in terms of social class. According to Kerckhoff (1974) people
marry homogamously not only because they encounter more similar
than dissimilar others, but also because they prefer to be with
socially similar others. It has also been suggested by Coombs
(1966) that similarity of social class indicates value consensus
between the partners, and fosters mutually rewarding interaction
which in turn leads to a greater tendency to continue in the relationship. In contrast to this, however, Golden (1954) and Smith (1966)
found that many partners who were socially heterogamous have
relatively lasting relationships and it has therefore been suggested

by them that, in such cases, the extent to which dissimilar partners
have freed themselves from the disjunctive forces of their social
backgrounds may determine the cohesiveness and duration of their
relationships.

A substantial number of informants in the survey were unable to
give the occupation of their spouse's father or of the breadwinner
in their spouse family of origin (16% D and 8% CM could not provide
this data about their spouses). Among those whose backgrounds could
be compared, however, there was no evidence to suggest that D marriage
partners were less likely than CM to be from similar social backgrounds, since 72% D and 72% CM came from broadly similar social
class groups (non-manual or manual), and 36% D, 38% CM came from
identical social classes of origin.

Homogamy of social class at marriage

It seems probable that homogamy of social class, as defined by the
occupations of each individual spouse at marriage, would be less
prevalent than homogamy of social class of origin. This is because
women from working-class backgrounds are more likely than men from
similar backgrounds to go into non-manual occupations on leaving
school, and women from non-manual worker homes are less likely than
men from equivalent social classes to be in high grade occupations
or in the professions. As might be expected, it was evident from
the survey data that homogamy of social class at marriage was not
the case for the majority of survey informants. However, a slight
contrast was evident between D and CM regarding husband/wife occupations, in that wives in divorced marriages were more likely than
the wives in continuing marriages to be in higher grade occupations
than their husbands at the time of marriage. This can be seen in
Table 19.

TABLE 19   Homogamy of social class at marriage

	D n=520	CM n=570
Wife higher social class		
By 1 class	26	21
By 2 classes	8	7
By 3 classes	4	1
By 4 classes	Ø	−
Husband higher social class		
By 1 class	18	20
By 2 classes	3	6
By 3 classes	1	1
By 4 classes	−	Ø
H and W same social class	23	30
Not stated	18	14

SOCIAL MOBILITY AND DIVORCE

Various writers have noted that social mobility, whether upward or
downward, may lead to interpersonal stress (Blau, 1956; Durkheim,
1952). The consequences of moving from one social class to another,
in terms of the ease with which new social norms and behaviour
patterns are acquired, will obviously vary according to an
individual's ability to negotiate any differences in norms, values
and expectations between the social class in which he grew up and
the new social class which has been acquired as a result of education, occupation or marriage. Conflict between the culture in which
an individual has grown up and the culture he has since moved into
in adulthood, have been described by Merton (1957) and Lipset and
Bendix (1959). It seems probable that the greater the social class
change which is made, then the more marked may be any socio-cultural
gap and, therefore, the greater the possibility of disaffection,
embarrassment and, in the extreme, of 'anomie', a loss of identity.
     It might be expected that since D in many other instances show
evidence of having been more at risk than CM to personal and
environing stress, then they would also be more likely than CM to
have been socially mobile and therefore to have experienced more
interpersonal stress because of this. However, this was not the
case. When informants' social class of origin was compared against
their social class at marriage (as defined by their own occupation)
there were few differences between D and CM. D were slightly more
likely than CM to have been upwardly mobile (36% : 34%) and slightly
less likely to have been downwardly mobile (24% : 26%). As might
be expected, women were more upwardly mobile than were men (40% DW;
37% CMW; 28% DM; 26% CMM). Overall, 60% of D and 60% CM were in a
different social class at marriage from their social class of origin,
but generally, the movement was by only one social class and therefore the negative effects of social mobility would probably not be
particularly marked among survey informants, and D appeared to have
been no more at risk to such stress than were CM.

EDUCATION

It is known that concordance with respect to educational level is
greater than that for social class, for in one study, 45% of couples
came from the same social class but 71% of couples reached a similar
educational level (Berent, 1954). Winch, using Hillman's analysis
of American census data (Hillman, 1962), has noted that there is an
inverse relationship between the educational level of husbands and
divorce - the more educated the husband, the less likely it is that
his primary marriage will end in divorce. There is also some
evidence from Komarovsky's work (1967) which suggests first, that
the higher the husband's educational level, with its connotations
of increased verbal communication skills, the more self-disclosure,
empathy and sympathy there is likely to be between him and his wife;
and second, that the husband in higher occupational levels is
apparently less rigid in his role playing within marriage; he has
more confidence within himself, and is able to swap roles when
necessary, for instance in respect of child care, domestic chores,

or in enabling his wife to pursue her own career. Along similar
lines, Barry (1970), in a review of factors associated with marital
breakdown, noted that a pattern does seem to be emerging from the
research literature on marriage, which indicates that those characteristics generally considered to lead to a stable male identity
are also associated with marital stability, and he cites a high
educational level as one of these characteristics.

Since educational level is closely linked with job status and
overlaps considerably with social class, the mechanisms whereby
educational level is associated with marital stability are not
clear. Komarovsky's work seems to suggest that it is educational
level in itself, namely the greater degree of awareness which is
gained from being educated longer and to a higher level, which
permits this flexibility and understanding observed in more highly
educated husbands. Equally, however, since, in the USA, being
highly educated is likely to be associated with a financially
rewarding job which may well confer high status in the community,
it may be this status, combined with job satisfaction, and the
feeling of being a success (at least in his wife's eyes) which
enables highly educated husbands to be more understanding towards
their wives.

According to Levinger (1976) a husband's educational or occupational rank has traditionally determined his family's place in
society and this still appears to be so in the 1970s (Rossi et al.,
1974). Levinger postulates that a wife's attraction to her husband
may be positively related to his education for reasons of social
status. Whilst it may be that higher education encourages better
marital communication placing higher value on marital companion-
ship, more importantly, the husband's education appears to be
positively related to his financial income and therefore to the
couple's living standard. Cutright (1971) has demonstrated that
the association between high husband education and low divorce
proneness could be mostly accounted for by variations in the level
of husband income; he found no overall association between husband's
education and marital durability, nor did high status alone reduce
proneness to divorce, unless associated with high income.

However, the associations noted previously, particularly those
from American census data, are between marital stability and educational level and not between marital happiness and educational
level. It may be that the marriages of highly educated men are no
happier than those of less educated husbands but simply more stable
(Cuber and Harrof, 1962); there are certainly sound economic reasons
for them to keep their marriages intact, since, for them, divorce
is likely to be more disruptive because so much is invested in
joint property and possessions. After divorce, both husband and
wife are likely to be poorer, he because of alimony costs, she
because she is unlikely either to earn the equivalent of her pre-
divorce income or to receive as much in alimony. For less educated
men, in lower status occupations, the financial effects of divorce
are not so devastating, since both husband and wife generally have
less to lose.

Another interesting finding regarding the relationship between
educational levels and marital stability is that of Bumpass and
Sweet (1972) who noted that the effect of education on marital
disruption is minimal when age at marriage is controlled.

THE SURVEY FINDINGS ON EDUCATION

Informants' education

In the light of the US findings on education and divorce, it was
expected that, in this survey, D would be less likely than CM to
have had a selective education (i.e. a grammar school or technical
school education) and this was the case; 18% CM compared with 11% D
had attended selective schools.

With regard to further education, men were at least twice as
likely as women to have had any sort of further education, and CMM
were the most likely to have done so (24% DW, 24% CMW, 48% DM,
55% CMM were educated beyond statutory requirements). As well as
being the most likely of the four survey sub-groups to receive
further education, CMM were slightly more likely to have had a
university or professional training and DM were the least likely
to do so (8% CMM, 3% DM, 6% DW, 6% CMW).

It is to be expected that individuals with non-manual backgrounds
would be more likely to receive further education generally and
particularly to have had a university or professional education;
this was very much so for CM but was far less marked for D, for
40% of CM n-m who went on to further education went to university
or into a profession, whereas only 26% D n-m who received any
further education did so. This data on social class suggests
perhaps that D with non-manual backgrounds are less typical of their
social class of origin, with regard to educational achievement.

Educational backgrounds of the marriage partners

When comparing the educational backgrounds of spouses, homogamy of
education during the period of compulsory schooling has more
relevance as a possible indicator of shared educational   experiences
than has homogamy in relation to further education. This is because
the probability of a girl receiving further education is considerably
less than that of a boy with an equivalent educational record
during the statutory period of education. Having said this, however,
full comparisons between the survey marriage partners in terms of
their education could not be made because a substantial number of
D informants could not say anything about their spouses' schooling.
17% D, 4% CM did not know which school (either name of or category
of school) their partner last attended; those most unaware of this
aspect of their partners' life were D informants with non-manual
worker backgrounds (23%). Furthermore, a fairly high proportion of
D did not know how old their ex-spouse was when he or she left
school; this was so for 13% D and 2% CM and finally, 9% D and 2% CM
could not say whether or not their spouse had received any further
education.

There were two consistent features of this category of informants
(whether D or CM) who knew nothing about their spouses' or their
ex-spouses' educational background. First, the later the age at
marriage then the higher the incidence of such ignorance concerning
the spouse's background, and second, informants from earlier
marriage cohorts were relatively more prevalent amongst these
'don't knows'.

These two features do suggest that time factors may be accounting for the 'don't knows', partly in the sense that the events in question took place progressively longer ago, and partly because a spouse's educational history may be less relevant to older couples generally, in contrast to teenage brides and grooms who have more recently left school, and whose school experiences and school friends might feature in their courtship conversation and even in social and work spheres of their activities.

Notwithstanding these two possible influences, there were still a substantial number of D who were married relatively recently, or who were partners within a teenage marriage, who claimed to know nothing about their spouses' educational background; for instance, this was so for 13% D who were married in 1960-9, 10% D in cohort 1950-9, 24% D married 1940-9, in relation to the school last attended by their ex-spouse. Similarly, 10% of informants in D marriages in which the bride was under 20 years, 12% in which the bride was aged 20-4, 22% in which the bride was 25-9 years old, did not know how old their ex-spouse was when he or she left school.

The prevalence amongst D of this ignorance about their spouses' schooling perhaps points to a lack of involvement with their ex-spouse prior to their marriages. This ignorance, however, cannot be largely accounted for by a cultural disinterest in education amongst lower social classes, since it was relatively more prevalent amongst informants with non-manual worker backgrounds. This interesting group of informants who were unable to give information about key aspects of their spouses' background are considered further at the end of this chapter.

Comparisons between the educational backgrounds of those D and CM for whom sufficient data was available indicated little difference between D and CM partners with regard to homogamy of educational background. For instance, 83% D, 80% CM marriage partners were educated in broadly similar types of schools (i.e. either both in selective schools or non-selective schools). However, partners in D marriages were slightly more likely than partners in CM marriages to have had equivalent durations of schooling, for 74% D spouses as opposed to 66% CM left school at similar ages. With regard to further education, whilst CM partners were more likely than D partners to have had further education (13% D : 18% CM), there was little difference between D and CM marriages with regard to dis-similarity of educational levels, since in 35% D, 37% CM marriages only one partner had received any further education.

RELIGION

The extent to which the religion in which an individual grew up may be an important influence upon his life obviously depends upon the intensity of any religious experience within his background and upon his own response to that experience. Questions to informants on religious upbringing were confined to asking whether or not they were brought up in any particular religion and if they were, which religion it was. As with many other areas of the survey enquiry, any questioning in depth was avoided because it was felt that a large scale survey could not satisfactorily be used to elicit such data.

Religious adherence during marriage was also explored (again in outline), since this could have relevance to the decision to divorce in the event of serious marital difficulties; informants were asked first, whether, at the time they were married, they would have described themselves as belonging to any particular religion, and if so to which religion. Second, they were asked whether during their marriage they ever went to church apart from occasions such as christenings, weddings and the like; and if so, how often did they attend church during their marriage. They were also asked about the religious background of their spouses.

Religion in which informants grew up and were affiliated to at marriage

It was evident from the survey data that the majority of informants grew up with some kind of religious influence upon them, but no marked differences between D and CM in relation to any formal religious barrier to divorce were apparent, although there was a slight tendency for CM to belong to 'other protestant' denominations (who may frequently take a less lenient view of divorce), and for D to have had no religious influence within their backgrounds, which perhaps suggests that the notion of divorce would have been a slightly more acceptable course of action for D than for CM in the event of serious marital problems. Table 20 shows the religion in which informants grew up.

TABLE 20   Religion in which informants grew up

	D n=520 %	CM n=570 %
Particular religion	92	94
C of E	60	58
Other Protestant	19	24
Catholic	12	11
Other	1	1
No religion	9	6

Whilst the vast majority of informants, whether D or CM, grew up with a religion, by the time they married, however, 71% D and 77% CM claimed that they regarded themselves as belonging to a particular religion.

The partners' religion at marriage

Religious similarity has frequently been linked with marital dura-bility and Bumpass and Sweet (1972) reported confirmation of this linkage, although in this study, D were no more likely than CM to have married partners of a dissimilar religion. However, similarity of no religion has been found by Landis (1963) to be more related to divorce proneness than has a mixed faith marriage and this was

evident from the survey data. The survey findings are shown in
Table 21.

TABLE 21   The religion of both partners at marriage

	D n=520 %	CM n=570 %
Both partners with a religion	47	66
One partner only with a religion	30	17
Neither partner with a religion	23	16

It can be seen in Table 21 that the chances of both D partners being
adherents of some religious group were apparently substantially less
than for CM partners. This, together with the figures for the total
absence of any religious commitment by either marriage partner,
suggests that the chances of a religious barrier to divorce being
present would be relatively less likely for D survey informants.
Whilst the significance of the claimed religious affiliation is not
known, it seems likely that divergence between spouses in an area
such as religious affiliation may well be indicative of other
barriers towards mutual understanding.

Churchgoing during marriage

American research studies have shown that non-attendance at church
is associated with divorce, for like-faith couples who attend church
regularly have been found less likely to break up their marriage
than those who do not (Locke, 1951; Goode, 1956; Chesser, 1957).
The mechanisms whereby churchgoing may protect against divorce are
not known. It is likely, for instance, that the groups within which
churchgoers move tend not to sanction divorce. It may also be that
individuals who are churchgoers are also conformist and would themselves not wish to use divorce as the means of dealing with marital
conflict. Also, it could be that churchgoers either have less
marital conflict than non-churchgoers, or they may be helped to
overcome their marital difficulties because of the support and
direction which they may either find personally in their religion
or in the wider religious community. Each of these possibilities
seems likely to apply to some individuals, but the relative
importance of each is not known. Table 22 shows the survey findings
on the prevalence of churchgoing for informants.

TABLE 22   Churchgoing during marriage - informants

	D n=520 %	CM n=570 %
Churchgoer	31	44
Not a churchgoer	69	56

TABLE 23 Marriage cohort and churchgoing

| | Before 1940 | | 1940-9 | | 1950-9 | | 1960-9 | |
	D n=41 %	CM n=32 %	D n=75 %	CM n=142 %	D n=149 %	CM n=159 %	D n=255 %	CM n=221 %
Both partners churchgoers	31	38	15	32	13	30	9	25
One partner churchgoer	36	35	25	23	26	24	16	19
Neither partner churchgoer	34	28	60	45	60	46	75	56

(All Divorced)

It is apparent that CM were, not surprisingly, more likely than D to be churchgoers. Churchgoing by both partners was more than twice as likely for CM as for D (13% D : 28% CM), and there was an expected generational effect upon churchgoing, with informants from earlier cohorts being more likely to be churchgoers. This can be seen in Table 23.

It is apparent from Table 23 that churchgoing is associated with progressively earlier marriage cohorts but, within a given cohort, D are always less likely than CM to be churchgoers.

It can also be seen in Table 23 that relatively more CM came from earlier marriage cohorts and the much greater prevalence of church-going observed amongst CM generally, to some extent results from this. Hence, the overall difference between D and CM will be accentuated by their lack of parity in terms of marriage cohort but, as the cohort analysis has shown, there appear to be genuine differences between the two main survey groups of D and CM.

Frequency of churchgoing during marriage

Although it has been shown in the previous section that D were less likely than CM either to have any religious affiliation or to be church attenders, amongst those informants who did claim to be churchgoers, D were more frequent attenders than were CM. This can be seen in Table 24.

TABLE 24   Frequency of churchgoing among D and CM - informants who claimed to be churchgoers

Frequency	D n=159 %	CM n=252 %
Once a week or more	33	22
Every few weeks	14	15
Every few months	38	42
Less often	15	21

Catholics, as might perhaps be expected, described themselves as the most frequent churchgoers and the differences between D and CM who attended church at least once a week are to some extent accounted for by the higher representation of Catholics among D churchgoers.

Although the differences between D and CM partners on religious allegiance and church attendance are not particularly marked, the data do suggest that D may be less likely than CM to share their partners' values and beliefs, and perhaps, therefore, be more likely to experience marital conflict because of such differences.

MARITAL DIFFICULTIES AND IGNORANCE OF SPOUSES' BACKGROUND

It will be recalled that a substantial number of informants were unable to provide information about their spouses' early backgrounds, in terms of either their partners' social class of origin, or their

TABLE 25   The timing of the marital difficulties for D related to ignorance about their spouse's social class and education

Difficulties started	Social class		Education (class)	
	Information n=436 %	No information n=84 %	Information n=441 %	No information n=79 %
Within 6 months of marriage	23	32	23	33
6 but less than 12 months	12	13	12	9
1 but less than 2 years	15	13	16	10
2 but less than 5 years	21	20	20	25
5 but less than 10 years	20	8	18	18
10 but less than 15 years	6	8	7	4
15 years or more	3	5	4	1

education. This lack of knowledge is perhaps indicative of a lack of
involvement between the spouses in the pre-marital period, and D who
appeared to know little about these two aspects of their partners'
earlier influences did experience an ear ier start to their marital
difficulties, as can be seen in Table 25.

SUMMARY

Social class

It is evident from official statistics that social classes V and
IIIn-m have far higher divorce rates than other social classes.
Certain data from this study have indicated that the relatively high
divorce rates of social class V may be interpreted in terms of the
relatively acute and widespread environing disadvantage among this
group. In contrast, the divorce proneness of social class IIIn-m in
general appears not to result from such disadvantage but may rather
be due to their greater risk of stress arising from their aspirations,
'marginality' and ambiguity of social position.
    Social mobility did not emerge in this study as a correlate of
divorce. Nor, unlike American findings, was there any evidence from
this survey data to link dissimilarity of social class background
with divorce. However, marriages in which the wives were in a higher
grade occupation (at marriage) than were their husbands, appeared to
be more prone to divorce.

Education

Marriages in which the husband is highly educated appear from this
and other studies to be relatively stable. A variety of factors may
be causing this association between high husband education and low
divorce proneness. For example, being highly educated may also be
indicative of a high status job, or of a highly paid job, and either
of these may act as a barrier to divorce.
    Any link between divorce and dissimilarity of the marriage
partners' educational backgrounds was not apparent in this study.
However, being ignorant of the educational background of one's
spouse seems a predictor of divorce; but this association was not
explicable in terms of social class, nor located solely in earlier
marriage cohorts, so that it may be reflecting a lack of involvement
between 'divorce-bound' partners, both prior to and during marriage.

Religion

Marriages in which both partners were affiliated to a particular
relgion, and especially those in which the partners were churchgoers,
appeared in this and other studies to be most set for marital
stability, although the mechanisms whereby religiosity may protect
against divorce are unclear. For example, such marriages may be
just as unhappy as those of non-religious couples but the barriers
to divorce may be much stronger for them. Alternatively, there may

be less marital unhappiness within marriages of religiously active
couples because of the security, support or direction which they
may find in their religion.

Chapter 4

THE COURTSHIP PERIOD

This part of the study explored some aspects of the informant's
courtship period with their primary marriage partner, a period
defined as the interval between the first date and the marriage.
Data was collected for items which, it was considered, would have
consequences for the partners' marital adjustment in terms of the
ease with which they would be able to assume their respective marital
roles. Features such as short courtships, the lack of a formal
engagement or honeymoon, the breakdown of the relationship between
the spouses during their courtship, and the existence and persistence
of strong familial and parental opposition to the marriage, were
regarded as possible high risk factors in the sense that they were
likely to indicate on the one hand, inadequate preparation for the
changes in life style and responsibilities implicit in marriage, or,
on the other hand, the absence of a support system likely to facilitate and ameliorate the couple's adaptation to their new marital
roles.

OPPOSITION TO THE MARRIAGE

The presence or absence of parental support systems was explored
because it was believed to have considerable relevance to the marital
outcome of the offspring. Informants were asked whether or not they
had experienced strong opposition to their marriage taking place and
about the outcome of any opposition. Table 26 shows the prevalence
of reported opposition (almost always parental) to the marriages of
survey informants.

TABLE 26 Percentage of D and CM marriages in which marital opposition
was reported

	All D n=520 %	DW n=336 %	DM n=184 %	All CM n=570 %	CMW n=371 %	CMM n=199 %
Opposition	43	51	29	13	13	14
No opposition	57	49	71	87	87	86

It can be seen that the survey D apparently experienced considerably
more marital opposition than did those who were still continuing with
their marriages. Evidence of sustained parental opposition seems
likely to be an indicator of the possible lack, at the start of the
marriage, of one support system regarded by many as important.
According to Burgess and Cottrell (1939) and Locke (1951), where
there is in-law approval of the marriage, there is likely also to be
marital happiness. Nevertheless, it must not be overlooked that the
presence of certain kinds of parental support or 'silver cord'
involvement, does not necessarily augur a satisfactory marriage for
the offspring, since it may in some instances inhibit marital
socialisation by preventing the child's independence (Komarovsky,
1967).

It has to be borne in mind that a variable such as marital
opposition might be particularly susceptible to distortion of recall.
Opposition to a successful marriage might well be forgotten, whereas
those whose marriages were unsuccessful might be more inclined to
remember parental efforts to prevent the wedding or, indeed, to have
later been reminded of such attempts by their parents. For survey
informants opposition to marriage was certainly significantly
correlated with marital dissolution, but how this may be interpreted
in causal terms is problematic, for marital opposition may contribute
to marital breakdown via one or more intervening variables. First,
lack of parental support may make marital adjustment more difficult
for young people who may be going through an identity crisis (53%
of D marriages in which the bride was teenage experienced marital
opposition),or for pregnant brides who may be in need of maternal
support (54% of D informants in such marriages reported opposition).
Second, opposition may actually create conflict between the new
marriage partners because of the stresses caused by the hostile
attitude of in-laws should a partner's loyalties become divided
between the family of origin and a husband or wife; for instance,
Barry (1970) has suggested that in-law problems may result in
conflict between the spouses, particularly over their basic values.
He bases his suggestion upon findings by Ackerman (1963) and Zelditch
(1964) who showed that higher divorce rates occur in societies in
which spouses retain separate ties to their families of origin;
where spouses develop mutual ties to both families of origin there
are lower divorce rates. However, the relationship between opposition to a marriage and divorce may in fact be spurious, since some
other factor (for example the unsuitability of the couple *per se*),
may have caused both the marital opposition and also the marital
breakdown.

Another point of interest worth noting in Table 26 is the finding
that DW were far more likely than DM to have experienced opposition
to their marriages. This may be reflecting a variety of causes.
For instance, the male respondent in the divorce case (the respondent
was considered the guilty party prior to the 1969 Divorce Reform Act)
may have generated far more in-law hostility than did the wives of
survey DM and may have demonstrated (at least in his in-laws' eyes)
characteristics which were clearly incompatible with those of his
intended spouse.Alternatively, it may be that women are far more
likely to be given advice about marriage than are men and more
control is exercised by their parents over their choice; according

to Mueller and Pope (1977), parents do attempt to control mate
selection outcomes of women more closely than those of men, since
a woman's future status critically depends upon the husband she
marries.   In the survey most of the marital opposition apparently
came from the informant's own family of origin and DW were therefore
more likely than DM to be in conflict with their own parents.   There
is some evidence from other studies which suggests that, after
marriage, women retain far closer ties with their families of origin
than do men and this behaviour is possibly related to the wife's
need for support in her new role.   Hence, many DW can be considered
as having been relatively isolated at the start of their marriage.

The reasons for the marital opposition

In the survey, informants who had experienced opposition to their
marriage were asked to suggest the reasons for this.   The data from
the open-ended questions did, in some cases, indicate a direct
causal connection (in informants' minds) between opposition and
divorce, since some informants believed that the marital opposition
had been a contributory factor in their own marital problems and,
therefore, in their eventual marital breakdown.   However, in other
marriages, the marital opposition and the eventual marital breakdown
each seem to have been independently related to the same apparent
characteristics of one partner, and generally, it was not possible
to assign the various explanations offered by informants to the
alternative explanations of the relationship between marital opposition and divorce suggested previously.   What can be said, however,
is that where there is marital opposition then the newly-weds may
lack a substantial potential support system.
    When comparing the prevalences of the various reasons for the
opposition suggested by DW, DM, CMW and CMM, the relatively small
cell-base sizes of CMM and CMW must be borne in mind.   There were
considerable differences between the reasons for the opposition
most frequently mentioned by D and those put forward by CM.   By far
the most frequently given reason by both groups, but especially by
D, was that their parents disliked their future daughter- or son-in-
law, but with no specific reason for the dislike being instanced by
informants.   This non-specific parental personal dislike of their
spouses was expressed by as many as 57% of DM reporting opposition,
compared with only 30% of CMM, and by 43% of DW compared with 35% CMW.
    A further 12% of DW were more specific about the reasons for their
parents' dislike of their prospective son-in-law.   This dislike
centred upon perceived negative characteristics.   These apparent
defects ranged from vague labels of selfishness and fears of
irresponsibility and laziness, to specific concerns about the son-
in-law being 'work shy' or having been 'in trouble with the police'.
DW alone mentioned such specific focuses for parental opposition.
Whether or not such characteristics were accurately recognised by
parents, the expression of hostile views towards the prospective son-
or daughter-in-law and the promotion of pre-marital discord, sometimes
resulted in a hardening of the determination to go through with the
marriage, the so-called 'Romeo and Juliet' effect noted by Driscoll
et al.(1972).

'They found out that he had lied about his age. They said he
couldn't keep a steady job. I had a row with my parents which
made me more determined to marry him!' (Pre-maritally pregnant
DW, aged 17 at marriage)

'My parents didn't approve of my wife. This made me want to marry
her all the more.' (DM, aged 24 at marriage)

Another interesting difference between the two survey groups in the
reasons given for parental opposition can be seen along the dimension
of responses which ranged from parental protectiveness, with expressed
concern about possible inheritable physical defects, through those
who wanted someone 'better' for their child (characterised by the
phrase 'they didn't think he was good enough for me'), to a jealous
possessiveness with its connotations of unwilling relinquishment to
a marriage partner. Among those who reported opposition, almost a
third (32%) of CMW gave replies which could loosely be described as
stemming from a concerned, even if possibly over-protective, parental
background, compared with only 10% of the DW. It is suggested that,
although there are obviously many aspects of over-involvement and
concern by the parents, it is likely that possessive parents will
attempt to provide a support system for their child, and possibly
thus reduce their initial hostility towards the marriage partner
once the wedding has taken place. Further research in depth is
needed to explore the various aspects of this suggestion.

The age of the brides and grooms at marriage was also the cause
of some opposition. Parental opposition allegedly due to the
youthful age of the couple was relatively frequently mentioned by
DM (21%) but relatively infrequently by DW (8%). The married group
showed no such marked difference: 16% of CMW and 19% of CMM reported
that their parents thought they were too young. A small number of
women mentioned their parents' concern over the age discrepancy
between them and their prospective spouse, the age difference in
such instances usually being about ten years. 12% of DW and 4% of
CMW claimed that the parental opposition was because of a concern
about a marriage precipitated by pregnancy.

It was mentioned earlier that reported opposition for the divorced
sub-sample was most pronounced for marriages in which the bride was
teenage or pregnant. It was also progressively more prevalent amongst
more recent marriage cohorts. Although the relative lack of reported
opposition to the marriage from earlier cohorts may have been due to
inadequate recall, it might also be reflecting the greater emphasis
in the past upon institutional marriage, with its predominantly
instrumental role. More recent marriages are perhaps more likely
to have been approached with more demanding expectations and a
greater emphasis upon the affective role of the marriage partner,
thus requiring more selectivity and hence more parental criticism
of partner choice.

Whatever the connection between opposition to a marriage and
subsequent divorce, opposition to the marriage, especially if it is
parental opposition, indicates that the courtship period with the
spouse will have been characterised by parent-child conflict, with
possible negative repercussions upon the couple's own relationship
during their courtship.

Informants who reported opposition to the marriage were also
asked about their relationship with those expressing opposition,
after the marriage had taken place, and the results of this are shown
in Table 27.

TABLE 27 The development of the relationship between the new marriage
partners and those who had opposed the marriage (Base: those reporting
opposition)

	All D n=226 %	All CM n=76 %
Reconciled and on good terms	26	49
Reconciled but no affection	26	9
Situation slowly improved	4	20
Situation initially better but soon deteriorated	7	3
Situation never improved	36	16
Can't remember	1	3

The survey data on marital opposition suggest first, that relative
to CM, D experienced more hostility to their marriage, and that this
hostility was more likely to continue after the wedding. Second,
that within D, the type of bride most likely to be in need of a
support system following marriage was the least likely to have been
offered such support from her family of origin. The marriages of
D teenage brides appear to have experienced the most sustained
opposition of all, with 43% of them (i.e. of those who experienced
opposition), claiming that the situation between them and those who
opposed the marriage never showed any improvement. The figure for
marriages of D pregnant brides was 33%, slightly less than for D as
a whole, which suggests that rather more reconciliation occurred for
this group.

PROBLEMS BETWEEN THE COUPLE DURING COURTSHIP

In the present study, there was interest in the extent of pre-marital
conflict between the couple themselves. Informants were asked
'During your courtship with your (former) husband/wife, did the two
of you ever have difficulties serious enough to cause you to split
up or to come to the point of splitting up?' Such difficulties were
reported by 29% of D and 19% of CM.
    It is recognised that the presence of serious pre-marital conflict
does not necessarily presage serious conflict within the marriage.
Indeed, it may be that confrontation and the resolution of difficulties in the pre-marital period is indicative less of future
strife than of deep involvement and commitment, and may possibly
augur an easier marital adjustment. What seemed to be the more
likely sources of future serious marital conflict were unresolved
areas of conflict in the courtship, which could recur during the
marriage, particularly at times of stress. Thus the number of times

a couple split up, or almost did so, during the courtship period, was taken as one possible index of on-going unresolved conflict.

Table 28 shows that D had more instances than CM of such pre-marital break-ups. More than twice as many D as CM claimed three or more (27% D : 11% CM) pre-marital break-ups with their eventual spouse.

TABLE 28   Number of pre-marital break-ups for informants reporting at least one break-up

Number of pre-marital break-ups	D n=149 %	CM n=106 %
1	49	70
2	23	18
3 or more	27	11
Don't know	1	1

D informants from the particularly 'high risk' categories of teenage brides and pregnant brides (see Chapter 5) reported the highest proportion of break-ups during their courtship (55% of the former and 54% of the latter who admitted to serious difficulties with their spouse claimed to have broken up more than once). Not surprisingly, perhaps, those D couples who had experienced pre-marital problems, and especially those who had 'broken-up' more than once, were more likely than those who had not to note an early start to their marital difficulties. This is shown in Table 29.

TABLE 29   The relationship between the number of pre-marital break-ups and the start of the marital problems which were to lead to divorce

Number of pre-marital break-ups	Divorced informants	
	Marital problems started by first anniversary n=192 %	Marital problems started after first anniversary n=328 %
None	67	74
1	13	15
2	8	5
3 or more	11	5
Don't know	Ø	Ø

The reasons given by informants for their pre-marital difficulties

The reasons for the pre-marital difficulties were culled from an open-ended question, and although inevitably restricted in scope, some interesting differences did emerge both between the divorced and the continuing married groups and also within the divorced group

itself. D, and particularly DW, were far more likely than CM to
cite negative aspects of the spouse's personality as the main reason
for the pre-marital difficulties (40% D : 15% of CM reporting pre-
marital difficulties).

'He was childish and stubborn.' (DW aged 19 at marriage)

'Because I found out he was a boaster.' (DW aged 19 at marriage)

'My husband was always telling lies. He told me my sister's
little boy had been run over and killed. I later found out this
was untrue. At the time he really upset my parents and me.' (DW
aged 17 at marriage)

'He was gambling. Once he borrowed money from me and didn't pay
it back. Also over the engagement ring, he didn't get one when
he promised.' (DW aged 21 at marriage)

Whilst it is clear that, in some cases, the pre-marital difficulties
stemmed from the immaturity of both partners, there is evidence
which suggests a category of DW for whom perceived basic negative
personality features in the spouse would be likely to persist into
marriage and be a constant source of trouble. There is also evidence
from the open-ended questions that some of the pre-marital difficulties were due to one partner's feeling pressurised by the other
into a marriage for which he or she was not yet ready. This seemed
particularly true for some DM.

'I think it was my attitude to life. I enjoyed going out with
the lads and deep down I felt I was being rushed into marriage.
She chased me really. She wanted me to spend all my time with
her.' (DM aged 21 at marriage)

'I wanted my freedom. I was too involved with sport and my
mates, and women didn't enter into this.' (DM aged 21 at marriage)

This notion of uneven pace in the relationship was not confined to
the men, but the differing perceptions of the same concept by the
women perhaps highlight the different, and possibly opposing ideas
about marriage which men and women may have and which need deeper
exploration. The two responses below from DW illustrate, albeit
superficially, this aspect:

'He said he wasn't ready to get married, and I said I was. He
wanted to call it off and I had had my dress made.' (DW aged 18
at marriage)

'I was undecided about marrying him. I just couldn't make up my
mind whether I wanted him or not.' (DW aged 21 at marriage)

This experience of uncertainty about the marriage was also claimed
by a substantial proportion of CMM and CMW, but the emphasis with
them, unlike for D, seemed to be upon mutual uncertainty rather than
upon one partner being unsure and the other being set upon marriage,

so that this shared uncertainty presented no threatening unevenness
of pace within the relationship.

Unfaithfulness was also cited, especially by D, as a cause of pre-
marital break-up, and was particularly mentioned by DM (22%).   D,
however, mentioned only their partner's infidelity as the sole cause
of the problems, whereas their own infidelity was cited by some CM
informants, illustrating perhaps a greater mutual recognition of
responsibility.

'He was double-crossing me, he was going out with other girls,
but denied it.' (DW aged 20 at marriage)

'She went out on several occasions with someone else.' (DM aged
22 at marriage)

'I found her with another chap.' (DM aged 20 at marriage)

'A fortnight before we were married I went out and had intercourse
with someone else, and I thought it was the end of C....(spouse)
but it was not.' (CMW aged 20 at marriage)

'I was flattered by the attentions of this other man.   He was a
manager and spent money on me, and bought me presents.   I just
came to my senses.' (CMW aged 23 at marriage)

There was obviously a degree of overlap between the two survey
groups, so that none of the reasons for the pre-marital difficulties
was exclusively related to either D or CM, although some reasons
were given mainly by D, e.g. the partner's violence or bad temper,
whereas others were cited predominantly by CM, e.g. restricted
opportunities for meeting due to the partner's absence or unsocial
working hours.   When the reasons were considered overall, the aspects
which tended to emerge as clues for further investigation were the
mutuality and the shared responsibility for problems more apparent
among CM, in contrast to the complaints against the partner more
usually found with D.   Furthermore, a sub-category of D seemed to
be delineated, which could be described as those who were not yet
ready for the sustained relationship of marriage, and for whom the
inevitable tensions of early marital adjustment and parenthood might
have been particularly difficult for them to come to terms with.

PREPARATION FOR MARRIAGE

The following factors are examined in this section: first, the
duration of the courtship, second, the presence of a formal engagement and third, the taking of a honeymoon.   These latter two items
are part of the ritual preparation for marriage which, it is thought
by many, facilitates the couple's transition from the single to the
married state by publicly formalising their future plans and so
reinforcing both their own and other's acceptance of their new
marital roles.   The presence of a church wedding, whilst undeniably
a ritualistic event, has deliberately not been included in this
section because of its possible overlap with religious affiliation.

The duration of the courtship

The duration of the courtship can be considered as one basic
indicator of readiness for marriage, since it describes the length
of time during which the partners could get to know one another.
Table 30 shows the length of the courtships of the survey groups
D and CM.

TABLE 30   The duration of the courtships of D and CM

	D n=520 %	CM n=570 %
Less than 6 months	6	1
6 but less than 12 months	14	7
1 year but less than 2 years	39	34
2 years +	41	57

This table shows that D tended to have shorter courtships than CM
and this tendency was also noted by Gorer (1971); in the present
study, 20% of D but only 8% of CM had known each other for less than
one year. Pregnant D brides knew their grooms the least time of all
(25% of them had known each other for less than a year, compared
with 9% of CM pregnant brides). This suggests that pre-marital
pregnancy may not have had the same consequences for D and CM. It
is likely to have had a vastly different impact in a longer courtship
where the partners knew each other well (and may indeed have found
pregnancy the reason for marrying then, rather than at a later date),
than for partners who were relative strangers to each other, and who
may have found an unexpected pregnancy a traumatic event forcing
them into a marriage for which they were unprepared, and which they
might not even ever have considered.
    It was apparent from some of the responses by D to the open-ended
questions, that marriage, and possibly even pre-marital pregnancy,
which would precipitate a marriage, were the consequences of a desire
to escape from an unhappy parental home, so that short courtships in
this context acquire a new significance, an indication of the haste
to leave the parental home. The following quotations illustrate this:

'I didn't have a very good home life so I wanted to get out of
it.' (Pre-maritally pregnant DW, aged 18 at marriage)

'Well, really why I wanted to get married was to get away from
my father, who I detested.' (DW, aged 20 at marriage)

'My father didn't want me to marry till I was 21. I decided to
become pregnant and force the issue.' (Pre-maritally pregnant
DW, aged 18 at marriage)

None the less, however much short courtships may reflect the urge
to change environments, they inevitably imply restricted knowledge
of one's partner and less knowledge of oneself in relation to that

person. In a marital environment in which there are clearly defined
normative roles and expectations, and where there is adequate social
education for such roles, the partners' lack of knowledge of one
another may matter relatively little. However, in our present society,
in which there is little formal or ritualistic preparation for
marriage and where there is a growing emphasis upon marriage as an
important source of personal happiness and fulfilment, adequate time
in which to get to know each other would seem to be very important,
since each marriage is so highly individualistic. This movement
away from the more rigid marriage of the past, with its unambiguous
expectations, to a more fluid relationship which requires a greater
awareness of personal needs, is likely to make the pre-marriage
period one of crucial importance for the development of the marriage
relationship.

Formal engagements and honeymoons

Another event which was taken in this study to reflect the extent
of preparation for marriage was the presence of a formal engagement.
It seemed probable that a courtship which was ritualised by an
engagement ring or celebratory party, with its connotations of
social advertisement of the commitment, might facilitate the transition from the single to the married state, with a consequent reduction in the number of areas of possible marital conflict. Substantially more CM apparently had a formal engagement (79% CM : 61% D).
This difference is not altogether surprising, since formal engagements are likely to be less common where there is pre-marital
pregnancy, and D were more likely than CM to be pre-maritally
pregnant.
    The taking of a honeymoon, like the presence of a formal engage-
ment, is part of ritualistic preparation for the new marital roles.
38% of D compared with 52% of CM went on a honeymoon. Teenage D
brides were far less likely than older D brides to have taken a
honeymoon (30%), and pre-maritally pregnant D brides were the least
likely to have done so (23%). The figure for CM pregnant brides
(27%) suggests, again not surprisingly, that pregnancy is very much
a limiting factor in the decision whether or not to take a honeymoon. A lack of money was the reason most frequently given for not
taking a honeymoon, and was particularly associated with D (56% of
D : 44% of CM who did not take a honeymoon). It is also interesting
that 25% of CM, but only 11% of D apparently had sufficient funds
for a honeymoon but preferred to spend this money on their homes.
    Although the ritual preparation for marriage is likely to have
consequences for early marital adjustment by affirming and pro-
claiming the individual's new marital status, the duration of the
courtship can, perhaps, be regarded as the underlying determining
factor of any ritual pathway to marriage. With very short courtships not much marital preparation of any kind, but especially
ritualistic preparation, seems likely.

SUMMARY

There were several ways in which the courtship periods of the
divorced in this study appeared markedly different from the courtship periods of those who were continuing with their marriages.
Marriages preceded by short courtships, or without any informal
engagement or honeymoon, and towards which there was strong opposition (usually parental) to the marriage taking place, all had an
increased risk of ending in divorce. Opposition to the marriage
was a particularly strong discriminant between D and CM, especially
in marriages where the bride was teenage or pre-maritally pregnant,
and in the former there was usually little experience of reconciliation after the wedding, so that it is likely that these brides, who
may have been relatively vulnerable, lacked an important source of
support.

   Additionally those marriages which ended in divorce appeared to
have had more break-ups in the relationship preceding marriage, and
these repeated conflicts may well have been unresolved and caused
later marital stress. They could also have been reflecting the
seeming unevenness of pace in the courtship relationship where one
partner only firmly wished to marry, a characteristic more frequently
displayed in marriages which ended in divorce.

Chapter 5

TWO HIGH RISK FACTORS: Teenage Marriages and Pre-marital Pregnancy

This chapter focuses upon the two features which individually are known to increase the risk of divorce and, when present together, are likely to compound this risk considerably. Each is discussed in turn, both in relation to the present survey data and also with reference to other research findings.

TEENAGE MARRIAGES

It is evident from the Registrar General's returns that teenage brides and grooms are over-represented in the divorce courts (HMSO, 1967). This finding also applies to the USA (Glick, 1957) and the marriages of a teenage bride or groom, but especially those of teenage partners, appear considerably more likely to end in divorce.

Tables 31, 32 and 33 show the survey data for the proportions of teenage brides, teenage grooms and teenage partners, and demonstrate a striking difference between D and CM.

TABLE 31   Percentage of D and CM marriages in which the bride was under 20 years of age

	D n=520 %	CM n=570 %
Bride under 20	44	28
Bride aged 20 or over	56	72

TABLE 32   Percentage of D and CM marriages in which the groom was under 20 years of age

	D n=520 %	CM n=570 %
Groom under 20	16	7
Groom aged 20 or over	84	93

TABLE 33   Percentage of D and CM marriages in which both partners were under 20 years of age at marriage

	D n=520 %	CM n=570 %
Both under 20	13	7
Both aged 20 or over	53	70
One under 20	34	23

Interpretations of this association between teenage marriage and divorce are problematic, although one interpretation, namely that the association may largely be reflecting the increment of risk due to longer durations of marriage has been discounted by Monahan (1953).

Many observers point to the possibility that early marriage will tend to be unstable because the young spouses are themselves changing at a faster rate than are older partners. For instance, Rutter and Madge (1976) noted that the predisposition of teenagers to marital breakdown may well in part stem from the likelihood that, since the individual partners are still developing emotionally, they may develop at different rates and in different directions after marriage. In a similar vein, Dominian (1968) believes that the wider significance of the marital relationship, beyond the physical component, is less capable of developing in teenage marriages. Also, Winch (1971) notes that adolescence in Western societies seems to be a period during which personality is in a state of flux, so much so in fact, that the kind of mate teenagers would most wish to choose may actually vary from one year to the next.

There is, however, conflicting evidence from the very small amount of research that has been carried out on the question of the emotional maturity of teenage marriage partners. Two studies (Martinson, 1955; Moss and Gingles, 1959), demonstrated that girls who married earlier appeared less stable on personality tests, and had less satisfactory relationships with their parents than did girls who did not marry early. There was, however, no such difference in the data from Burchinal's study (1959).

Two other factors have to be borne in mind when considering the implications of early marriage; first that there is an over-representation of pre-marital pregnancies in teenage marriages and second, that there is also an over-representation in teenage marriages of social class V, the unskilled manual group; both of these factors in themselves are known to increase the risk of divorce, and the disentanglement of which of them may actually be the intervening variable is problematic.

Teenage marriage and pre-marital pregnancy

According to Christensen and Rubinstein (1956), pre-marital pregnancy seems to be part of a 'divorce-producing syndrome' and Winch (1971) suggests that where pregnancy forces a choice between abortion, single parenthood and marriage, and when marriage is the course taken, it is probable that such marriages will contain an

over-representation of poorly matched couples. Table 34 shows the
survey findings regarding pre-marital pregnancy (Pmp) and age of
the bride at marriage.

TABLE 34   Teenage brides and pre-marital pregnancy

	All D n=520 %	D under 20 n=230 %	D 20 yrs or over n=290 %	All CM n=570 %	CM under 20 n=161 %	CM 20 yrs or over n=409 %
Pmp	32	47	21	19	30	14
No Pmp	68	53	79	81	70	86

It can be seen from Table 34 that the marriages of teenage brides,
whether D or CM, were more than twice as likely to include pre-
marital pregnancy than were the marriages of older brides. Marriages
involving pre-marital pregnancy are discussed in more detail later
in this chapter.

Teenage marriage and social class

Chester in the UK (1972b) and Winch and Greer in the USA (1964) have
suggested that the association between teenage marriage and divorce
may actually be reflecting a social class factor. It has been
clearly shown in the USA (Udry, 1966), that divorce is inversely
related to social class, with the lower the social class the greater
the risk of divorce. Although this clear inverse relationship is
not apparent in the UK, social class V, as has already been mentioned,
has, in this country, been shown to be the most divorce prone
(Gibson, 1974). It is known that the working classes tend to marry
earlier than the middle classes (General Register Office, 1965), and
hence one would perhaps expect relatively more teenage brides in the
overall divorced population.
    The survey data on teenage brides was analysed by social class
and the results are shown in Table 35.

TABLE 35   Percentage of brides from social classes II-V* who were
under 20 years of age

	II n=72 %	IIIn-m n=38 %	IIIm n=224 %	IV n=85 %	V n=50 %
D – Under 20	38	32	43	52	58
D – 20 or over	62	68	57	48	42
	n=88 %	n=41 %	n=284 %	n=86 %	n=53 %
CM – Under 20	27	22	30	28	36
CM – 20 or over	73	78	70	72	64

* Social class I has not been included since the numbers were too
  small (18 for CM, 1 for D)

What is particularly interesting in Table 35 is the difference
between the prevalence of teenage brides in D and CM marriages of
the *same* social class. It can be seen that D from social classes
II, IIIn-m and IIIm were far more similar to CM from social classes
II, IIIn-m and IIIm in terms of the proportions of teenage brides
than were D and CM from social classes IV and V; D marriages from
social classes IV and V were far more likely than CM marriages from
these two social classes to include a teenage bride. Although Table
35 demonstrates that survey D brides from all social classes marry
younger than their CM counterparts, it is apparent that the
differences between D and CM are most marked for social classes IV
and V; since the survey data about CM are taken to represent the
norms for the social classes, the data on social class and the
bride's age at marriage indicate that D of these social classes
appear to be relatively atypical.

It was also evident from the survey data that CM marriages from
the five social classes were more or less equally as likely to have
included a pregnant teenage bride (9% II; 10% IIIn-m; 11% IIIm;
12% IV; 10% V), but this was not the case for D, for D marriages
from social classes IV and V were far more likely than were other
D social classes to have included a pregnant teenage bride (26% II;
14% IIIn-m; 28% IIIm; 37% IV; 34% V). The data therefore suggest
that, whilst the combination of teenage marriage and pre-marital
pregnancy generally does not appear to have a social class bias (as
evidenced by CM), when this combination is present in lower social
classes, then it becomes a high risk combination. This may be
because the marriages of those in the lowest social classes, perhaps
generally more stressful because of their lower incomes, and less
adequate housing, cannot accommodate the tensions in the marital
relationship which result when youth and pre-marital pregnancy are
combined.

Other features associated with teenage marriages

Apart from pre-marital pregnancy and social class, certain other
features distinguished survey teenage marriages from those of
informants who married when older, and these data point to the
greater probability both of underlying tensions in the childhood or
adolescence of informants in teenage marriages, and of relatively
greater environing disadvantage during such marriages. For instance,
those informants (whether D or CM), who were members of teenage
marriages, were slightly more likely than those who married later,
to have been hospitalised whilst growing up, or to have experienced
fears or emotional difficulties during their adolescence. The
relevance of such aspects of health during childhood and adolescence
has been discussed in Chapter 2, in which it was suggested that such
items, if present, can be considered as indicative of increased risk
of stress whilst growing up and hence of a greater risk of impeded
emotional development which may have implications for emotional
maturity at marriage.

It was also evident from the survey data that informants who were
teenagers at marriage were slightly more likely than those who married
when older, to have had either unhappily married parents or to have

75   Chapter 5

had divorced or separated parents. This can be seen in Table 36
and gives some support to the view that early marriage in the offspring may, in some instances, be precipitated by unhappy or broken
parental marriages.

TABLE 36   Informants' age at marriage and the prevalence of parental
marital unhappiness (evidenced either by divorce, separation or the
opinion of informants from intact homes)

	Age at marriage			
	Under 20 yrs		20 yrs or over	
	D	CM	D	CM
	n=236	n=180	n=284	n=390
	%	%	%	%
Parents unhappy	22	16	13	9
Parents happy	67	71	75	79
Inadequate recollection	11	13	12	12

Whereas the data on health and parental marital status indicate that
D informants who were under 20 years at marriage appear to be similar
to (although more disadvantaged than) their CM counterparts, there
was a striking difference between this D sub-group and all other
informants (including teenage CM informants) with regard to parental
preference. It can be seen in Table 37 that teenage D informants,
of whom the vast majority were DW, were the most likely to express
a preference for their father. The interpretation of this difference
between teenage D and other informants is problematic, but it may be
that, in the context of youthful marriage in particular, a strong
father-attachment may be a source of marital difficulties; first,
because it could be evidence of a continuing need for a father
figure and a corresponding inability to assume marital roles, and
second, it may lead to dissatisfaction, if the husband does not
compare favourably with the bride's father.

TABLE 37   Informants' age at marriage and their parental preference

	Under 20 yrs		20 yrs or over	
	D	CM	D	CM
	n=236	n=180	n=284	n=390
	%	%	%	%
Preferred father	24	14	14	14
Preferred mother	28	33	26	31
No preference	39	42	47	47
Inadequate recollection	9	11	12	8

It was also evident from the survey data that teenage marriages,
whether D or CM, experienced more opposition than did those of
informants who married at a later age, but it was D teenage marriages
which experienced by far the most opposition (53% D under 20 experienced strong opposition to their marriages, compared with 35% D over
20, 19% CM under 20, 11% CM over 20). More importantly, perhaps,

after marriage, D under 20 were the least likely to be on good terms
with those who opposed their marriage, whereas CM under 20 were the
most likely to be so. The exact nature of the relationship between
the opposing parties prior to the prospect of marriage is not known,
but the survey data does suggest far less hardening of parental
attitudes towards CM under 20 than was the case for D under 20,
which possibly indicates relatively better parent-child relationships in general for CM under 20. Whatever the quality of the
parent-child relationship, however, it is apparent that D under 20
were far less likely than CM under 20 (or any other D age group), to
have had access to a familial support system in the early period of
their marriages.

Furthermore, with regard to the circumstances of their marriages,
it is evident that there was a greater probability of stress
resulting from environing circumstances within the marriages of
teenage informants, and this likelihood was greatest for D under 20.
For example, with regard to housing experiences: informants in
teenage marriages moved home more often in the early years of
marriage; they were less likely to be in self-contained accommodation,
were therefore more likely to be sharing their accommodation and
were more likely to report that there was friction between them and
the people with whom they were sharing – this latter feature being
particularly marked for D under 20. In general, the accommodation
pattern for teenage marriage partners indicated that their housing,
especially in the first year, appeared to be less independent and
also relatively unstable, in that there was a tendency for more
frequent moves from shared to shared accommodation, this tendency
being most apparent for D under 20.

Another feature of teenage marriages which emerged from the
survey data on parenthood, was the greater fertility of these
marriages. Teenage brides had relatively more children than did
older brides which may, to some extent, be reflecting higher proba-
bilities of conception due to longer duration of marriage. However,
they had children both earlier in their marriage and with shorter
intervals between pregnancies. There are no data about any contraceptive practices of survey informants, so that it is not known
whether or not older brides may have been more successful at avoiding
pregnancy or less successful at achieving it. What is apparent,
however, is that the marital environment into which the children of
teenage brides, and particularly those of D under 20, were born,
was relatively less likely to show the hall-marks of planning. This
is evidenced by several features; first, teenage parents were more
likely themselves to be still dependent upon their own parents for
a home; second, the work record of the husband was relatively
erratic (more job changes, more unemployment), which is perhaps
indicative of a less secure financial situation; and third, the
courtships of teenage brides, in particular D under 20, were
relatively shorter and lacking in features of ritual preparation,
which, together with their greater prevalence of pre-marital
pregnancy, is suggestive of their having had a relatively unplanned
pathway to marriage.

PRE-MARITAL PREGNANCY

According to Gibson (1974) the Registrar General's returns show that
the marriages of pregnant brides are more at risk than those of non-
pregnant brides and Christensen and Meissner (1953) noted that, in
the USA, marriages in which the bride was pregnant had twice the
rate of divorce as that found amongst wives who conceived after
marriage. Amongst survey marriages, one in three D marriages
compared with one in five CM marriages involved pre-marital
pregnancy (Pmp).

It is generally accepted that pre-marital pregnancy greatly
increases the probability of eventual marital dissolution (Monahan,
1960; Lowrie, 1965). Coombs and Zumeta (1970) noted that, of
couples who conceived pre-maritally, 41% were no longer together
five years later, compared with 18% who had not conceived pre-
maritally.

There are several reasons why pre-marital pregnancy may predispose
a couple to divorce. According to Christensen (1960), pre-marital
pregnancy may cut short the process of preparing for married life.
Couples who marry precipitately may not be ready for the responsibilities of marriage and may not be particularly committed to their
spouse. Havighurst (1961) and Winch and Greer (1964) found that pre-
maritally pregnant couples frequently lacked kinship support. A
further disadvantage which a precipitated marriage may experience is
likely to be an economic one, since there may be no benefits of
accumulated savings, nor the contribution of a wife's income in the
case of a pregnant bride. There is also evidence to suggest that
the abrupt introduction of a child can prevent the formation of
solidarity between partners that might otherwise develop during the
early years of marriage (Pohlman, 1969).

In an attempt to disentangle the relationship between pre-marital
pregnancy and divorce, Furstenberg (1976) found that one connecting
link was the weak economic position of the father of the pre-
maritally conceived child. He found no confirmation of the possibility of different cultural standards amongst the Pmp, nor of the
negative contribution of what he describes as 'accelerated family
building'. Furstenberg's data did, however, confirm that both the
disruption to the courtship process caused by Pmp and the economic
disadvantage experienced by such marriages, tended to account for
the high rates of disintegration of Pmp marriages.

Survey marriages which had a pre-marital pregnancy

The reports of D concerning the start of their marital problems,
indicated that these difficulties started sooner in D Pmp marriages,
for 44% of these, compared with 33% of D NoPmp, claimed that their
serious marital problems, which were to lead them to divorce, started
in the first year of marriage. There were certainly features of D
Pmp marriages which indicated a greater probability of stress
developing within these marital relationships, than within other
survey marriages. First, there is the evidence from the work record
of the husband; the husbands of D Pmp were more likely than those
who were not pregnant at marriage to have been unemployed during the

early years of marriage, but there was, however, no significant
difference between the two CM groups. Additionally, D Pmp husbands
changed employment more frequently than D NoPmp husbands, but here
again, there was little difference between CM marriages involving
Pmp and those which did not.

There were many differences between D and CM marriages which had
a pre-marital pregnancy and the survey data suggested that pre-marital
pregnancy may not have had the same impact upon the early marital
environment of CM Pmp compared with that of D Pmp. In particular,
the marital relationship of CM Pmp appears, relative to D Pmp, both
to have developed from a sounder base and to have begun in an
atmosphere more helpful for marital adjustment. For example, D
Pmp had far shorter courtships than their CM counterparts (25% D Pmp
had courtships lasting less than one year, in contrast to 18% D
NoPmp; 9% CM Pmp; 9% CM NoPmp). Second, marital opposition appeared
to be unrelated to pre-marital pregnancy for CM but disproportion-
ately associated with it for D (54% D Pmp experienced strong
opposition to their marriages compared with 39% D NoPmp; 15% CM Pmp
and 13% CM NoPmp). Third, D Pmp were the most likely to have had
serious pre-marital problems with their spouses (pre-marital problems
were evident for 33% D Pmp; 27% D NoPmp; 16% CM Pmp; 19% CM NoPmp).

It was also evident from the survey data that CM pregnant brides
came from smaller families of origin than did D pregnant brides.
The relatively larger families of origin of D pregnant brides may
have meant that they received relatively less attention at home,
which may in turn have made them less close to their parents, and
therefore less able to draw upon them for support during their
marriage. Also, the relatively larger family sizes of D pregnant
brides may have made them more eager to marry in order to leave home,
and therefore less careful in their choice of mate. The size of the
family of origin of pregnant brides is shown in Table 38.

TABLE 38   Pre-marital pregnancy and the size of the family of origin

| Number of children | DW | | CMW | |
	PmP n=128 %	NoPmp n=208 %	Pmp n=61 %	NoPmp n=310 %
1	11	15	25	14
2	18	24	16	22
3	22	14	21	18
4 or more	49	47	38	46

Another important difference between D Pmp and CM Pmp was in the
prevalence of post-puerperal depression. Although it is not known
to what extent post-puerperal depression may have either a physiological or a psychological origin, nor can it be presently ascertained
to what extent factors within the environment may influence or even
cause the condition, when a wife is post-puerperally depressed there
is an increased risk of stress developing within the marital relationship. It is interesting that CM Pmp (who had relatively more
children than those in the other three sub-groups), had the shortest
overall duration of post-puerperal depression, whereas D Pmp had the

longest duration. If, as some workers believe, post-puerperal
depression tends to arise because of stress (irrespective of any
additional stress its presence may create), then the marriages of
CM Pmp in contrast to D Pmp, would appear to have contained
relatively low levels of underlying tension.

Although there is evidence from the survey data which suggests
that D Pmp and CM Pmp were in some ways very different, there
were, however, three survey variables which demonstrated the
relative similarity of D and CM individuals who conceived pre-
maritally. First, and not surprisingly, perhaps, informants in
marriages involving pre-marital pregnancy (whether D or CM), were
different from their counterparts who did not conceive pre-maritally,
both with regard to aspects of their pre-marital and extra-marital
sexual experience, and also in their attitudes towards the sexual
side of marriage. Informants in Pmp marriages were slightly more
likely than their non-Pmp counterparts to have had a pre-marital
sexual partner (other than their spouse), or to have had an extra-
marital affair. Also, they were, relative to their counterparts
who were not Pmp, slightly more likely to have been immediately
satisfied with the sexual side of their marriage.

Another difference between individuals in Pmp marriages and those
who were not, was in the pattern of their religious affiliations.
Pmp informants were less likely than their non-Pmp counterparts to
claim that they had a religion at marriage (63% of D Pmp; 68% CM
Pmp; 74% D No Pmp; 79% CM No Pmp), and were more likely to have
ceased to follow the religion into which they were born. Given
this, churchgoing during marriage was, not surprisingly, less
prevalent amongst Pmp informants (27% D Pmp; 28% CM Pmp; 32% D No
Pmp; 48% CM No Pmp) but especially any churchgoing by both spouses
(8% D Pmp; 17% CM Pmp; 15% D No Pmp; 31% CM No Pmp).

Informants in D and CM Pmp marriages also shared some socio-
economic characteristics. They were slightly more likely than their
non-Pmp counterparts to be working class (80% D Pmp; 77% CM Pmp;
72% D No Pmp; 71% CM No Pmp), and less likely to have had a selective
education (11% D Pmp; 11% CM Pmp; 14% D No Pmp; 20% CM No Pmp).
These factors may have been likely, in part, to account for pre-marital
conception, either because they are reflecting less awareness of
contraceptive methods (Cartwright, 1976), or because they are indicative of greater social acceptance of pre-marital pregnancy amongst
lower social classes.

SUMMARY

Teenage marriages

Marriages in which one or both partners is teenage are widely
regarded as being more at risk, and in the present study more
marriages of the divorced group had teenage partners. A variety of
inter-related factors appear to distinguish these partners from those
who married at a later age, and it is problematic to locate the
dominant contributor to the divorce proneness of teenage marriages
or define the precise relationship between them.

In this study, as elsewhere, teenage marriages tended to include

a pre-marital pregnancy, and to be working-class, and when these
two features were in combination, the marriage seemed particularly
likely to founder. Additionally, the overall background of the
courtships and marriages of teenage brides and grooms, though
especially those who divorced, showed evidence of an increased
risk of both personal and environing stresses. However, two factors
were present in teenage marriages within the continuing married
group, which may have mitigated their vulnerability and to some
extent protected them against divorce. They, in sharp contrast to
the teenage marriages in the divorced group, experienced relatively
strong parental support both prior to and during marriage.
Additionally, teenage brides in marriages which did not break down
were more attached to their mothers than their fathers when they
were young, which could indicate both a stronger maternal identification and more maternal support within the marriage. Correla-
tively more teenage brides who divorced described a preference for
their fathers in their formative years, and this strong attachment
may have implications for marital stress and be a source of marital
difficulty.

Pre-marital pregnancy

Many studies have shown that a pre-marital pregnancy greatly
increases the risk of divorce; several factors which are associated
with pre-marital pregnancy may be causally influencing this increased
risk, although the relative importance of each factor is not, at
present, known. For example it appears that marriages precipitated
by pregnancy tend also to have had a short courtship, to lack
kinship support, and to be economically disadvantaged.
    In this study pre-maritally pregnant marriages which ended in
divorce were similar to CM Pmp marriages but different from marriages
not involving a pre-marital pregnancy on three variables; first, in
having had a greater tendency to sexual experience (apart from any
with spouse) both prior to and during marriage; second, in having had
less prevalance of religious allegiance whilst growing up and also
during marriage; third, they shared certain socio-economic characteristics such as social class of origin and type of education. However,
there were many features of pre-maritally pregnant marriages which
ended in divorce which were not shared by pre-maritally pregnant
marriages which appeared to be stable. In particular, courtship
disruption, lack of kinship support and other personal and environing
stresses both prior to and during marriage seemed far more typical
of pre-maritally pregnant marriages which had ended in divorce and,
overall, the marital relationship of stable pre-maritally pregnant
marriages seemed both to have developed from a sounder base and to
have begun in an atmosphere more conducive to marital adjustment.

Chapter 6

HOUSING DURING MARRIAGE

It has been shown by Wedge and Prosser (1973) that dissatisfaction with housing is not strongly linked with the objective quality of the housing occupied. The extent to which the objective quality of the marital accommodation may constitute a stress within the marriage, will be influenced by the couple's own expectations about housing, and these expectations are likely to result from cultural and peer group influences, as well as revealing individual preference or tolerance for certain types of housing. Nevertheless, whilst acknowledging that the type of housing regarded by couples as acceptable or desirable may vary, it is a clinical impression that certain kinds of accommodation may be intrinsically stressful. In particular, accommodation which does not allow a couple the privacy to develop their marital relationship appears, clinically, to have relevance to the inability to form a firmly based marital relationship, and in the survey, marital difficulties tended to start earlier for those without 'a place of their own' at marriage (38% of D without a place of their own, 30% of D with a place of their own, claimed that their difficulties started in the first year).

This impression, that privacy will tend to ease marital adjustment and generate marital solidarity, implicitly affirms the importance of the affective side of marriage and, in a sense, posits the companionate marriage as a more 'ideal' type with its emphasis upon interpersonal involvement between the spouses. There is, however, a wider sense in which privacy may be said to be important in reducing the risk of marital stress, namely, that it allows the individual more control over his immediate environment, both in spatial terms and in the freedom to organise the domestic patterns of his own life.

At the planning stage of the survey, the main interest was to discover whether there were any objective types of housing or patterns of accommodation which were more typical of D rather than of CM. Informants were asked only about certain objective characteristics of their housing history and not about their subjective responses to that accommodation or its effect upon their marriage. With hindsight, this emphasis upon the objective characteristics is regrettable, since it limits considerably any overall interpretation of the significance of informants' housing histories in relation to marital stress.

Informants were asked to describe the following characteristics
of each of the accommodations they occupied during their marriage:
first, was it somewhere they were buying, renting or living in rent-
free; second, was it an entire house, a self-contained flat, one
room, caravan, etc; third, was it fully furnished, partly furnished,
or unfurnished; fourth, were they living there alone or were they
sharing; fifth, if they shared, with whom, and was there any
friction or trouble between the parties sharing.

At the analysis stage three types of housing were differentiated;
these three types were similar to those used by Pierce (1963).

Type I   -   *Independent living* in an unfurnished, self-contained
              entire house or self-contained flat.

Type II   -   *Semi-independent living* in a partly or fully
              furnished entire house or self-contained flat.

Type III -   *Dependent living* in a furnished room, rooms or non-
              self-contained flat.

Type III accommodation may be largely equated with that category of
housing regarded as intrinsically unhelpful for marital adjustment
and, therefore, more associated with D than with CM, especially in
the first year of marriage. This expectation was borne out amongst
survey informants: 54% D but 40% CM went into Type III housing
immediately following their marriages, and after one year of marriage
43% D but 32% CM were still without 'a place of their own'.

This discrepancy between D and CM continued to be shown during the
early years of marriage, though to a diminishing extent, until, by
the sixth anniversary, D and CM were occupying broadly similar types
of housing and were more or less equally likely (83% D : 85% CM) to
be in independent accommodation. However, during the first five
years of marriage some two-fifths of D informants had ceased to
cohabit and 60% of these had been living in Type III housing during
their first year of marriage.

There is some evidence from the survey data which suggests that
the greater tendency of D towards more disadvantaged housing cannot
largely be attributed to the economic disadvantage which is likely
to be associated with either a teenage marriage, a pre-marital
pregnancy or a manual worker background; CM informants who were
members of either teenage marriages, pre-maritally pregnant marriages
or from a manual worker background were consistently less likely than
those CM informants without these characteristics, to have a place
of their own, either at marriage, or in the early period of their
marriages. However, in contrast, the differences between D teenage
marriages compared with older D, between pre-maritally pregnant D
and D marriages not involving pre-marital pregnancy, between D with
manual worker backgrounds and those with non-manual worker backgrounds,
with regard to independent housing in the early stages of their
marriages were slight or even non-existent (see Appendix III). The
survey data also showed that home-ownership at marriage, whilst less
typical of D generally, was relatively less likely for D non-manual,
in relation to their CM counterparts, for they fell considerably
below what may be considered typical of this broad social class group

(as defined by the husband's occupation at marriage). This can be seen in Table 39.

TABLE 39   Home-ownership immediately following the wedding related to social class

	D		CM	
	Non-manual n=111 %	Manual n=409 %	Non-manual n=147 %	Manual n=423 %
Buying	24	12	39	18
Renting	64	74	49	65
Rent-free	12	14	11	17

SHARED HOUSING AND FRICTION

Housing was regarded as shared if any facilities, whether bathroom, kitchen or living quarters, were not for the sole use of informants or their children. Although Type III housing, the so-called dependent living, is frequently shared, this is not necessarily always the case. Similarly, in Type I or Type II accommodation, the owners or renters are usually the sole occupants, but in the present survey there were a few instances of family or lodgers living in the new marriage partner's own home.

For each accommodation informants were asked, 'were you and your (former) husband/wife living there alone or were you sharing with anyone - not counting your own children?' If sharing was reported then, 'and was there any friction or trouble between you and them during the time that you and your husband/wife shared the accommodation with these people?' Finally, the identity of the party or parties with whom the accommodation was shared was established.

Whilst D were slightly more likely than CM to share their housing, both at marriage (59% D : 51% CM), and by the first anniversary (40% D : 34% CM), (a feature which, in itself, may be taken to indicate a greater risk of stress during the early phase of marital adjustment), they were considerably more likely than CM to have been in actual conflict with the shared party. For instance, of those who shared their first marital home, 50% of D but only 27% CM reported friction between them and those with whom they shared; 22% D, compared with 9% CM claimed that there had been a lot of friction. A similar overall pattern of increased risk of stress for D emerged from the data on the early housing experiences of D and CM, both with regard to the prevalence of sharing and in relation to the extent of any friction between the sharing parties (see Appendix III).

HOUSING AND PRE-MARITAL PREGNANCY

Those who were pre-maritally pregnant may be regarded as a particularly vulnerable group for whom housing might be of special importance. Whilst there was little difference between D Pmp and CM Pmp in terms of the prevalence of independent accommodation (33% D, 30% CM had a place of their own on marriage), there were some differences between them with regard to the kind of independent accommodation occupied. For instance, CM Pmp were more likely to be living in a house (25% CM : 14% D), whereas D Pmp were more likely to be occupying a flat or in some instances, a caravan (19% D : 5% CM).

Whilst D and CM who were pre-maritally pregnant appeared similarly at risk to stress when their overall prevalences of sharing were considered, it was evident that CM Pmp had less overt stress than D Pmp from sharing, for 28% D Pmp, but 11% CM Pmp who shared reported a lot of friction, and 41% D Pmp, but 68% CM Pmp reported no friction at all.

In view of the extent of this friction, it is perhaps hardly surprising that substantial percentages of both groups, but especially D Pmp, stayed only a relatively short time in their first accommodation, with 16% CM Pmp but as many as 28% D Pmp moving before six months was up (i.e. when the birth of the child was probably imminent, or had just occurred). However, considered overall, CM Pmp tended to display a greater stability of accommodation, for approaching one half of them (47% CM Pmp) stayed in their initial marital accommodation two years or more, compared with only 27% D Pmp.

HOUSING MOVES

There is evidence from the survey to suggest that CM tended to have had a more stable history of marital accommodation than did D, particularly in their first year of marriage. Substantially fewer D remained in the same accommodation during the first year and those D who did move, moved more frequently. This can be seen in Table 40.

TABLE 40   Number of different accommodations reported by the first anniversary

	D n=478 %	CM n=564 %
One accommodation only throughout	56	65
Two accommodations	31	30
Three accommodations	10	4
Four accommodations or more	3	1
Don't know/can't remember	Ø	1

THE REASONS FOR MOVING HOME

Since the initial accommodation after marriage may well be a temporary measure only, perhaps enabling the newly-wed couple to save up for, or negotiate, more suitable longer-term accommodation (which may be bought or rented), it thus may be that a move to a second accommodation within the first year may be part of a careful plan, rather than a hasty change made necessary by unsatisfactory

initial living conditions. Analysis of the changes in accommodation concentrated upon women of the survey, for, in general, where
one lives usually impinges more upon women than men, and, additionally, the contrast between DW and CMW in terms of housing experiences
appeared to be more marked than among the men. When the data from
women who changed their accommodation at least once during the first
year was examined, some differences emerged. For instance, it
appeared to be more likely for CMW than for DW that the first move
would be from initial sharing with parents or relatives to an
independent existence. Some 42% of CMW who had shared in this way
at the start of their marriage, compared with only 11% of DW, left
in order to 'have a place of our own'. However, this difference is
not found when those who moved from sharing with a relative to
renting a property are compared, for similar percentages (23% DW
and 21% CMW) ceased sharing in order to rent a house or flat on
their own.

Further investigation of the reasons which were given for moving
home showed certain broad similarities between D and CM, although
upon more detailed examination of the data from the open-ended
questions some interesting differences emerged. For instance, the
most frequently given reasons for moving in the first year by both
groups were 'because of husband's job' or wanting an improved
accommodation more in keeping with their requirements (e.g. 'bigger
house'; 'better area'). However, as was found with courtship
behaviour, CMW overall seemed more likely than DW to show evidence
of planning and foresight in their housing pattern, irrespective of
whether their move was to buying or renting a property. Typical of
such responses amongst the CMW were:

'Living with my parents was just temporary accommodation until
we got our own house.'

'We moved because our own house was now ready for occupation.'

'We wanted our own house - we'd saved hard.'

'Because of living with my mother-in-law - so crowded - we got
our own council house.'

It appeared, in contrast, that DW who had shared with parents or
relatives and who moved to a place of their own, showed less
evidence of such forward planning in their arrangements. Many of
their moves seemed determined more by problems arising out of their
shared accommodation rather than through any positive decision to
move. Some CMW had indeed also experienced difficulties in sharing,
but these were, where cited by them as the reason for moving, more
often described in fairly muted language, such as 'relative trouble'
or 'family arguments' or 'I just didn't get on with my mother-in-
law', whereas DW, in contrast, were more likely to describe their
friction in words which suggested a stronger and more persistent
discord:

'His mother finally told us to get out.'

'.. trouble all the time, my husband wouldn't work and his
mother gave him money.'

'My parents turned my husband out on doctor's advice, causing
my mother to be ill with a nervous breakdown.'

When the housing history overall was considered, but particularly
that of the first year of marriage, the response from DW suggested
that they were less likely than CMW to be in command of their
choices, and more at the mercy of external events. This is highlighted by the experience of eviction, or having to leave the
accommodation, an event mentioned by several DW, and described as
'being in arrears with the rent and had to leave'; 'asked to leave -
his drinking', and 'we had to get out - children weren't allowed in
the flat' (this last from a Pmp DW). Such an experience of forced
or precipitated departure was only once mentioned by CMW, which
perhaps suggests that, in some measure, their housing experiences
in the first year were more ordered, or at least less traumatic,
than were those for DW.

Some other distinct differences did emerge with regard to the
accommodation changes of D relative to CM. It was apparent that CM
more often seemed to change their accommodation in line with what
they considered an improvement-flow, that is to say, they might
start by sharing and move to non-sharing (rented or home ownership),
with subsequent moves due to reasons of husband's job requirements,
or more suitable or better quality housing. D as a whole, on the
other hand, seemed less likely to display this particular pattern,
and conversely they exhibited certain types of housing experience
which were much less often found among CM informants. One pattern
which, in any marked form, was almost exclusively found in the
divorced group, was that of oscillations between various sets of
relatives, which we have termed 'shuttlecock accommodation'. During
the first year this shift from one set of relatives immediately to
another (most commonly from one set of parents to the opposite
parents), was found in as many as 14% of DW who moved, but in as few
as 5% of CMW, and although such 'shuttlecock accommodation' was very
much a rare occurrence in the CM group after the first year, this
was not so in the divorced group. The following D early housing
histories are perhaps extreme illustrations, but they portray one
particular pattern of stress and uncertainty posed by accommodation
difficulties for some of the divorced group, who thus had to grapple
with problems which were rarely faced by the CM. First, an 18-year-
old DW married to a lorry driver, who spent the first six months
with her parents but 'moved because of trouble with mum'; then spent
four months with his friends but was forced to leave 'because his
friends caused trouble'; this was followed by eight months with his
parents, ended 'because we wanted a home of our own'. Second, a
17-year-old DW Pmp married to a shoemaker, who spent the first three
months of married life with his parents then 'his mother didn't
speak and she told us to get out'. After this, one year with her
parents which ended because 'my mother didn't get on with my husband'.
Third, a DW Pmp married to a grinder at a colour mill, who went to
live with her aunt after the marriage but this only lasted six months
since 'she got a council house and we had to leave'. Then two months

with his mother, but 'his father made us go' and then two months
with her step-mother which ended because 'my step-mother couldn't
stand it any more'. Fourth, an 18-year-old DW Pmp married to a
miner, where the first year was spent with her parents but 'my
husband and mother didn't get on'. They then moved to the husband's
parents but after only one month 'his mother didn't want us to stay
there'. They next spent eighteen months with an old lady until 'I
was having another baby, and we got a council flat'.

SUMMARY

Disadvantaged housing, especially in the early years of marriage,
appeared to be more typical of those who divorced rather than of
those who were continuing with their marriages, as did friction
between the parties in shared accommodation. In general in this
study, marital stability and a stable accommodation history in the
first year of marriage tended to go hand in hand. When housing
patterns were considered overall those who were continuing with
their marriages tended to change their accommodation less frequently,
and when a move was made it was more through choice and represented
a planned move and an overall improvement in their housing. In
contrast, those housing problems which arose because of difficulties
with landlords or neighbours and which tended to result in a
haphazard or even forced move, rather than one which reflected more
conscious planning, were almost exclusively associated with marriages
which ended in divorce.

Chapter 7

THE ARRIVAL OF CHILDREN

Although the precise reasons for any couple having children may vary, there appears to be a prevailing generalised belief that children are essential to married life, to the extent that in one study (Busfield and Paddon, 1977), having children emerged as the major, if not the only reason, for getting married. In the light of such strong normative pressures towards parenthood, the vast majority of any decisions about it would seem more likely to be concerned with the timing of the births of children, rather than with the advantages or disadvantages of having children at all.

According to Winch (1971) the burden of evidence tends to support the conclusion that children are, on the whole, perceived as 'sources of gratification', since it does appear that the majority of parents do not regret having had children. For instance Freedman et al. (1959) found that only 1% of people interviewed would prefer not to have had children if they could live their married life over again. The more recent study by Busfield and Paddon (1977) found rather less direct evidence of the benefits of parenthood, but none the less noted that a majority (some two-thirds) of those able to give a definite answer felt that life would be worse without children.

Notwithstanding the benefits which both parenthood and parenting may bring to a couple, the marital relationship will inevitably be affected by the arrival of children, and in particular by the arrival of the first child. There is consistent evidence from the USA which indicates that couples with children in the home have lower marital happiness levels than those living alone; they also have greater financial burdens and more inter-personal stress (Burr, 1970; Rollins and Cannon, 1974; Campbell, 1975).

Freedman et al. (1959) found that the presence of the first child changes people's views about the size of family they would like, for the number of children wanted a year after the birth of the first child was found to be considerably lower than at the time of marriage, or at the time of an interview some time later. This is perhaps indicative of the stresses generated by the first child, and Freedman et al. believe that the depressive effect the first child has upon people's intended family size, is a consequence of the wives' first experiencing the cares of motherhood.

Other workers have found that the arrival of the first child can mark a crisis point in the marriage: in a study by Le Masters (1957), the majority of the couples interviewed had experienced the arrival of their first child as a crisis and Dyer (1963) reported similar findings. However, since Hobbs (1965) and Beauchamp (1969) did not report such negative effects of the first child upon the marriage, the extent to which first parenthood is usually experienced as a crisis is at present uncertain.

The reasons why children do not, on the whole, appear to enhance the personal relationship between the spouses are not, at present, fully understood. At the simplest level of explanation, it seems inevitable that children will channel both time and energy away from one or both spouses and, even if this switch of emphasis is not resented, the couple's relationship is likely, in one sense, to be weaker simply as a result of a lessening of contact between them. The care which children, and especially young children require may be tiring for many wives, and this fatigue, in itself, may detract from the quality of the marital relationship.

According to Le Masters (1957), the adverse affect which the first child had upon the marital relationship appeared to be due to poor preparation for parental, and especially maternal, roles and was not related to the child being unwanted, to the parents being neurotic, or to an unstable marital relationship. There is also evidence which indicates that the period in the marriage when young children have to be looked after may be a particularly stressful time for many mothers: Richman et al. (1975) noted that depression was common in mothers of pre-school children and Brown et al. (1975) found that depression was the most prevalent amongst mothers with a child under 6 years.

It is also a clinical impression that parenthood may constitute a stress upon the marital relationship by crystallising underlying emotional difficulties in one or both parents, to such an extent that the child may actually constitute a threat to the emotional security of a parent (Dominian, 1978).

PARENTHOOD AND DIVORCE

Given that children may constitute a stress for the marital relationship, it might be anticipated that, in general, divorced people would be more likely than those who do not divorce, both to have children, and to have more of them. Neither supposition at first sight appears to be the case. The Registrar General (1964) has noted that those divorcing are relatively infertile and Jacobson in the USA (1959) has estimated that in 1955 there were 1.6 divorces among childless couples for every divorce occurring among couples with children; furthermore, the divorce rate varies inversely with the number of children a couple has. In this survey, D marriages were more than twice as likely as CM marriages to be childless (19% : 8%). However, whilst on average D marriages had 1.8 children and CM marriages 2.1, the mean number of children born to fertile D marriages was 2.3, identical to the mean number of children born to fertile CM marriages. Although the Registrar General's returns appear to indicate an association between childlessness and divorce, it is uncertain whether or not there are genuine differences in the

fertility patterns of those who divorce compared to those who remain
married. This is because, as Chester (1972c) points out, the
definition of children used in these calculations is different for
those who divorce and for those who are married. Census data which
enumerates all live births forms the basis of the calculations of
the fertility patterns of married couples, whereas divorced couples
are only counted as fertile if they have dependent children.
Therefore, married couples are credited with children who may have
died or who may no longer be dependent, whereas divorcing couples
are not. Further complications in determining the relative fertility
patterns of divorced or married couples arise because of the differential inclusion of illegitimate and adopted children, and Chester
(*ibid.*) concludes that:

> We cannot currently know whether the fertility of divorced women
> is understated or exaggerated in divorce court returns, but
> certainly the issue is problematic, and our knowledge of the
> total fertility experience of divorcing women is unsatisfactory.

The contribution which re-marriage has upon the question of the
relative fertility of divorcing and non-divorcing couples has also
to be borne in mind. Several writers (Rowntree and Carrier, 1958;
Chester, 1972c) consider that fertility comparisons would be less
problematic if they were based upon primary marriages only since,
among other considerations, the way in which children are defined
for the purposes of the divorce courts means that re-marriages which
end in divorce are likely to contribute 'more than their share of
divorces and less of their share of fertility' (Chester, 1972c).
     In this survey the fertility patterns of D and CM marriages can
be compared since first, the same definition of children (namely,
live children born to the marriage) applied to both D and CM
marriages, and second, all survey marriages, whether D or CM, were
primary marriages. As mentioned previously, the survey data
suggest that D marriages were, relative to CM marriages, more likely
to be childless, although fertile D couples had, on average, as many
children as fertile CM. The distributions of the number of children
born to the marriages of D and CM, were however different, in that
fertile D were more likely than fertile CM to have had either
only one child (36% : 27%) or to have had four or more children
(17% : 14%).

CHILDLESSNESS AND DIVORCE

As is often the case with a correlate of divorce, this relatively
higher degree of childlessness amongst divorced couples may be
interpreted in opposing ways. It can be argued that the survey
findings demonstrate the void which may be created in a marriage
where there are no children, thus increasing the risk of marital
breakdown. Conversely, it may be that children do indeed reinforce
the stability of a marriage, although not by lessening any risk of
marital unhappiness but rather by making unhappily married parents
more reluctant to divorce because of an overriding sense of obligation to remain together for the sake of their children. A further

interpretation of the association between childlessness and divorce
is that divorced couples may have had less opportunity to conceive
than continuing married couples have had, and the apparent association may largely be reflecting differential opportunities to conceive,
rather than genuine differences between D and CM in terms of either
their reproductive capabilities, or their contraceptive practices.
The possibility that the association between childlessness and
divorce may, in reality, be a statistical artefact obscuring an
opportunity factor, has been noted by Jacobson (1959), Davis *et al.*
(1950), Winch (1971) and Chester (1972c). The contribution of such
an opportunity factor is, however, difficult to elucidate, since
differential coitus rates and contraceptive practices as well as
differing periods of marital cohabitation make comparisons problematic.

It was to some extent possible to compare the survey D and CM in
terms of differential periods of cohabitation (data on coitus rates
or contraceptive practices were not available), although not, however, for cohabitations which lasted two years or less, since all
CM had been married for at least two years. The survey data suggest
that the relative infertility of D must, in part, be due to their
having had unequal opportunities to conceive, since 54% of D
marriages which lasted *de facto* less than one year were infertile,
and 47% of those which ended between the first and second anniver-
saries were also infertile. For marriages in which cohabitation
lasted between two and three years, D marriages were actually more,
rather than less likely than CM marriages to have been fertile
(75% : 71%), and a similar higher incidence of fertility was apparent
for D couples who had cohabitated for between four and five years,
relative to CM marriages of the same *de facto* duration (83% of such
D marriages, 76% of such CM marriages were fertile). Table 41 shows
the relative fertility of D and CM marriages of equivalent *de facto*
durations.

TABLE 41   *De facto* duration of marriage and fertility

	D		CM	
	Fertile	Infertile	Fertile	Infertile
De facto duration	n=419	n=101	n=523	n=47
(years)	%	%	%	%
Less than 1	3	14	–	–
1 but less than 2	5	17	–	–
2 but less than 3	7	10	3	13
3 but less than 4	6	5	3	11
4 but less than 5	6	18	3	13
5 but less than 10	27	21	20	19
10 but less than 15	21	10	15	11
15 but less than 20	11	5	14	9
20 or more	13	1	42	25

It can be seen in Table 41 that an opportunity factor is likely
to account, in part, for the relatively high rate of infertility
noted for D relative to CM.

DIVORCE AND FERTILITY TRENDS

Notwithstanding the difficulties previously noted in using official statistics to compare the fertility patterns of couples who divorce with those who remain married, certain trends in the 'fertility' of divorcing couples are apparent. According to Leete (OPCS, 1976), there are two main trends. First there is a decline in the proportion of childless couples; in 1960, 33% of divorcing couples were childless but in 1973 this was so for 25%. A second trend apparent within official statistics is an increase in the average family size of divorcing couples with children; in 1960, fertile divorced couples had a mean of 2.0 children, but by 1973 this had risen to 2.3. Whilst it may, at first sight, appear that there is thus an increasing trend towards divorce for couples with children, the trend may, however, as Leete notes, 'merely reflect changes in fertility and marriage amongst the population as a whole'.

PARENTHOOD AND THE MARITAL RELATIONSHIP

Although it is the case that the survey D were more likely than CM to be childless, and therefore less likely to be at risk to any stresses which might be associated with having children, nevertheless the vast majority of both D and CM did have children (81% D : 92% CM). According to Dominian, the earlier into the marriage pregnancy and the birth of a child occurs, then the more likely it will be that these events will have a disorientating effect upon the marital relationship. This is because marital roles and responsibilities take time to learn and to adjust to, and for the majority of couples it will probably be at least one year before anything like a stable equilibrium will have developed. The physical, emotional and financial needs of a pregnant wife, new mother and infant, and the re-orientation required by the father, may constitute stresses both for the partners individually, and for the marital relationship at any stage in the marriage, but very particularly if they occur during the very early stages of the marriage.

When D and CM patterns of the timing of the birth of children were examined, it was evident that D were more likely than CM to have had a child very early in their marriages. For instance, 51% DW compared with 32% CMW had a child in their first year of marriage, and 69% DW but 45% CMW had had their first child by their second anniversary. Hence, D marriages may be regarded as being more at risk to stress, on this account, in the early stages of marital adjustment than were CM marriages. When the timing of the marital difficulties of the divorced was considered in relation to marital fertility some interesting differences emerged. First, both very early fertility and infertility were each associated with a very early start to the marital difficulties. This can be seen in Table 42 where it can also be seen that fertility arising out of pre-marital pregnancy is most closely associated with early marital problems. (Note: the following tabulations about childbirth in relation to the stage in the marriage, are derived from the reports of female informants only. This was because the pilot work had indicated that fathers often do not know the exact dates of birth of their children whereas women, not surprisingly perhaps, recall such details accurately).

TABLE 42   Fertility and early marital difficulties

	Divorced Women			
	Fertile in 1st year		Fertile after 1st year	Infertile during primary marriage
Difficulties started	Pmp n=126 %	NoPmp n=41 %	n=107 %	n=59 %
In first year	52	49	32	47
Later	48	51	68	53

Second, marriages of briefer duration were associated, on the one hand, with very early fertility, and on the other hand, with infertility. This can be seen in Table 43.

TABLE 43   The *de facto* duration of marriage and fertility

	De facto duration			
	Less than 5 yrs n=131 %	5-9 yrs n=75 %	10-14 yrs n=55 %	15 yrs + n=75 %
Fertile in 1st year	57	48	40	45
Fertile after 1st year	12	36	49	68
Infertile	31	16	11	7

Whilst the data from Tables 42 and 43 suggest that, for fertile DW, the early arrival of children may have constituted a definite stress upon the marital relationship leading to early marital dissolution, it seems unlikely that infertility *per se* would actually have contributed to marital stress at such an early stage in the marriage. The association between infertility and marital problems is therefore more likely to be reflecting the conscious decision to avoid conception, or perhaps less opportunity to conceive due to less frequent coitus either because of sexual difficulties, or because of the impingement of other marital difficulties upon the marital sexual life.

It was also evident that the marital difficulties of fertile D largely arose whilst the wife was still involved with infant care. When, at the analysis stage of the study, the start of the marital difficulties was related to the age of the youngest child, in 80% of cases the youngest child was under 12 months old. It therefore seems likely that, whatever the causes of the marital difficulties may have been, their resolution during the early period of infant care, with its attendant stresses for the mother, would seem unlikely.

POST-PUERPERAL DEPRESSION AND THE MARITAL RELATIONSHIP

Whilst depression following the birth of a child will inevitably

affect the marital relationship, it may to some extent be less
traumatic for the relationship than other forms of depression might
be. This is because it is relatively easy in such instances to
locate a proximate cause and origin of the depression, and this may
make the 'depression' more acceptable to the husband, since he may
perceive it as entirely associated with the birth and unrelated to
him. He may thus be able to accept his wife's post-puerperal
depression and indeed give support to her during this period, which
may even strengthen the marital relationship. Notwithstanding this
possibility, that post-puerperal depression may create less stress
for the marital relationship than might other forms of depression,
none the less its presence, particularly if prolonged, may be
regarded as increasing the risk of stress within a marriage. During
the survey informants were asked:

> 'As you may know, most women are thrown a bit out of their stride
> after having a baby and many of them find that it takes some time
> to get back to their old selves. Doctors call this the maternal
> blues and mothers suffering from this feel weepy and depressed
> for some time after they have had a baby. Could you tell me if
> you/your wife ever suffered with your/her nerves at all after the
> birth of any of your children?'

Those who had were asked to say for how long it had lasted.

In the survey there was little difference between D and CM in the
prevalence of post-puerperal depression; 25% D, 27% CM wives had
apparently experienced post-puerperal depression (Ppd) after the
birth of their first child. There were, however, some differences
between D and CM regarding the reports about post-puerperal
depression made by women about themselves, as opposed to those
reports given by men about their wives; CMM and CMW reported more
similar proportions of post-puerperal depression after the birth of
the first child than did DM and DW; this can be seen in Table 44.

TABLE 44   Gender differences in the reporting of the post-puerperal
depression after the birth of the first child

	DW n=276 %	DM n=140 %	CMW n=338 %	CMM n=185 %
Post-puerperal depression	28	19	29	23
No post-puerperal depression	71	76	70	74
Can't remember	1	5	1	3

The interpretation of the difference between the reports of DW and
DM is problematic; whereas the variations may be taken as an indication that DM may have been less sensitive to Ppd in their wives,
nevertheless the possibility that their wives may, in fact, have
experienced less Ppd than did women who petitioned for divorce, has
also to be borne in mind.

It is known that the severity of post-puerperal depression can
range widely, from bouts of weepiness requiring no medical treatment

at all, through to a psychotic condition necessitating hospitalisation. The actual severity of any post-puerperal depression could
not be gauged during the survey, nor could its effect upon the
husband and the marital relationship be assessed. Clinical
impressions, however, had indicated that the duration of any post-
puerperal depression was a measure of its severity and therefore
this was examined in this survey. Although the presence of any
post-puerperal depression following the birth of the first child was
virtually identical for fertile DW and CMW (28% : 29%), any
depression tended to last longer for DW (mean of 5.7 months compared
with 4.9 months for CMW).
  Although the prevalence of Ppd after the birth of the first child
was similar for DW and CMW, DW were nearly twice as likely as CMW
to have experienced Ppd during their first year of marriage (16% DW :
9% CMW). Since DW were more likely than CMW to give birth during the
first year of marriage, then their greater prevalence of Ppd may be
regarded as simply due to their increment of risk. However, the
intensity of Ppd during this period, as indicated by its duration,
was even more marked for DW relative to CMW than was the case for
Ppd associated with the first child in general; the mean duration
of Ppd which started in the first year was 7.5 months for DW who
were pre-maritally pregnant; 3.0 months for DW NoPmp; 4.3 months.
for CMW Pmp and 4.9 months for CMW NoPmp.
  With regard to any post-puerperal depression following the birth
of the second child, again there were little differences in its
incidence between D and CM; 21% D, 19% CM wives were apparently
depressed. However, as was the case for the first child, the
duration of any post-puerperal depression was longer for D; 32% D,
16% CM were apparently depressed for more than six months after the
birth of their second child and the mean duration of this depression,
associated with the second child, was 9.8 months for D, 5.1 months
for CM.

SUMMARY

Other research studies have shown that there are strong normative
pressures towards parenthood, but there is also consistent evidence
to suggest that children probably do not enhance the marital relationship, since couples with children living at home appear to have
lower marital happiness levels than those living alone; they also
have greater financial burdens and more interpersonal stress. The
arrival of the first child has been shown in several studies to
mark a critical turning point in the marital relationship and it
may even constitute a crisis within the marriage. The reasons for
the disruptive effect of the first child are unclear but it may, in
part, be due to poor preparation in our society for parental and
especially maternal roles.
  The fertility patterns of those who divorce noted in official
statistics provide an unsatisfactory statement of their total
fertility experiences, for a variety of reasons. The data from
this study indicated that marriages which have ended in divorce
were more likely than those which were ongoing to be childless.
However, fertile divorced couples tended either to have had only

one child, or to have had four or more children. Furthermore, the
relative childlessness of those who divorced may, to a large extent,
be due to their relatively short periods of cohabitation and may
not represent genuine differences between divorcing and non-divorcing
couples either in willed contraception or in inability to conceive.

Those who divorce seemed more likely than those who were continuing
with their marriages to have had a child within two years of the
wedding, and especially in the first year of marriage. Early
fertility, especially when this arose because of pre-marital conception, was also associated with serious marital difficulties arising
in the first year of marriage. Furthermore, for divorced couples,
the vast majority of their marital difficulties arose when the wife
was still involved with infant care. Therefore, whatever the causes
of these marital problems, the chances that they may have been
resolved in their early stages would seem unlikely, since the early
period of child care itself appears to be associated with stresses
upon the mother.

Post-puerperal depression seemed equally likely to arise for
'divorce-bound' mothers and for those in stable marriages. However,
any depression experienced by wives who divorced tended to last
longer.

Chapter 8

THE SEXUAL DIMENSION
OF MARRIAGE

The implications of the sexual dimension of marriage extend far
beyond the sexual arena. Dominian (1968) has emphasised the
psychological importance of intercourse, both as a means of communication and as a process of mutual reassurance between a couple. It
is Dominian's view that the sexual act may serve as a focus of an
individual's personality difficulties and, in some instances, may
even precipitate latent difficulties, which are not necessarily
sexual in nature. Consequently, the sexual dimension of the
marital relationship may generate feelings of exploitation, degrada-
tion or manipulation, rather than being experienced as a mutual
source of affirmation and reassurance for the partners. Dominian's
view of the contribution which sexual difficulties may make to the
overall syndrome of marital breakdown, is that whilst there can be
sexual problems within an otherwise harmonious relationship, these
tend to have arisen largely because of ignorance of sexual anatomy
and technique or because of transient environmental stresses,
whereas the sexual problems which are part of the marital breakdown
complex, tend to be due to the poor quality of the non-sexual
dimension of the marriage. This is also a view shared by other
workers in the field (Kubie, 1956; Wallin, 1960; Pierce, 1963) and
it does appear that the causal contribution to marital failure of
difficulties specifically sexual in nature is small, save in cases
of perversion. The relationship between dissatisfaction with the
sexual side of marriage and serious marital problems has been summed
up by Dominian (1968) as follows:

> The majority of persistently serious sexual complaints are the
> end result of personality conflicts manifesting themselves in
> this extremely sensitive area.

Three factors associated with the sexual side of marriage were
explored in the survey: first, the extent of satisfaction with the
sexual side both at the beginning of marriage and later on, together
with the reasons for any dissatisfaction; second, attitudes towards
sex within marriage in terms of (a) a rating of its importance, and
(b) opinions as to whether men and women derive equal pleasure from
sex; third, the extent of pre-marital and extra-marital affairs.

SATISFACTION WITH THE SEXUAL SIDE OF MARRIAGE

The questions in the survey relating to sexual satisfaction referred simply to the extent to which the sexual side of their marriage was regarded by survey informants as satisfactory. In the interest of validity there were no specific questions about frequencies of intercourse or orgasm. Consequently, patterns of sexual activity which might be associated with either D or CM marriages cannot be delineated, and marriages which were regarded by informants as sexually satisfactory may well be reflecting a wide variety of sexual activity and practice (including none at all).

SEXUAL SATISFACTION AT THE START OF MARRIAGE

The majority of informants claimed that, at the beginning of their marriage, the sexual side of their relationship was satisfactory. However, CM were more likely than D to claim so and men, whether D or CM, were more likely than women to have been satisfied with the early sexual side of their marriage. This can be seen in Table 45.

TABLE 45   Sexual satisfaction at the start of marriage

	DW	CMW	DM	CMM	All D	All CM
	n=336	n=371	n=184	n=199	n=520	n=570
	%	%	%	%	%	%
Satisfactory	76	85	84	94	79	88
Not satisfactory	24	15	15	6	21	12
No answer	-	-	1	-	Ø	-

Further analysis showed that informants in marriages involving pre-marital pregnancy were more likely than those in marriages in which the bride was not pregnant to claim that their early marital sexual life was satisfactory. This can be seen in Table 46.

TABLE 46   Sexual satisfaction at the start of marriage related to Pmp (women only)

	DW		CMW	
	Pmp	No Pmp	Pmp	No Pmp
	n=128	n=208	n=61	n=310
	%	%	%	%
Satisfactory	81	73	92	83
Not satisfactory	19	27	8	17

Although the extent to which the absence of pre-marital pregnancy may be due to sexual abstinence is not known, the probability that non-Pmp partners first experienced intercourse within marriage is obviously higher than in the case of Pmp partners, and hence the latter's greater degree of sexual satisfaction may be due to their

being more sexually adjusted to their partners at the start of
marriage. However, since pre-marital pregnancy can result from a
single and even unsatisfactory act of intercourse, the higher
incidence of sexual satisfaction claimed by Pmp brides may not
necessarily be a result of their being more generally sexually
adjusted to their partner. It is also possible that the actual
state of being pregnant at the very start of marriage may be the
cause of this higher claimed incidence of satisfaction, for several
reasons; first, because the fear of becoming pregnant and thereby
experiencing the loss of income or of freedom did not exist; second,
because they were more relaxed, perhaps due to hormonal influences,
or third, because their pregnant state provided them with legitimate
excuses for sexual abstinence or less frequent intercourse.

Sexual satisfaction at the start of marriage in relation to marriage
cohort

Kinsey (1953) noted that the prevalence of female orgasm was lower
among women from earlier birth cohorts. The present survey data,
however, did not show significant differences between different
marriage cohorts (whether D or CM) with regard to satisfaction with
the sexual side of marriage, and hence there appeared to be no
generational effect. If, as Kinsey found, female orgasm is progressively more prevalent in more recent cohorts, then the survey
findings do, perhaps, indicate the strength of the prevailing
societal norms upon individuals' perceptions of their own sexual
identity, in the sense that wives from earlier marriage cohorts may
have been less sexually aroused or fulfilled than those who married
more recently; but if they had lower expectations in this area, then
they would be unlikely to be dissatisfied with their sexual life.

The reasons for any claimed dissatisfaction with the sexual side at
the start of marriage

Informants who found the sexual relationship at the start of their
marriage unsatisfactory in some way (24% DW; 15% CMW; 15% DM; 6% CMM)
were asked to give their reasons why they considered this was so,
and the replies from D and CM showed very different perceptions of
the problem, possibly indicating different characteristics of the two
survey groups. It must, however, be noted that relatively few of
CMM said they were dissatisfied, and therefore the replies from CM
came principally from CMW.
    When considering the reasons for dissatisfaction, it is necessary
to treat the answers with some caution, for not only is this retrospective data, but it concerns a particularly sensitive area of
marital experience, and its presentation may additionally be affected
by the climate of feeling about the marriage overall, a factor which
may account for some of the complaint in the replies from D.
    Predominantly, in their answers regarding dissatisfaction with the
sexual dimension of marriage, D, both men and women, complained about
their partner's sexual behaviour, whereas this was much less
frequent the case with CM. This 'blaming approach', which so

characterised some of the D replies, encompassed three principal
themes: *'partner selfish or inconsiderate in lovemaking'*; *'partner
cruel or brutal in lovemaking'*, and *'partner frigid or unresponsive'*.
When these three are grouped together, this accounts for 58% of all
reasons given by DM and 38% of those given by DW, but for only 13%
of CMW and less than 1% CMM. As has been suggested, this emphasis
upon blame is probably inevitable for D, who were, it will be
remembered, all petitioners to the divorce, and who could, therefore,
perhaps be expected to highlight any failures or inadequacies they
may have perceived in their partner's sexual behaviour.

When these three categories are separated out, there were marked,
albeit expected, differences between DM and DW: *'partner selfish'*
was mentioned by 26% DW but only 4% of DM (and 2% CMW), whereas
'partner cold' was a complaint made by 54% of DM but only 6% of
DW. "Partner cruel' was entirely mentioned by women, 6% DW and 7%
CMW. Typical of these complaints against the partner were the
following:

'Partner selfish/inconsiderate'
'He thought only for himself and not for me - it (sic) was like
a dog.' (DW, married in 1961 aged 20 at marriage)

'My husband didn't seem to bother. I might just as well not have
been there.' (DW, married in 1962 aged 21 at marriage)

'Partner cruel'
'He was very brutal. I was horrified after our first night - he
was only affectionate when he felt like it - other times he was
cruel.' (DW, married in 1963 aged 18 at marriage)

'Partner cold'
'Unresponsive partner - she was frigid.' (DM, married 1959, wife
aged 21 at marriage)

'He was not able to satisfy me - he was not interested in the
physical side of marriage, when I wanted him to make love to me
he would tell me to "get off to sleep".' (DW, married 1957 aged
19 at marriage)

'She was very frigid - wooden really - I tried to find out why
but I drew a blank.' (DM, married 1966, wife aged 20 at marriage)

These differences, namely the women's focusing upon their partner's
selfishness in pursuing their own satisfaction only, and the men's
complaining of their wife's non-responsiveness, are echoed later in
this chapter when there is discussion about perceived gender
differences in relation to the expressed enjoyment of sex.

In marked contrast to the overall blaming approach of D, those
in the CM group who had not found the sexual side of their marriage
initially satisfactory, were strikingly more likely to attribute it
to their being *'both tense/uncertain'*, often stressing their mutual
lack of experience, and this type of response was given by 65% of
CMW, and over two-thirds of CMM, but by only 16% of DW and 4% of DM.
The overall picture which thus tended to emerge, was one of the

continuing married group being apparently more likely than the
divorced to accept a joint responsibility for initial sexual difficulties, as is illustrated by the following quotations:

'I was a virgin, we were both rather ignorant about the subject.
It took quite a while before either of us achieved any satisfaction.' (CMW, married 1955 aged 20 at marriage)

'Could not quite get adjusted to each other's needs.' (CMM,
married 1963 aged 22 at marriage)

'I think I wasn't relaxed enough about it. As you go on I think
you get into each other's ways and it makes marriage more satisfactory.' (CMW, married 1946 aged 19 at marriage)

A reason which was given with some frequency, particularly by DW,
was their own recollections and conviction that they *derived no
pleasure from sex*': 18% DW, 9% CMW said this, together with 4% of
DM who complained about their wives in this way.

'I married because I was pregnant. I realised I had no feelings
for him so I couldn't enjoy the physical side of marriage.' (DW,
married 1965 aged 19 at marriage)

'It never came up to my expectations. I was never completely
satisfied with this side of marriage.' (DW, married 1950 aged
25 at marriage)

'It didn't interest me very much. My husband didn't help me at
all. I didn't enjoy intercourse at all.' (DW, married 1959 aged
24 at marriage)

'I just couldn't reach a climax. I wasn't completely satisfied'.
(CMW, married 1969 aged 19 at marriage)

This reason in some measure echoes the non-responsiveness mentioned
earlier, which DM had complained of in their wives, although it
seems probable that it also conceals resentment or disappointment
in the women, due to what they regarded as their husband's inability
to arouse them sexually.
   Another aspect of sexual dissatisfaction which was expressed by
informants was the presence of fear, sometimes arising out of
ignorance of the sex act itself (5% DW, 9% CMW : 11% DM) as can
be seen in such comments as:

'I was scared of lovemaking. It was never talked about when I
was young. I didn't know what to expect.' (CMW, married 1947
aged 18 at marriage)

'I didn't know anything - it was awful. We didn't see anything
like that at home.' (DW, married 1962 aged 17 at marriage)

'My wife was brought up to believe that sex was rude and was only
to be suffered to propagate the species.' (DM, married 1958,
wife aged 26 at marriage)

At other times this fear was related to the possibility of an unwanted pregnancy, and this was mentioned particularly by DM (5% DW, 2% CMW : 11% DM).

Difficulties with a physiological component affecting the sexual relationship, such as premature ejaculation or the need for the wife to have a 'stretching operation', were mentioned by more CMW than by any other group (6% DW, 9% CMW : 7% DM), and the only references to non-consummation of the marriage were always from DW.

It was interesting that the lack of privacy due to sharing was given as a reason more frequently by CMW than DW (4% DW, 7% CMW), despite the earlier information, at the housing questions, that the divorced group experienced more difficulties through sharing their initial accommodation. This may once again reflect the past shyness on the part of some CMW:

'My husband never touched me until after two weeks - we were so tired - and we were in a strange place - sharing with other people in the house - bells under the bed - they played jokes on us.... Well - you could hear every movement we made - I felt awful.' (CMW, married 1946 aged 20 at marriage)

It seemed as if perhaps D informants were less willing to attribute responsibility for difficulties to external factors such as sharing accommodation, for where DW did focus upon something outside the sexual relationship (6% DW), it tended to be on the total lack of compatibility with their spouses which they felt prevented a satisfactory sexual relationship, epitomised by one DW who said: 'You don't enjoy sex if you don't get on with someone do you?'

Subsequent improvement in the sexual dimension of their marriages for those who had claimed initial dissatisfaction

All informants who had been disappointed with the physical side of marriage in the early stages, were then asked if at any point things had improved. The vast majority of CMW (91%) and almost all CMM who had mentioned initial problems, said things had subsequently become much better, but most of those D (86% DW, 96% DM) who had had early sexual problems, presented a sharp contrast to the CM, for they found no such improvement.

So far we have described those for whom the initial phase of the sexual relationship was felt to be unsatisfactory (largely D), and whether this unsatisfactory state of affairs later improved (which it did for most of the married group but not so the divorced). Problems in the sexual relationship which appeared to have manifested themselves at a later stage in the marriage are now considered.

SEXUAL SATISFACTION LATER IN THE MARRIAGE

Although almost all the continuing married group (96% CMW : 98% CMM) claimed that the sexual side of their marriage had both started and continued in a satisfactory fashion or had resolved any earlier difficulties, outstandingly fewer of D, especially DW, considered

this to be the case with them.   Some 38% DW and 30% DM, whose
initial sexual relationship had been without difficulties, said
that they experienced problems within, or affecting the sexual
relationship, later on in their marriages.

The reasons for later deterioration for those who had been initially
satisfied with the sexual side of marriage

When the reasons which the divorced group gave as being responsible
for this deterioration were examined, a certain similarity was
apparent between these later problems and those which had been
encountered by divorced informants whose sexual relationship had
foundered early on in the marriage.   Divorced women spoke strongly
against what they considered their husbands' over-frequent sexual
demands and his selfishness and lack of affection in the sexual
arena (18%).

> 'My husband was very over-sexed - he wanted intercourse every
> night and used to say I didn't satisfy him.   I began to feel as
> though I was just a body being used by him - there seemed to be
> no love.' (DW, aged 25 at marriage)

> 'A selfish lover.   He just went to bed and made love when he
> wanted it and then went to sleep.   He just treated me like a
> housekeeper.' (DW, aged 23 at marriage)

This complaint was not, however, confined to DW, for 7% of DM also
considered their partners selfish and demanding.   The reason most
frequently mentioned by DW for later deterioration in the sexual
relationship was that the husband was drinking heavily and 22% of
them complained of this, usually in conjunction with some associated
problem:

> 'He always used to come in drunk and demand his rights.' (DW,
> aged 18 at marriage)

> 'In later years his conduct to me became loathsome and repugnant.
> He was an alcoholic.   Because he started to drink heavily and
> tried to force himself on me.' (DW, aged 23 at marriage)

Further evidence of the impairment of the marital sexual relationship
was provided by the substantial proportions of both DM and DW who
cited their partner's unfaithfulness (18% DW and 26% DM).   For both
sexes, this pattern of affairs appeared most often to consist of
casual encounters rather than any one particular rival involvement:

> 'My wife wanted to go out a lot.   She used to get very drunk and
> started going out with other men.' (DM, aged 22 at marriage)

> 'She thought I wasn't sexy enough for her.   She started going
> off with other men.' (DM, aged 24 at marriage)

'He started going out with other women. He used to leave me in
on my own every night while he was gadding off.' (DW, aged 23 at
marriage)

Of course, in no way can cause and effect be disentangled in such
situations, for these affairs (as indeed the heavy drinking earlier)
may themselves have caused the friction, or they may have been an
attempt to seek relief caused by disinterest or rejection whether
sexual or general, on the part of the spouse.
    The partner's loss of interest in sexual matters was a reason
given by 24% of DM and 12% of DW. The men tended to use words like
'cold', or phrases such as 'cooling off all the time'.

'Sometimes she wouldn't let me near her - wouldn't let me touch
her - she'd turn over - used to laugh at me.' (DM, aged 22 at
marriage)

The women portrayed men who had lost their sexual drive, for instance:

'He didn't seem to bother. He always went out on his own, drank
quite a lot and sex-wise he didn't want to know.' (DW, aged 20
at marriage)

'We were all right up to the first 12 months. He never bothered
about my feelings much in bed - just his own. Then at the latter
end of our marriage he never bothered with sex with me at all.
I thought he must have another woman but I never found out.' (DW,
aged 26 at marriage)

Some men dated their wife's loss of interest in sex from the birth
of a child, a reason mentioned by twice as many DM as DW; 9% DW :
17% DM. (This is particularly interesting in the light of Chapter 6
where we discuss the finding that 51% DW compared with 32% CMW had
a child within their first year of marriage.) From the answers
which were given to this question it was clear that the birth of a
child could have a disruptive effect upon the marital and sexual
relationship in many ways. Sometimes the reason appeared to be
connected with the birth itself.

'I lost interest in sex after my first baby. I had to have
hospital treatment to bring on the birth, and had to have tablets
afterwards.' (DW, aged 24 at marriage)

'After my second baby I went frigid - I was very frightened of
getting pregnant again. I went completely off sex altogether.
My husband didn't understand.' (DW, aged 18 at marriage)

'She never bothered after the baby was born. She just wasn't
interested. All she wanted was to cling to the child and no one
else was allowed to get near him or take him out or anything.'
(DM, aged 20 at marriage)

'It took a pattern. When the second baby was coming and she got
the fixed home she wanted, she just didn't want to make love as
frequently.' (DM, aged 20 at marriage)

Allied to this reason was the associated one where sexual problems
were due to the wife's ill health or tiredness: 9% DM, 4% DW.

'I was tired with work and not well either working 18 hours a
day - too tired with a young baby to satisfy him in that way.'
(DW, aged 24 at marriage)

It can be seen that a marked impact may be made on the quality of
the sex life by factors apparently external to it, although these
factors may themselves spring from the personality or behaviour of
the partner. Divorced men in particular (24% DM, 6% DW) referred
to the poor non-sexual relationship they had with their wives which
adversely affected the later quality of their sexual life.
Interestingly, a small group of DW (5%) claimed that it was their
husband's refusal to work or look for a steady job which caused the
deterioration in their relationship, an indication of the way in
which the sexual relationship can reflect the total well-being of
the marriage. In contrast, the sexual problems of CM tended not to
be the reflection of underlying difficulties in the relationship in
the same way that this appeared to be the case for D. Other reasons
given by DW and DM included absence of the husband (away on work or
Army service); non-sexual physiological reasons (e.g. husband's
spastic attacks) and sexual incompatibility.
      Considered overall, the principal difference between the reasons
given by D and CM for their dissatisfaction with the sexual side
of married life, was the tendency for CM to believe that the difficulties were caused neither by negative personality traits in the
partner, nor by underlying difficulties in the marital relationship,
whereas for D the dissatisfaction was seemingly firmly based in
just these areas.
      It is important to note, however, that overall the extent of
claimed satisfaction with the sexual side of marriage was high.
When informants who had had early sexual difficulties but had
resolved them, were added to those whose marital sexual life was
always satisfactory, it appeared that 96% CMW, 98% CMM, 51% DW,
60% DM were always content with the sexual side of their marriage.
      These figures of claimed satisfaction for D are a little
surprising, for in view of the breakdown of their marital relationship, difficulties in the sexual side of their marriage might
perhaps have been expected for the vast majority rather than for
only half of them. However, given that there are always difficulties in gathering data about individuals' sex lives, but especially
about their sexual problems or associated difficulties, a degree
of reticence in a survey interview is to be expected. Also, it
is a clinical experience that the admission of sexual problems
often occurs only after much discussion with clients about general
marital problems and, in some instances, the sexual 'problem' is
one of abstinence, a situation finally occurring after progressively infrequent acts of intercourse between the spouses.
      It is therefore possible that the level of claimed sexual
satisfaction by some survey informants may be indicative of the
relatively minor role that sex may have played within their marital
relationship. If sexual attraction between the couple is not there,
then the absence of sexual intercourse between them is unlikely to

be regarded by them as a problem, although such marital relationships
can be considered as being deprived of an important source of
personal satisfaction, which can reinforce the closeness and unity
of the partners, and in this sense abstinence is a 'problem' although
not necessarily perceived as such by the couple themselves.

ATTITUDES TOWARDS SEX

Informants were asked first, to rate the importance they attached
to the sexual side of marriage, and second, to say whether they
regarded one sex as deriving more pleasure from lovemaking than the
other. The questions were phrased as follows:

  (a) How important would you say the sexual side of marriage is?
       (Card)   Very important
                Fairly important
                Fairly unimportant
                Not at all important

  (b) In general, who would you say derives more pleasure from
       lovemaking, the man or the woman?
       (Card)   The man   ⎫
                The woman ⎬ Ask → (c)
                Both equally ⎭

  (c) Why is this so, do you think?

It can be seen from these questions that informants were not asked
either how important the sexual side of their own marriage was to
them, nor whether they felt that it was they or their partner who
derived more pleasure from lovemaking. The 'general', rather than
specifically 'personal' phrasing of the question, was so designed
because it was felt that, in a survey interview, direct questions
about informants' sex lives might be inhibiting or even cause
offence. It was clear from the reasons given for believing in any
gender differences in deriving pleasure from sex, that informants
were largely interpreting the question in a general sense, but those
who did refer to their own marriages appeared to regard their
experiences or beliefs as typical of the general population, rather
than the reverse.

The importance of the sexual side of marriage

Table 47 shows the results of survey informants' rating of this
aspect of the marital relationship.

TABLE 47

Sexual side	DW n=336 %	CMW n=371 %	DM n=184 %	CMM n=199 %	All D n=520 %	All CM n=570 %
Very important	59	41	51	47	56	43
Fairly important	38	54	45	51	40	53
Fairly unimportant	2	4	3	2	3	4
Not at all important	1	1	2	–	1	1
No answer	–	–	–	1	–	Ø

Table 47 shows, not surprisingly perhaps, that the sexual side of marriage was regarded as important by the vast majority of informants. It can be seen that DW were the most likely to rate the sexual side of marriage as very important and CMW were the least likely to do so. Informants were not asked the reasons for their rating and hence it is not known whether DW (who were the most likely to be dissatisfied with the sexual side of their marriages), believed that this side of the marital relationship was very important because sexual problems tended to be a feature of their marital difficulties, or whether DW were, as a group, more sexually active. However, an analysis of dissatisfaction with the sexual side of marriage and opinions about the importance of sex in marriage, indicated that those informants who had, at some point, been dissatisfied with the sexual side of their marriages were consistently more likely than those who had never expressed dissatisfaction, to rate the sexual side of marriage as very important. This was especially so for DW as Table 48 shows.

Opinions about gender differences in deriving pleasure from lovemaking

In the region of two-thirds of all women and nearly three-quarters of all men, believed that men and women derive equal pleasure from lovemaking. Those who felt that there were gender differences in the enjoyment of lovemaking, generally felt that it was the man who derived more sexual pleasure, and this belief was the most marked amongst CMW, as Table 49 shows. It will be recalled that the question referred to pleasure from lovemaking and not to orgasm *per se*.

TABLE 49   Perceived gender differences in deriving pleasure from lovemaking

	All D n=520 %	All CM n=570 %	DW n=336 %	CMW n=371 %	DM n=184 %	CMM n=199 %
The man derives more pleasure	26	32	31	37	17	22
The woman derives more pleasure	4	1	1	1	9	3
Equal pleasure	69	67	67	63	73	75
No answer	Ø	–	1	–	–	1

TABLE 48   Sexual dissatisfaction and opinions about the importance of sex in marriage

Sexual side	D		DW		DM		CM		CMW		CMM	
	*S n=278 %	*D n=241 %	S n=168 %	D n=168 %	S n=110 %	D n=73 %	S n=548 %	D n=21 %	S n=354 %	D n=17 %	S n=194 %	D n=4 No
Very important	51	61	54	63	47	56	43	52	40	53	47	2
Fairly important	46	34	43	33	50	37	53	43	54	41	51	2
Fairly unimportant	2	3	2	2	2	4	4	–	5	–	2	–
Not at all important	1	2	1	2	1	3	1	5	1	6	–	–

* S = satisfied
* D = dissatisfied

In the light of the previously mentioned Kinsey findings (which
demonstrated that there appeared to be generational differences in
the incidence of female orgasm) and the findings from this survey
(which showed no significant differences between informants from
different marriage cohorts regarding satisfaction with the sexual
side of their marriage), beliefs that men experience greater sexual
pleasure than do women would perhaps be expected to be more prevalent
amongst earlier marriage cohorts. This was so for CM, but not for D.
For example, 42% of CM who married in the 1940s, but only 28% of CM
who married in the 1950s, believed that the man enjoyed sex more than
the woman. However, within the D sample, informants marrying in the
1940s, 1950s or 1960s were all more or less equally likely to believe
that this was so (29%; 25%; 27%). The trend noted for CM with regard
to beliefs about gender differences in sexual pleasure does appear
to accord with changes in societal norms relating to beliefs about
female sexuality. The relatively high incidence, among D from
earlier cohorts, of the belief that men and women derive equal
pleasure from lovemaking, however, suggests that D informants from
these earlier marriage cohorts may have been less influenced by the
prevailing stereotypes of sexuality which were typical of their
generation. D from earlier cohorts would also have grown up and
married during periods when beliefs in the permanence of marriage
were more universally held and it is also possible that such D may
have been less conformist in their attitudes towards marital
dissolution.
    Those survey informants who believed that it is the woman who
derives the greater pleasure from lovemaking were very much in the
minority. It can be seen in Table 49 that men were more likely than
women to believe this and that DM were the most likely to believe
so. There was no generational pattern regarding this belief, either
for D or for CM. The extent to which a belief in unequal enjoyment
from lovemaking may be reflecting personal disappointment with
intercourse is of course, unknown. In the case of DM, who believed
that women experienced more sexual pleasure than men, however, other
survey data suggested that those men were relatively passive types
who believed that they had married highly sexed women and it is
possible that their perceptions of their wives' sexuality may have
been influenced by their own less pronounced sexual needs.

The reasons given for believing in gender differences in deriving
pleasure from lovemaking

It has to be borne in mind that only a minority of the sub-groups
believed that there were gender differences in deriving pleasure
from lovemaking (32% DW; 38% CMW; 26% DM; 25% CMM). None the less,
when the answers from D and CM were compared, some interesting
differences emerged. The reasons most frequently given by informants
were those connected with what was perceived as the innate nature of
male sexuality. Some 62% of CMW and around half of all the others
(48% DW; 54% DM; 57% CMM) to whom the question applied, referred to
such characteristics as: 'men need sex more'; 'men are more easily
aroused' and 'men are more easily satisfied'.
    'Men need sex more/it's man's nature' was more frequently given

as a reason by CM than by D: 20% DW; 34% CMW; 24% DM; 31% CMM.   It is interesting that both men and women held this opinion.   Closer examination of the responses showed a difference between the two groups of women: CMW expressed no overt resentment about what seemed to be accepted by them as a biologically 'given', almost gender, identity:

> 'Because a man is made that way.' (CMW, married in 1957 aged 20 at marriage)

> 'With men intercourse is as essential as having a pint.' (CMW, married in 1942 aged 22 at marriage)

> 'The nature of the beast - the male of the species are supposed to be that way inclined aren't they?' (CMW, married in 1960 aged 23 at marriage)

Although some DW held this same view, yet there were others whose replies suggested a degree of resentment about heightened male sexuality, as evidenced by comments such as:

> 'Men seem unable to do without sex.' (DW, married in 1961 aged 19 at marriage)

Another aspect of masculine sexuality, *men are more easily aroused*, was mentioned more frequently by CMW than DW, but most of all by DM: 8% DW; 11% CMW; 14% DM; 8% CMM.   Once again, considered overall, there was a tendency for CM to comment upon this as an accepted, almost 'neutral' fact, whereas the responses from D hinted at irritation:

> 'A man is more easily aroused. It takes longer for a woman to relax.' (CMW, married in 1959 aged 18 at marriage)

> 'A woman is too slow to respond - they want too much petting first.' (DM, married in 1967 aged 22 at marriage)

The third characteristic of masculine sexuality which was mentioned was *men are more easily satisfied*: 20% DW; 17% CMW; 16% DM; 12% CMM.   Here also among the female informants there was an indication of greater acceptance of this by CMW than DW; CMW responses which illustrated this include:

> 'I think they must reach a climax every time. I don't think that the woman does, although I personally don't let my husband know that.' (CMW, married in 1965 aged 20 at marriage)

> 'A man is more receptive and reaches a climax very quickly.' (CMW, married in 1947 aged 24 at marriage)

Among DW responses there was evidence which suggested some resentment at the ease with which a man achieved sexual satisfaction:

'A man must have physical satisfaction, but it can happen that
the woman has none - the man's had his and just turns over and
goes to sleep.' (DW, married in 1930 aged 23 at marriage)

'The man gets his satisfaction easier, and is not so susceptible
to conditions which easily affect how a woman feels.' (DW, married
in 1952 aged 18 at marriage)

One possible explanation of the different balance of responses
discussed so far, with CM apparently more accepting but D appearing
to reveal resentment at the unequal pleasure, could be that for CM
the belief that differential pleasure is due to innate gender
identity may be an opinion neutrally held, whereas for D such an
opinion could well be reflecting a personally unhappy sexual experience.
    Another way in which D and CM differed was that three reasons were
given by D which were relatively infrequently mentioned by CM. The
first of these was a response, made predominantly by DW, which echoed
some of their 'complaint' at the earlier questions which dealt with
sexual dissatisfaction: *men are selfish/don't care for women's needs'*
(17% DW; 5% CMW; 2% CMM and no divorced men). DW expressed their
resentment in replies such as the following:

'Men are selfish - they'll get what they want.' (DW, married in
1968 aged 19 at marriage)

'As long as he was satisfied himself he could not have cared less
about me.' (DW, married 1957 aged 21 at marriage)

A second reason, this time given principally by DM (no divorced
women, 1% CMW; 16% DM; 4% CMM) conveyed the belief that *the sex act
is a lengthier/deeper experience for a woman'*, and was reflected in
such comments as:

'A woman gets a later climax, therefore a longer period of enjoyment.' (DM, married in 1965, aged 22 at marriage)

'Because it goes much deeper for a woman it means more to her,
therefore she must get more out of it.' (DM, married in 1959 aged
24 at marriage)

It is impossible to know whether or not these men were envious of
their wives' perceived greater sexual pleasure, although another
reason mentioned almost exclusively by DM (6%), *'man always has to
take the initiative/is the dominant partner'*, at times implied
resentment:

'Because the man has to do all the work.' (DM, married in 1953
aged 23 at marriage)

The reasons so far discussed have all highlighted differences between
D and CM, but similar percentages of both D and CM female informants
raised aspects which were less often mentioned by the men: *'women
worry about pregnancy'* (8% DW; 9% CMW; 4% all men) and *'women are*

too tired/preoccupied to enjoy sex' (5% DW; 7% CMW; 2% DM; 4% CMM).

As one might expect, the fear of an unwanted pregnancy was more likely to be mentioned by informants from earlier cohorts, but a third of those who mentioned it as an inhibitor to the enjoyment of sex, were from marriages which took place in 1965 or later, so that greater availability of contraception knowledge and methods has not dispelled it entirely.

The second reason which concerned women more than men, *'women are too tired/preoccupied to enjoy sex'*, in some cases referred to the tiresomeness of children, and in others to the demands of a full-time job. It was interesting that more CMM than DM appeared to be aware of the woman's problems; typified by one CMM who commented 'very often the woman is too tired - children are very wearing and need lots of attention'.

One reason which was given only by women informants was the belief that *'a man requires physical pleasure only - a woman needs emotional involvement as well'*: 6% DW; 2% CMW; and DW tended to comment on the way 'a man's pleasure comes far more easily, there does not need to be any affection there', or 'a man needs sex, a woman needs love'. One further reason for greater enjoyment by one partner which was given either by female informants, or DM speaking about their wives, *'self/wife derived little or no pleasure from sex'* (4% DW; 4% CMW; 6% DM - no CMM gave this reason).

It is difficult to draw any firm conclusions from the total reasons given for believing in the disparity between male/female enjoyment of sex. However, one theme which emerged was an apparently greater acceptance by CM of unequal pleasure due to seemingly innate gender differences. A trend opposite to this, which runs throughout, is the greater complaint and discontent inherent in the reasons advanced by D. It is not possible to say whether this discontent may be due to the stronger sexual identity of D, or whether it could be that they were simply more disappointed in their sexual experience, having perhaps had greater initial expectations which were not fulfilled in their marital relationship. Overall, however, the differences between the reasons of D and CM are greater than the differences between the replies from male and female informants.

PRE-MARITAL SEXUAL EXPERIENCE

One American study (Locke, 1951) found that the marriages of individuals who had had pre-marital sexual relationships were more likely to end in divorce than were the marriages of those who had no such relationships. This was to some extent a finding of this survey: 22% DW; 8% CMW; 52% DM; 27% CMM claimed that they had made love before marriage with someone other than their eventual marriage partner.

The kind of relationship in which this pre-marital sexual activity took place, in the sense of whether it was in a casual or in an on-going relationship, is not known, but since relatively few pre-marital sexual partners were claimed by informants, this suggests that pre-marital sexual relationships can rarely be equated with promiscuity, at least for women (16% DW; 5% CMW;

9% DM; 9% CMM had made love with only one person prior to meeting their eventual spouse). Men were more likely to claim several pre-marital sexual partners and DM claimed the greatest number (32% DM; 13% CMM; 2% DW; 1% CMW reported having had three or more sexual partners prior to their courtship with their spouse).

The significance of having had a sexual experience with someone other than one's spouse is, however, difficult to define. Informants in marriages involving a pre-marital pregnancy were, relative to their non-pregnant counterparts, more likely to have had a sexual partner (other than their spouse) prior to marriage, and this contrast was most marked for CM (35% D Pmp; 32% D NoPmp; 21% CM Pmp; 13% CM NoPmp). There was also an interesting generational difference between D and CM which can be seen in Table 50.

TABLE 50   Experience of pre-marital sexual partners analysed by cohort in which the marriage took place

		All D		
	Before 1940	1940-9	1950-9	1960-9
	n=41	n=75	n=149	n=255
	%	%	%	%
Sexual partner prior to spouse	15	40	34	33
No sexual partner prior to spouse	83	60	66	67
No answer	2	-	-	∅

		All CM			
	Before 1940	1940-9	1950-9	1960-9	1970 +
	n=32	n=142	n=159	n=221	n=16
	%	%	%	%	%
Sexual partner prior to spouse	6	11	13	18	6
No sexual partner prior to spouse	94	89	87	82	10
No answer	-	-	1	-	-

It can be seen in Table 50 that the pattern for CM is in line with social trends towards increasing sexual permissiveness, whereas that for D is not. The figure for the D 1940s cohort is particularly striking and the similarity between reports from D who married in the 1950s and 1960s suggests that D, as a group, and particularly those from earlier cohorts, can perhaps be regarded as less affected by prevailing societal norms.

Not surprisingly, those informants who claimed that they had no religious affiliation at marriage were apparently more likely to have had a sexual partner prior to marriage (excluding any sexual relationship which they may have had with their eventual spouse) and this was particularly so for CM as Table 51 shows.

TABLE 51

	D		CM	
	Religious affiliation n=367 %	No religious affiliation n=153 %	Religious affiliation n=441 %	No religious affiliation n=128 %
Sexual partner prior to spouse	30	39	12	23
No sexual partner prior to spouse	70	61	88	77

It is a strong clinical impression that, for some people, sexual
experience prior to marriage is a reflection of their need for
affection rather than the simple manifestation of sexual drive.
The extent to which this was so for survey informants, in particular
for D, with their greater prevalence of pre-marital pregnancy, could
not be assessed directly during the survey. However, at the
analysis stage of the study, pre-marital sexual experience was
considered in relation to the quality of the parental marriage. It
was felt that growing up against a background of parental conflict
would increase the likelihood of an unsatisfactory emotional
environment for the offspring, which might cause them to turn more
readily to sexual experiences, but there was, however, no evidence
from the survey data to support this.

EXTRA-MARITAL SEX

The effect which extra-marital sexual experience may have upon the
marital relationship is unclear. Although adultery has long been
legally considered sufficient cause for marital dissolution, only
12% of married informants in one survey (Gorer, 1971) said that they
would consider ending their marriages were they to discover that
their spouse had been unfaithful. Extra-marital sexual activity
may represent a wide variety of causes and effects. It may indicate
deep or fleeting involvements; it may be clandestine or overt; it
may reflect the desire to change partners or merely the need for
more variety of partners. At present little is known regarding its
extent and significance and only very superficial consideration was
possible in this survey.
    Informants were asked the question: 'And during your (former)
marriage did/have you had any affairs or brief sexual relationships
with another man/woman?' 24% DM; 8%CMM; 16% DW; 2% CMW said that
they had had an extra-marital sexual relationship. Divorced
informants, whether DW or DM, who claimed to have had an extra-
marital sexual partner, were more likely than those who did not to
note a very early start to their marital difficulties, as Table 52
shows. However, whether such affairs were a causal factor to the
marital difficulties or whether they were a necessary source of
consolation, either during the marital difficulties or after
cohabitation ceased is not known.

TABLE 52 The start of the marital difficulties related to the prevalence of extra-marital sexual experience

Marital difficulties started	D		DW		DM	
	Extra-marital sex n=100 %	No extra-marital sex n=418 %	Ems n=55 %	No Ems n=281 %	Ems n=45 %	No Ems n=137 %
In the 1st year of marriage	50	43	58	50	40	28
1 but less than 5 years	23	29	18	29	29	29
5 but less than 10 years	15	16	13	12	18	23
10 but less than 15 years	9	9	9	6	9	14
15 years or later	3	4	2	3	4	6

SUMMARY

Overall, the extent of claimed satisfaction with the sexual side of marriage reported by informants in this study was high. However, those who divorced seemed more likely than those who were continuing with their marriages to have been dissatisfied with the sexual side of marriage, either initially or experiencing a later deterioration in this aspect of their marital relationship. Furthermore, those who divorced tended to perceive the causes of their sexual difficulties rather differently from those whose marriages appeared stable, for they adopted a more blaming attitude towards their partner, in contrast to the latter's greater emphasis either upon both partners sharing the responsibility for the sexual difficulties, or referring to the effect of environmental factors such as lack of privacy.

The majority of the people interviewed in this study considered that men and women derive equal pleasure from lovemaking. However, those who thought that there are gender differences in this respect generally regarded the man as obtaining more enjoyment; the small minority who believed that it is the woman who gains more sexual pleasure tended to be divorced men. Innate gender differences in sexuality were cited as the main reason for the man's greater enjoyment of sex, and this belief tended to be accompanied by more acceptance and rather less resentment by those in on-going marriages in contrast to those who had divorced.

The marriages of those who had pre-marital sexual relationship, and in particular a sexual relationship with someone other than their eventual spouse, appeared relatively divorce-prone, although the vast majority of those with such experience had very few other partners. Those without any religious affiliation at marriage were more likely than those with a religion to claim a pre-marital sexual relationship (other than with their spouse).

Very few people claimed to have had an extra-marital sexual relationship but those who did so tended also to have divorced. However, the meaning of such affairs, and the extent to which the extra-marital affair may have been a causal factor in the marital difficulties, or whether, alternatively, it represented a necessary source of consolation, either during cohabitation or after the marriage broke down, is not known.

Chapter 9

THE TIME DIMENSION
OF MARITAL BREAKDOWN

In the natural history of those marriages which end in divorce, four important landmarks in the process of dissolution can be discerned: first, the point in the marriage when the serious marital difficulties were first apparent; second, the point at which cohabitation ceased; third, the time when a divorce was decided upon; and fourth, the point at which the marriage was finally and legally dissolved (that is to say when the decree absolute was granted). These temporal points in dissolved marriages define certain critical phases or intervals in the lives of individual marriages. Such phases may be considered to be reflecting the variety of personal, social and environmental factors which are influencing on the one hand the marital relationship, and on the other hand, the decision processes affecting marital durability. Variations between individual marriages, for example in the tolerance of marital unhappiness, or in the duration of the period between separation and divorce, will thus reflect the total range of these influences.

At the present time, only the interval between marriage and its legal dissolution (the *de jure* duration), is publicly recorded, and these statistics, whilst providing an accurate picture of one aspect of trends in divorce behaviour, will not reflect actual marital duration (in the sense of a couple's personal commitment to their relationship), because cohabitation will have ceased some time prior to the granting of the decree absolute. Accordingly, the period between the wedding and separation (the *de facto* duration), may be regarded as more accuratly representing the temporal life span of a marriage. This period has been estimated both by Chester (1971a) using court records, and by ourselves using data from the present study.

Of particular importance also in the processes leading to divorce, is the duration of any marital satisfaction amongst those who divorce. This 'satisfaction' may be regarded as the period between the wedding and the noting of the start of the serious marital difficulties. Another important interval is that between the start of the marital difficulties and the time when the spouses actually separated; this describes the period during which the couple may be regarded as tolerating their marital unhappiness. Neither of these data can be known from official statistics and were therefore derived from the reports of the survey D.

Finally, the interval between separation and divorce is of
particular importance in the natural history of marital dissolution,
not merely as a measure of the speed of the legal machinery by
which the marriage may be finally terminated but, since many people
do not necessarily separate in order to divorce (Chester, 1972a),
this interval may mark a period of adaptation to the reality that a
marriage is truly over. Chester (1972b) has provided an estimate
of this interval between separation and divorce and the present data
also provide such an estimate.

The points in the marriage when the divorce was decided upon and
the divorce action was initiated also reflect important moments in
the natural history of the dissolution of a marriage. In this survey,
however, informants were not asked when they decided to sue for
divorce, a regrettable omission.

In this chapter each of the periods which have previously been
described as important in the mapping of any trends in the processes
associated with marital dissolution are discussed. It should be
noted that specific questions about the reasons for the marital
problems of the survey divorced were not asked. This was because,
as was mentioned in Chapter 1, the majority of the survey divorced
were relatively recent divorcees.

THE START OF THE MARITAL PROBLEMS

It was evident from the survey data that more than one third of D
believed that the serious marital problems which were ultimately to
lead them to divorce had started by their first wedding anniversary.
By the fifth anniversary these serious marital difficulties had
started for 73% of D. The overall pattern for D can be seen in
Table 53 together with the marked differences in the reports of men
and women.

TABLE 53 Year in the marriage and the start of the marital problems
of the divorced

	All D n=520 %	DW n=336 %	DM n=184 %
By 1st anniversary	37	44	23
2nd	15	15	15
3rd	9	10	8
4th	7	6	8
5th	5	5	5
6th	6	5	7
7th	5	4	8
8th	3	2	4
9th	2	1	3
10th	3	1	5
11th	3	1	4
12th	1	1	2
13th	1	1	1
14th	1	1	-
15th +	4	3	8
Mean duration of marital 'Happiness'	3.87 yrs	3.27 yrs	4.98 yrs

There are two points of particular interest in Table 53; first, the marked gender differences in the perception of when the marriage began to break down and second, the very early start of the marital difficulties for a substantial proportion of D informants. Each is considered in turn.

Gender differences in reporting the start of serious marital problems

It is evident from Table 53 that the reports of DW and DM about the timing of their marital difficulties did not coincide. For instance, DW were more than twice as likely as DM to believe that their marital problems were apparent by the first anniversary. The interpretation of these discrepancies is problematic since the reports are solely those of petitioners (the respondents, i.e. the other partners to the divorced marriages, were not interviewed). Therefore, it is not known how soon after the wedding the respondents (i.e. either the husbands of DW or the wives of DM) believed that their marital problems had started. Were it to be the case that divorced women, irrespective of whether they were petitioners or respondents, tended to notice marital difficulties earlier than their husbands, then this would indicate that gender differences do exist in the perception of marital problems.

Notwithstanding the possibility that women may be more alert than men to the tensions within marital relationships, it may also be that, for various reasons, women are more likely than men to be dissatisfied within marriage. In support of this latter possibility, there is evidence which suggests that marriage offers fewer immediate personal benefits for the wife. For instance, married men appear to be physically and mentally healthier than single men (Gove, 1972) but there are no such differences between single and married women. Furthermore, not only are married men less likely than single men to regard themselves as unhappy (Bradburn and Caplovitz, 1965) but they are less likely than married women to have any mental disorder (Gove, 1972); in the latter case there was no gender difference between single groups. Bernard (1964), Burgess and Cottrell (1939), Burgess and Wallin (1953), Landis (1946) and Blood and Wolfe (1960) observed that it is the wife who must make the greater adjustment to marriage. Additionally, the data obtained by Gurin et al. (1960) from a sample representative of the 'normal' adult population of the USA, indicated that marriage is a more stressful situation for women than for men.

Although a considerable number of research studies have shown that the observed gender differences with regard to personal adjustment and happiness tend in the main to be accounted for by married women, thereby indicating that the reasons may lie in social factors, and in particular, in some aspect of family life, other workers have found what seem to be overall male-female differences in adjusting to life in general. Johnson and Terman (1940), for instance, reported that fifty studies were almost unanimous in finding less emotional balance in women than in men. Other studies, Brim et al. (1962), and Kagan and Moss (1962) demonstrated that women tend to be more dependent and anxious, less confident and less self-sufficient, less

self-accepting and more aware of personal problems than are men.
The extent to which these findings indicate either a genetic predisposition, or merely demonstrate the inevitable outcome of the
processes operating upon women within their social situation is
not known.

The research evidence to date, however, does suggest that, whereas
marriage tends to satisfy men's physical and emotional needs, it
is less likely to do this for women and may for them actually
constitute a stress. It is not difficult to suggest reasons why,
both initially and in the longer term, marriage could be more
stressful for women. The transition from the single to the married
state will almost certainly require less adjustment for men. The
greater part of the husband's day will continue to be spent much as
it was before his marriage, whereas this is rarely so for the wife,
for if she continues to work, she is likely to have to combine the
job of housewife with that of full-time worker outside the home.
This may well produce conflicting requirements between her work
outside and inside the home. Additionally, and perhaps most
importantly, it is known that women who work full-time outside the
home undertake far more household tasks than do men (Young and
Willmott, 1973); this in itself may be a source of stress, partly
because of the fatigue ensuing from the additional workload, but
also, partly, because it means that she will have less opportunity
for relaxation. Notwithstanding the particular problems faced by
the working wife, even if the wife does not work following marriage,
there may be adjustment difficulties for her since she has to learn
to adopt a completely new life-style, and the absence of colleagues,
workmates and the loss of an independent income, will require
varying degrees of adaptation which may all contribute to a sense
of increasing isolation.

ADJUSTMENT DIFFICULTIES IN THE EARLY YEARS OF MARRIAGE

It is a clinical impression that the interaction of the couple in
the early years of their marriage critically affects marital stability,
and the start of marriage has been said to mark the beginning of a
period of disenchantment during which a transition from the myth to
the reality of married life occurs and a couple have to learn to
adapt to one another. Tension and conflict are inevitable in any
close relationship, and conflict within modern marriage, with its
emphasis upon the companionate nature of married life, seems highly
probable. There is some research evidence to suggest the widespread
presence of adjustment difficulties in marriage. For instance,
Landis (1946) reported problems of sexual adjustment among 50% of
his informants, and Pierce (1963) noted adjustment difficulties for
48% of her survey informants, largely to do with housing and finance.
Both of these studies took place in times when there were relatively
clear definitions of husband and wife roles and it seems probable
that more recent marriages, which place a greater emphasis upon
personal happiness, are likely to experience more, rather than less,
uneasy tension. It seems inevitable that such marital tensions will
be particularly marked in the early years of marriage because our
society offers little to its members by way of training for marital

roles; this may be due in part to the trend towards a breakdown in traditional ways of assigning marital roles in relation to employment, housework and the rearing of children, but most likely because the diversity of patterns of living conditions in modern society make such training difficult.   Therefore, in the absence of culturally sanctioned routines, couples are required to improvise what Winch (1971) calls 'marital folkways' and to develop their own private culture.

GENERATIONAL DIFFERENCES IN THE START OF MARITAL DIFFICULTIES OF THOSE WHO DIVORCED

The divorced petitioners in the present survey came from marriages which had taken place between three years and forty or more years before the divorce petition was heard.   This means that marriages of widely differing durations were being examined.   Table 54 shows the variations in the start of marital problems for different generations of D marriages.

TABLE 54   The start of the marital problems related to marriage cohort

	D Marriage cohort			
	Before 1940 n=41 %	1940-9 n=75 %	1950-9 n=149 %	1960-9 n=255 %
By 1st anniversary	37	25	26	46
2nd-4th	22	25	23	37
5th-9th	19	18	28	16
10th-14th	9	12	18	1
15th +	13	19	5	−
Mean duration	4.68 yrs	6.87 yrs	5.11 yrs	2.14 yrs

Although it is evident from the survey data that divorcees from more recent marriage cohorts were progressively more likely to note an early start to their marital problems, this does not necessarily mean that marriages are getting into difficulties progressively earlier. This is because many marriages, particularly those from earlier marriage cohorts, will have already ended in divorce by 1970 (the time from which the survey D sample dated), and many marriages, particularly those from more recent cohorts, have yet to be dissolved by divorce.

SOME FEATURES OF MARITAL DIFFICULTIES IN THE FIRST YEAR

Amongst D informants who claimed that their marital problems had started by their first anniversary, some differences emerged.   For instance, some 19% DW but 7% DM believed their marriages were in difficulty within one month of marriage.   Furthermore, it was

apparent that for DW, serious difficulties in the first year of
marriage were directly related to the prevalance of pre-marital
difficulties, since 62% of DW who had experienced serious pre-marital
difficulties with their eventual husbands, reported that the start
of their marital breakdown was evident by the first wedding anniversary, compared with some 40% of those without pre-marital problems.

Additionally, those marriages involving a teenage bride, and
particularly a pregnant teenage bride, emerged, relative to those
of older, non-pregnant brides, as more likely to be in difficulties
within the first year of marriage. This can be seen in Table 55.

TABLE 55   The relationship between two high risk factors: Pmp and
teenage brides, and the timing of the marital difficulties (DW only)

Marital difficulties started	Bride less than 20		Bride 20 or over	
	Pmp n=81 %	No Pmp n=72 %	Pmp n=47 %	No Pmp n=136 %
In the first year of marriage	53	48	40	34
After the first year	46	52	60	65
Can't remember	1	–	–	1

THE TOLERANCE OF MARITAL DIFFICULTIES

There is little evidence to suggest that couples whose marriages
terminate in divorce separate soon after their serious difficulties
start. The survey data indicate that marital difficulties may be
tolerated for a considerable time before cohabitation ceases, as
Table 56 shows.

TABLE 56   The tolerance of marital difficulties

Problems started	Duration of cohabitation				
	Less than 5 yrs n=186 %	5-9 yrs n=104 %	10-14 yrs n=101 %	15-19 yrs n=64 %	20 yrs + n=60 %
By 1st anniversary	58	24	19	28	30
2nd	19	15	12	10	10
3rd	10	13	7	5	7
4th	7	10	6	5	3
5th	6	5	6	3	3
6th	–	16	9	3	3
7th	–	12	10	3	2
8th	–	3	3	13	–
9th	–	2	6	2	2
10th	–	–	10	3	2
11th	–	–	8	3	5
12th	–	–	3	–	3
13th	–	–	2	5	2
14th	–	–	–	5	–
15th +	–	–	–	11	28
Mean duration to the start of the problems	1.4 yrs	3.3 yrs	5.2 yrs	5.8 yrs	7.9 yrs

It is evident from Table 56 that when their marriages began to get into difficulties, the majority of couples did not quickly separate; and the fact that there was cohabitation for some time after the start of the problems means that there had been the opportunity (at least in time), for the resolution of these difficulties within the marriage.

It can be seen in Table 56 that 50% of those married *de facto* 10-14 years claimed that the marital problems had started by the fifth anniversary, and for nearly a fifth of them the difficulties were apparent by the first anniversary. Many informants who cohabited for between 15 and 19 years after the wedding, experienced severe marital difficulties for at least a further 10 or 15 years after their onset; 28% of these informants claimed that the marital problems which were ultimately to end in divorce had started by the first anniversary, with 51% claiming that the problems were apparent within the first 5 years of marriage. A similar pattern can be seen within marriages which lasted *de facto* over 20 years; their difficulties often started soon after the wedding (nearly 30% claiming that within one year of marriage the problems were apparent), but cohabitation continued for very many more years.

DE FACTO DURATION OF MARRIAGE

The effective duration of marriage, that is the actual duration of marital cohabitation (the *de facto* duration) is obviously briefer than the legal duration. Chester (1971a) has noted that 38% of divorcees in his study had ceased to cohabit by their fifth anniversary, but that only 16% had divorced within this period. The present survey data showed that some 34% of D had separated by their fifth wedding anniversary and 11% had actually obtained a decree absolute by then. Table 57 shows the findings regarding the *de facto* durations of survey marriages.

The survey data in Table 57 indicate that, in marriages in which it is the wife who sues for divorce, cohabitation ceased sooner than in those marriages in which the husband was the petitioner. This differs from the findings of Chester (1971a) who noted that the mean *de facto* duration of the marriages of female petitioners was 9.4 years and that for male petitioners was 8.6 years. There may be several reasons for the differences between these two sets of findings. First, and perhaps most importantly, the female petitioners (DW) in the present study were more likely than the male petitioners (DM) to be from more recent marriage cohorts; 54% DW but 41% DM were married in the ten years preceding their divorce petition, and therefore shorter periods of cohabitation would be more likely for DW relative to DM. Second, and associated with this, the data from this present survey include both those petitioners who were eligible for divorce prior to the working of the 1971 Divorce Reform Act, and those who were only legally able to petition after January 1971 (a category not eligible for divorce at the time of Chester's study); the latter would particularly include those people who were petitioning under the five year separation clause, who would be more likely to be male and from relatively earlier marriage cohorts. An analysis of the present survey data indicated

TABLE 57   Year in the marriage when the final separation occurred

	All D n=520 %	DW n=336 %	DM n=184 %
By 1st anniversary	5	5	5
2nd	7	7	6
3rd	8 } 34%	9 } 37%	5 } 26%
4th	6	7	3
5th	8	9	7
6th	6	6	5
7th	5	5	5
8th	7 } 26%	8 } 26%	5 } 25%
9th	4	3	6
10th	4	4	4
11th	6	5	7
12th	3	3	5
13th	2 } 19%	1 } 16%	3 } 23%
14th	4	3	4
15th	4	4	4
After 15th	22	20	25
Mean *de facto* duration	9.3 yrs	8.3 yrs	10.2 yrs

that DM who petitioned after September 1971 (see Chapter 1 for discussion of the overspill of petitions from 1970 into 1971) had, on average, longer periods of cohabitation than those DW who petitioned during this same period, as Table 58 shows.

TABLE 58

	Petition presented			
	Before Sept.1971		After Sept.1971	
	Male petitioner n=80 %	Female petitioner n=100 %	Male petitioner n=104 %	Female petitioner n=236 %
Survey mean *de facto* duration	10.3 yrs	9.1 yrs	10.7 yrs	8.7 yrs

Other reasons which might help to account for the differences between Chester's findings and those in the present study relate, on the one hand, to the greater possibility of a response bias in this survey relative to Chester's study and, on the other hand, to the possibility of regional differences in divorce behaviour, since Chester's work related to Hull and this study to the West Midlands.

The factors associated with shorter *de facto* durations of marriage

Chester (1972d) in his study of marriages of brief duration (i.e. those lasting *de facto* less than two years), noted that variables such as young age at marriage and pre-marital pregnancy tended to lead to earlier break-up of marriage. In this study, there were few differences between marriages of such brief duration, but those marriages involving a teenage bride were more likely than those in which the bride was older, to have lasted *de facto* less than five years (37% : 28%), and overall, to have had shorter *de facto* durations (a mean of 8.6 years, compared to 10.2 years). Also, pregnant brides were less likely than non-pregnant brides to be still cohabiting with their spouse after five years of marriage (44% : 28%), and overall, they also tended to have had shorter *de facto* durations of marriage (a mean of 8.4 years, compared to 9.7 years).

It was also evident from the survey data that childless couples ceased to cohabit much sooner than did those with children, indicating that their relative infertility must, in part, result from their having had less opportunity to conceive. This can be seen in Table 59.

TABLE 59 The duration of cohabitation and fertility

Cohabitation lasted (years)	Fertile D n=419 %	Infertile D n=101 %
Less than 1	3	14
1-2	5	17
3-4	13	15
5 +	79	55

When the timing of children was related to the *de facto* duration of marriage, women who were fertile in the first year emerged as having had relatively shorter durations of cohabitation. This can be seen in Table 60.

TABLE 60 Early fertility and the *de facto* duration of marriage (DW)

	De facto duration			
	Less than 5 yrs n=131 %	5-9 yrs n=75 %	10-14 yrs n=55 %	15 yrs + n=75 %
Child in 1st year	57	48	40	45
Child after 1st year	12	36	49	48
Childless	31	16	11	7

Chester (1972d) has also noted that within marriages enduring less than two years there was a greater fertility than in continuing marriages of the same *de facto* duration. The data from this survey

indicate that marriages ceasing *de facto* within five years are
associated with both infertility and with relatively higher fertility:
53% of D marriages (DW and DM) lasting *de facto* less than five years,
were fertile by the first anniversary compared with 33% of CM
marriages of equivalent *de facto* duration. Also, by the second
anniversary, D marriages in which cohabitation had lasted less than
five years, had had relatively more children born to them than had
either D marriages which lasted longer, or than had CM marriages of
all durations, as Table 61 shows.

TABLE 61   Year in the marriage and the mean number of live children
born analysed by the *de facto* duration of marriage (calculation
included infertile marriages)

	Duration of cohabitation									
	Less than 5 yrs		5-9 yrs		10-14 yrs		15-19 yrs		20 yrs +	
	D	CM	D	CM	D	CM	D	CM	D	CM
By 1st anniversary	0.49	0.31	0.32	0.35	0.39	0.29	0.45	0.28	0.38	0.33
By 2nd anniversary	0.75	0.59	0.69	0.59	0.71	0.47	0.73	0.59	0.70	0.63

There is little evidence from the survey to suggest that the majority
of those with serious marital problems delayed separating until their
children were independent, since 60% of fertile couples separated
when their youngest child was under 5 years. In 88% of cases the
youngest child was under 11 years when the couple separated and only
18% of fertile divorcees delayed separating until all their children
were beyond statutory school leaving age.

THE INTERVAL BETWEEN SEPARATION AND DIVORCE

Contrary to popular belief, there is little evidence to suggest that
couples quickly seek a legal end to their marriages once cohabitation
ceases. According to Chester (1972b) it appears that, although the
prospect of remarriage may prompt a divorce action, couples tend not
to separate in order to divorce, and he noted a mean interval of
4.6 years between separation and divorce. McGregor (1970) found a
mean delay of five years from magistrate court action to divorce,
and the present survey findings show a mean interval of 5.2 years
from separation to divorce. Table 62 shows the distribution of this
interval amongst survey D, with particular reference to those
petitioning before and after September 1971.

TABLE 62   The interval between separation and divorce

Interval (years)	D n=520 %	DW n=336 %	DM n=184 %	Pre-Sept.1971 D n=180 %	DW n=100 %	DM n=80 %	Post Sept.1971 D n=340 %	DW n=236 %	DM n=104 %
Less than 1	11	9	15	18	14	23	8	7	10
1 but less than 2	20	21	18	23	28	17	18	19	18
2 but less than 3	19	18	19	17	15	20	19	20	18
3 but less than 4	13	15	9	7	8	6	15	17	11
4 but less than 5	8	9	6	4	5	4	10	10	9
5 but less than 6	5	6	4	7	9	4	5	5	4
6 but less than 9	9	10	7	9	12	6	8	9	7
9 but less than 12	4	4	5	3	3	4	5	4	6
12 but less than 15	3	1	6	2	1	4	4	2	8
15 but less than 20	3	1	5	3	2	4	3	1	5
20 +	5	5	7	6	3	9	5	5	5
Mean interval in years	5.2	4.8	5.9	4.8	4.2	5.6	5.4	5.0	6.2

THE *DE JURE* DURATION OF MARRIAGE

The *de jure* duration of marriage is defined as the interval between
marriage and the legal termination of the marriage, the decree
absolute. The mean *de jure* duration of survey marriages was 13.1
years (Chester, 1970, found a mean of 13.7 years). The Registrar
General's returns for successive marriage cohorts show a higher
incidence of divorce at given *de jure* durations of marriage,
indicating a tendency, in more recent years, for earlier legal
termination of marriage. This can be seen in Table 63.

TABLE 63 Percentage of marriages which had ended in divorce at
selected marriage durations (all brides under 45) (source: RG)

Year of marriage	Duration of marriage (exact years)						
	4	5	7	9	11*	13	15
1959	0.3	1.0	2.6	4.2	5.8	7.5	1.0
1961	0.4	1.2	3.0	4.9	7.1	9.9	
1962	0.4	1.3	3.2	5.4	8.3		
1963	0.5	1.5	3.6	6.0	9.1		
1964	0.5	1.7	4.1	7.3			
1965	0.6	1.9	4.7	8.3			
1966	0.7	2.1	5.7				
1967	0.7	2.4	6.4				
1968	0.9	3.3					
1969	1.5	3.6					
1970	1.9						

*   The figures to the right of the dotted lines are affected by the
    Divorce Reform Act, which came into effect in January 1971

The data in Table 63 indicate that the rise in divorce, especially
since 1971, has affected all marriage cohorts at all durations of
marriage. The Registrar General's statistics (OPCS, 1976) also
showed that the marriages of teenage brides, and especially those of
teenage partners, had relatively shorter *de jure* durations. This
was also a finding of the present survey, for teenage marriages had
a mean *de jure* duration of 12.0 years, compared to 13.7 years for
marriages in which the brides were aged 20-4, and 15.0 years if the
brides were aged 25-9. Interestingly enough, marriages in which the
bride was over 35 years had the second shortest *de jure* durations,
a mean of 12.3 years.
    In the survey, the marriages of pregnant brides emerged as having
a shorter legal duration, a mean of 12.0 years, compared with 13.6
years for D marriages in which there was no pre-marital pregnancy.
A social class variation in *de jure* duration of marriage was also
evident from the survey data, with social class V having the shortest
legal duration, a mean of 11.9 years, compared with 12.3 for social
class II; 14.1 for IIIn-m; 13.1 for IIIm; 14.0 for IV.
    Notwithstanding that factors such as young age at marriage, pre-
marital pregnancy or social class, are likely to lead to relatively
earlier legal terminations of marriage, it is, as Leete (1976)
notes, 'difficult to isolate the factors behind the new high level

of divorce'. Factors such as changes in the legislation have
undoubtedly led to a greater existential availability of divorce
but the influence of what Chester (1971c) calls 'normative'
availability, resulting in social and cultural changes in attitudes
towards marriage and divorce, seem likely to be highly relevant.

SUMMARY

Official statistics show that the rise in divorce has affected all
marriage cohorts at all durations of marriage but there is a tendency
towards both more divorce and earlier legal dissolution for more
recent cohorts. In this study, those marriages involving a teenage
bride or groom, a pre-marital pregnancy or those from social class
V had relatively shorter legal durations.

Marriages involving a teenage partner, a pre-marital pregnancy,
early fertility or which were infertile also had relatively shorter
periods of cohabitation. There was little evidence from this study
to suggest that the majority of couples whose marriage is breaking
down delay separating until their children are independent.

When their serious marital problems started, the majority of
couples did not quickly separate and marital difficulties, which
frequently started very early in the marriage, tended to be
tolerated for quite long periods. Nor did people quickly seek to
legally end their marriages once cohabitation had ceased.

More than a third of D believed the serious marital problems
which were ultimately to lead them to divorce had started by their
first wedding anniversary. Within five years, three-quarters of D
marriages had started to break down. Women reported a much earlier
start to their marriage breakdown than did men. These gender
differences, which were quite marked, may be due to a variety of
factors; first, they may simply be reflecting differences in the
marital experiences of male and female petitioners; second, they
may be indicative of gender differences in awareness that the
marriage is in difficulty. Furthermore it is possible that a wife
feels unhappy in a marriage where a husband is contented and this
may partly be because marriage *per se* appears to make more demands
upon women and to be more stressful for them. However, it could
also be partly because many studies have shown that women generally
appear less content than men, this being perhaps due to the kind of
socialisation processes in our society, which have tended to
preclude women from realising much of their potential.

Chapter 10

IN CONCLUSION:
The Characteristics
of those who Divorce

The question of who divorces is extremely complex. The findings
from this study have indicated that, in many ways, those who have
divorced may have had both more environing disadvantage and have
been more at risk to personal stresses. Divorce behaviour, however,
is inevitably affected by the macro-social system and whilst those
who divorce do so because they are unhappily married, other factors
will also influence the actual decision to divorce. According to
Levinger (1976), the private lives of marriage partners are inter-
twined with events in their surrounding social and economic environment and factors both internal and external to the marital relationship will influence marital dissolution. He has provided a 'social-
psychological' conceptual framework in which marital cohesiveness
is seen as the outcome of the attractions and barriers which impinge,
both internally and externally, upon the marital relationship.
Hart (1976), adopting an equally valuable approach, postulates a
model to explain marital breakdown in terms of those factors which,
first, act to reduce the level of commitment or *value* attached to
marriage; second, which tend to exacerbate conflict between spouses
or to inhibit their ability to manage tension, and third, which
increase the opportunities for individuals to escape from an unhappy
marriage.

Both the framework proposed by Levinger and the model suggested
by Hart recognise that being unhappily married may be insufficient
reason to prompt a divorce action; there may be legal, financial,
social or moral considerations which preclude divorce.

However, whereas in the past there may have been very little
overlap between those who were unhappily married and those who
divorced, this may nowadays be less so and it seems likely that those
who divorce and those who are unhappily married will, in the future,
tend to become a more homogeneous group. This is because certain
of the barriers to divorce are diminishing and the viable alternatives to remaining in an unhappy marriage are expanding; for example,
changes in the laws governing divorce have led to its widespread
availability, and there is evidence to suggest that divorce is
increasingly regarded as an acceptable solution to marital unhappiness and is therefore more normatively available within society
than it once was.

In addition to its being existentially more available because
of changes in the law, divorce is currently a more practicable
course of action than it used to be for most people. Whereas in
the past the prospect of marital dissolution and its aftermath may
well have been a less attractive alternative for a couple than the
prospect of continuing marital unhappiness, this is not so true
today. Although loneliness and social isolation may still follow
divorce, certain of the practical difficulties of life on one's
own have been comparatively tempered, and this is particularly so
for the male partner, for the everyday provisions and conveniences
found in a modern industrial society can enable and ease a more
efficient bachelor life. For the woman too, although there may
still be severe emotional trauma whose effects may persist for a
considerable period after the divorce, there are now more viable
alternatives to remaining unhappily married, although the day-to-
day care of and responsibility for dependent children will tend to
reduce the options open to women after divorce. None the less,
increased educational opportunities have meant that a wider range
of employment is now available to a woman, so that, after a divorce,
she is nowadays more often in a position to support herself
financially. Additionally, the availability of social security,
however limited this may be, does ensure that some financial
provision will be made for her and any children, should her husband
be unable or unwilling to provide maintenance.
Accompanying these legal and structural changes in society which
have extended the availability of divorce, there have been changes
in the structure of marriage itself, which will have been bound to
influence factors within the marital relationship. Perhaps the
most striking of these has been the decline in the extended family
network. This decline has resulted in the small family unit of
husband, wife and children, namely the conjugal family, becoming
increasingly the principal source of emotional support and gratification for its members. In particular, the notions of romantic love,
and of a marriage based upon exclusive love between husband and
wife, have meant that men and women will increasingly emphasise the
importance of the marital relationship, with each partner being
expected to recognise and satisfy the emotional needs of the other.
According to Dominian (1968), 'modern marriage is committed to the
goals of independence, freedom and the attainment of the highest
standards of personal fulfilment' and, if this is so, then it is
not surprising that the conjugal family unit is increasingly being
dissolved, since it now bears a heavy burden of demand and, relative
to the extended family, appears a fragile unit. Tension and conflict
are bound to arise in the normal course of events when two people
try to live together, but in modern marriage with its high expectations of personal happiness, relatively more tension and conflict
seems inevitable, and the conjugal family unit would seem to be
equipped with few buffers to withstand such strains.
In the light of the difficulties which might arise between
husbands and wives because of the nature of modern marriage, it is
the survival of the vast majority of marriages, rather than the
dissolution of the minority, which perhaps ought to evoke comment.
Nevertheless, in a society in which over 90% of the population
marry, comment has tended to focus upon the incidence of divorce,

perhaps because it has historically been regarded as abnormal and
even pathological. The notion of divorce as marital pathology
(a term frequently encountered in earlier literature on marital
breakdown) has always had strong connotations of failure, suggesting
that those who divorce have not only failed to sustain a marriage
but also the close human relationship it contains. Whilst clinical
work among unhappily married individuals tends to indicate that it
is their emotional immaturity which is the underlying cause of their
marital difficulties, this is not perhaps a very helpful basis for
locating the causes of marital unhappiness or dissolution, since
emotional immaturity in varying degrees is so common, and most
difficulties in human relationships, marital or otherwise, result
from this.

Research into the causes of marital dissolution, both in this
country and in the USA, has so far not enabled the firm identification of any one, or even several, dominant variables. It therefore
seems probable that the variables which characterise those who
divorce will not only be both numerous and subtle in their interaction with one another but also likely to be indicative of a wide
variety of differing pathways to divorce. However, the delineation
of any inter-relationship between the variables which are predictors
of divorce should permit the composition of typologies of who
divorces; this delineation was attempted in the present study using
two multivariate analysis techniques, namely cluster analysis and
AID (Automatic Interaction Detector).

The technique of AID tends not to be widely used in the social
sciences in this country, possibly because the SPSS package relating
to multivariate analyses does not provide this facility. The data
processing for this present study was almost entirely carried out
by a commercial agency which offers a wide range of multivariate
analysis techniques.

Attempts at compiling the profiles of those who divorce using
cluster analysis proved abortive, largely because the sample size of
D was too small; slightly more success resulted from AID analyses
and groups of inter-correlated survey variables were defined, first
using the *de facto* duration of marriage as the dependent variable
and second, with the *de jure* duration of marriage as the base. The
choice of the *de facto* and *de jure* durations of marriage as the
dependent variables was made because it was hoped that the AID
analyses which thus emerged would provide clues as to the factors
which were influencing the decisions to separate and legally to
terminate a marriage.

The AID programme automatically studied each of the 57 specific
variables which initial cross tabulations had suggested were
correlates of divorce, and progressively divided the divorced sample
into groups delineated by sets of these variables which were highly
inter-correlated. A list of the 57 variables, together with a more
detailed description of the AID programme and its limitations are
contained in Appendix IV.

'TYPOLOGIES' OF D MARRIAGES ACCORDING TO THE *DE FACTO* DURATION OF MARRIAGE

The 57 survey variables were finally grouped into 15 sets; each set consisted of highly inter-correlated variables, distinguished from other 'sets' by the mean *de facto* duration of the D marriages which composed the 'set'. Had the overall sample size of D been larger, then the AID analysis would probably have resulted both in more 'sets' being isolated and in more variables being correlated within the 'sets'. Unfortunately, however, the 'sets' or groups which did emerge are not comprehensive enough to be regarded as typologies; this outcome may reflect, on the one hand, the relatively small sample size of D and, on the other hand, the fact that a considerable number of variables which were felt to have relevance to who divorces could not be included in this study (see Chapter 1). Nevertheless, they can perhaps hint at combinations of stress factors within certain marriages which may have led to their dissolution at particular durations of marriage.

The variable which the AID analysis indicated was initially the most powerful in distinguishing D informants from one another in terms of the *de facto* duration of their marriages, was the size of their family of marriage. D marriages with 3 or more children and those with 0-2 children were distinguished from one another at the outset of the AID analysis, and the final 15 groups originated from these two main branches of the overall D sample.

Group 1 (n=24) was characterised by its relatively long *de facto* duration (a mean of 17.1 years) and was composed of only two inter-correlated variables; first, the presence of 3 or more children of the marriage and second, religious affiliation during marriage either to Catholicism or to Protestant denominations other than the Church of England. This group may perhaps typify those who hesitate to break up their marriages because of a religious commitment to marital stability. Their relatively large family size, however, may be indicative of a moral commitment to marital stability because of the presence of dependent children, or it could simply reflect an opportunity factor due to longer periods of cohabitation. The family size of this set may also be a contributory cause of the marital problems, but the absence of other survey variables within this group means that there are virtually no clues to the reasons for their marital unhappiness, so that it is likely that variables not included in the present enquiry would be necessary to enlarge the typology of this group.

Group 2 (n=43) consisted of informants with 3 or more children who either had no religion at marriage or who were Church of England (which, in some ways, could be regarded as a 'conventional' religious affiliation); a child was born in the first year of marriage, and the wife worked during marriage because she needed to financially, rather than through personal choice. The mean *de facto* duration of these marriages was 9.2 years. This group may perhaps be regarded as experiencing certain economic disadvantages (wife needing to work; a child very early in the marriage), and possibly there would be stresses resulting from having 3 or more children. Their relatively short period of cohabitation may have resulted from the severity of their marital stresses, but it may also be reflecting a weaker religious barrier to divorce, since they do not exhibit the stronger religious barrier which appeared to characterise Group 1.

Group 3 (n=42) consisted of those who had 3 or more children, and were similar to Group 2 in having had either no religious affiliation at marriage, or regarding themselves as Church of England. They did, however, have their first child at least two years after the wedding, and this may account for their longer period of cohabitation, a mean of 14.7 years.

Group 4 (n=25) were similar to Group 2 in the timing and extent of their fertility and their religious affiliation, but differed with regard to aspects of the wife's work. Whereas all the wives in Group 2 worked and did so because they needed the money, those in Group 4 either did not work, or if they did so it was because they 'wanted an outside interest'. Group 4 had a mean de facto duration of 14.5 years, compared with 9.2 years for Group 2, which suggests that economic stresses may well have led to the earlier de facto termination of the marriages in Group 2.

Group 5 (n=100). This relatively large group was distinguished from all other groups by only one factor, although a very precise one, the absence of any children in the marriage. It had the third shortest period of marital cohabitation, a mean of 5.5 years. None of the other 56 survey variables appeared to correlate with this group and were, therefore, not apparently highly relevant to the marital stress of childless couples. The reasons for, and the effects upon a marriage, of childlessness could not be explored in this study, and the inclusion of these variables would have been essential for there to be any further delineation of Group 5.

Group 6 (n=13) had the longest mean duration of cohabitation, 20.2 years. They had relatively small families of marriage (either 1 or 2 children) and their first (or only) child was born relatively late into the marriage, 7 years or more after the wedding. Such marriages would, by then, be likely to have accumulated substantial material assets, and their long period of cohabitation may well be due to the older age of the couple at parenthood, both of which factors might make them unwilling to separate; they thus may typify those who have an economic barrier to divorce. As to the causes of their marital problems, it may be that the birth of a child after a considerable period of married life (when marital habits would have been firmly established), may have exerted a disruptive influence upon the marital relationship.

Group 7 (n=52). This group, in sharp contrast to the previous group, had the shortest mean de facto duration of marriage, 4.5 years. The couple had either 1 or 2 children, the first of which was born in the early years of marriage, and the groom was teenage at marriage. It seems possible that this group reflects those divorcees who were, perhaps, not yet ready for a sustained relationship and whose marriage had foundered early as a result.

Group 8 (n=49). This group, with a mean de facto duration of 6.7 years, which is relatively short, is difficult to interpret in relation to the variables which are demonstrated by this analysis as inter-correlating. They had their first child (either 1 or 2 children were born to these marriages) in the early years of marriage, the groom was 20 years or older and the wife worked at the beginning of the marriage only. It seems likely that, as with

Groups 1 and 5, the other factors which contribute to the disruption of these marriages of relatively brief duration have not been included in this study.

Group 9 (n=42). The marriages in this group also had a relatively short mean de facto duration, 7.4 years, and were distinguished from Group 8 by the work pattern of the wife (who had worked continuously), as well as by the presence of marital opposition from the bride's parents. Opposition to the marriage was the most powerful discriminant in the survey overall between D and CM, so that it is interesting to find it highlighted as a variable for this Group in the AID analysis. It is possible that opposition specifically from the bride's parents, as seen in this group, together with the wife's continuous working, may indicate an important lack of parental support in a marriage which could be in financial need.

Group 10 (n=30) had a similar, and relatively short mean period of cohabitation to that of Group 9, 7.5 years; this group was also similar to Group 9 in fertility and age of the groom (over 20 years), but did not experience any marital opposition from the bride's parents; however, the wife miscarried in the first 3 years of the marriage, which may have constituted a stress early in the marriage. The experience of miscarriage had not emerged at any other stage of the survey as something which might have, in itself, any important implications for divorce, but it can be viewed as a time when some wives might be particularly vulnerable, and perhaps needing to rely strongly upon their husbands who may have failed to give adequate support.

Group 11 (n=15). This small group (mean de facto duration of 8.5 years) are distinguished from Group 10 by the timing of a miscarriage (after 4 years of marriage rather than in the first 3 years) and by the groom or the couple both being older than 16 when leaving school; they may well represent a middle-class group of D.

Group 12 (n=8). This group, also very small, is, in contrast, likely to be of low social status, since it differs from Group 11 on two factors: first, either the groom or the couple left school before they were 16 years of age, and the husband spent one or more of the first 5 years of marriage unemployed (a considerable spell at a critical period). The long mean period of cohabitation of this group, 17.5 years, is however difficult to understand in the light of the probable economic disadvantage experienced by the couples, although the small sample size may be the cause of this paradox.

Group 13 (n=4). This very small group is similar to Group 12 in terms of fertility patterns, groom's age at marriage (20+), most likely being composed of working-class people, and in the pattern of the wife's work (at periods other than just at the beginning). There was either no or little unemployment for the husband during the early years of marriage, and therefore no evidence of economic stresses resulting from this. However, such marriages were specific in that they had 3 or more pre-marital break-ups which may suggest a serious fragility in the relationship with the spouse, even before marriage. The mean de facto duration was 5.0 years, which must however be treated cautiously in the light of the small size of this group.

Group 14 (n=24). This group differed from Group 12 in having had either no or few pre-marital breakups (2 or less). It did,

however, consist of teenage brides and had a mean period of cohabitation of 9.8 years, and may be demonstrating the important vulnerability innate in many marriages with teenage brides.

Group 15 (n=45) with a mean *de facto* duration of 13.5 years had
identical characteristics to Group 14, but consisted of brides who
were 20 years or older, and perhaps highlights the differing
patterns of stress upon the marriages of teenage brides and those
of older brides. However, the absence of further qualifying
variables precludes any elaboration of the typologies of Groups 14
and 15.

'TYPOLOGIES' OF D MARRIAGES OF DIFFERING *DE JURE* DURATIONS OF
MARRIAGE

As with the sets of inter-correlated survey variables which distinguished D marriages according to their *de facto* duration, the
family of marriage size was also the variable which most powerfully
distinguished D in terms of the legal duration of marriage. D
marriages with 3 or more children, and those with 0-2 children were
again distinguished from one another at the outset of this AID
analysis, and the final groups therefore resulted from this
particular initial main division of the D sample.

Groups 1 (n=58) and 2 (n=76) typified those D marriages with
relatively large family sizes (3 or more children), and each
consisted of only one other variable, namely whether or not D
informants had been hospitalised during their childhood or adolescence. Group 1 consisted of those who had ever been hospitalised
and had a mean *de jure* duration of 14.6 years. Group 2, those who
had never been hospitalised, had a longer mean legal duration of
marriage, 18.0 years. The absence of any other survey variables in
these groups makes interpretation problematic. Having been
hospitalised did not emerge as a significant factor in determining
the length of cohabitation, and since the experience of hospitalisation is regarded (for the purposes of this study) as indicating an
increased risk of personal vulnerability, if it were associated with
marital dissolution it might have been expected to have been more
associated with the *de facto* duration of marriage than with the
legal duration. However, the lower mean *de jure* duration for those
D who were hospitalised when growing up may perhaps indicate that
their likely greater personal vulnerability could have made them
wish to end an unhappy marriage more quickly.

Group 3 (n=52) and Group 4 (n=18) were distinguished from each
other by the incidence of churchgoing during marriage. Both groups
had relatively small families (0 or 1 child), and the bride's
parents had opposed their marriages. However, the mean *de jure*
duration of Group 3 was nearly half that of Group 4 (6.6 years
compared with 11.1 years), and Group 3 were far less likely than
Group 4 either to have included those who were churchgoers at all
during marriage, and especially those marriages in which both
partners had attended church regularly.

Group 5 (n=42) consisted of marriages to which the bride's
parents had been opposed, and which also had two children; it had
a mean *de jure* duration of 11.7 years, compared with an overall mean

of 7.8 years for those who also had experienced opposition from
the bride's parents but who had either 1 or no children. As with
many of the groups which were finally delineated by AID analysis,
interpretation is difficult because of the limited number of survey
variables which comprise the group. The contribution to marital
duration of the higher number of children may be causal, in the
sense of being indicative of parental obligation to sustain a
marriage for the sake of the dependent children; on the other hand,
the higher number of children may merely be the outcome of increased
opportunity to conceive because of longer durations of marriage.

Group 6 (n=25) consisted of only 3 variables: first, those with
relatively small families of marriage (either none or 1 or 2
children); second, those for whom there was relatively little marital
opposition and third, who shared their second marital home with non-
relatives. The mean legal duration of marriages comprising this
group was 17.5 years (the second longest mean duration emerging
from this particular AID analysis), and this duration is difficult
to interpret in terms of the 3 inter-correlated variables.

Group 7 (n=28) and Group 8 (n=44) were delineated by 6 survey
variables, 5 of which were identical. First, those with relatively
small families; second, those for whom there was relatively little
marital opposition; third, the second marital accommodation was
either not shared or if it was, it was shared with family rather
than with strangers; fourth, there was a teenage bride or groom.
Groups 7 and 8 were then distinguished from one another according
to certain features of the bride's personality. For example, Group
7, which had a much longer mean *de jure* duration than Group 8
(12.0 years compared with 7.7 years) was more likely to include
wives whom their husbands considered* were stubborn, unable to take
criticism, not home-lovers, selfish, bad-tempered, not animal lovers,
cold personalities, untidy, sulky if annoyed, physically violent,
lazy, unfaithful, depressive, with a cruel tongue, a preference for
outsiders, a show-off, a heavy drinker and not very talkative.
Group 8's shorter mean *de jure* duration of marriage was seemingly
typical of wives whose husbands regarded them as pessimistic,
lacking in confidence, critical of others, indecisive, moody,
unaffectionate, jealous, easily hurt and secretive. Groups 7 and 8
are composed entirely of male petitioners to the divorce and the
perceived traits of their wives do, in general, seem to distinguish
between more outgoing, extroverted perhaps more confident, independent wives of Group 7 marriages and the more demanding, insecure,
possibly introverted wives of Group 8 marriages. The differences
in the overall legal duration may mean that husbands who perceive
their wives as demanding or clinging, may find that such characteristics prompt a desire for earlier marital termination.

Group 9 (n=21) consisted of the first 4 variables associated with
Groups 7 and 8; perceived personality qualities in the spouse, had

* Informants' perception of their spouses' personality qualities
  was not included in the earlier discussion of factors which
  distinguish D from CM because the marked differences between them
  seemed likely to be reflecting a tendency of D to over-emphasise
  their partners' negative qualities. It was felt that the differences between D informants in the perception of their spouses'
  personality qualities would be more informative.

no relevance to this group, and the fifth variable which highly correlated, namely marital opposition, makes the relatively long mean *de jure* duration of 14.4 years quite difficult to interpret.

Groups 10 (n=47) and 11 (n=26) each consisted of marriages between partners who were not teenagers. In both cases the families of marriage were relatively small, and marital opposition was likely to have occurred but rarely; if the second accommodation had been shared, then sharing was with family, rather than with strangers. These two groups diverged in terms of the pattern of the wife's work. Group 10 wives either worked part-time or not at all during their marriage, whereas Group 11 wives only ever worked full-time (and Group 11 were also home-buyers). The much shorter mean legal duration of Group 11 of 8.7 years (17.0 years for Group 10) may reflect several causes; first, there may have been more economic pressures within these marriages; second, there may have been more stresses resulting from the wife trying to combine a full-time job with the running of a home; third, wives who did work full-time may more likely have had a satisfying career outside the home and may, on the one hand, have been financially more independent; fourth more continual working outside the home may have provided more opportunities to find another partner.

Groups 12 (n=13); 13 (n=13); 14 (n=8); 15 (n=45) shared 6 characteristics. First, neither partner was teenage; second, their family of marriage size was relatively small; third, accommodation sharing was unlikely, but if it did occur it was with family; fourth, the wife worked full time during marriage; fifth, parental opposition was relatively rare and sixth, they were in rented accommodation rather than home owners, and were, therefore, more likely to be working class.

Group 12 had a mean legal duration of 17.5 years and although the wife worked full-time during the marriage, she did not work continuously. The relatively long *de jure* duration of this group may be reflecting relatively few external stresses upon the marital relationship.

Group 13 (n=13) also had a relatively long mean *de jure* duration of marriage, 16.3 years, and differed from Group 12 both in the pattern of the wives' work and in churchgoing, in that wives in Group 13 were more likely only to work at the beginning of their marriage and the divorce petitioner was a churchgoer; the latter feature may have been particularly influential in causing a relatively long legal duration of marriage.

Group 14 (n=8) differed from Group 13 in that the petitioner was unlikely to be a churchgoer and the husband was unemployed at the time of the marriage. This group had the shortest mean legal duration of marriage, 6.2 years, and economic disadvantage coupled with no religious barrier to divorce, seem factors likely to contribute to such a short *de jure* duration.

Group 15 (n=45) was identical to Group 14 except that the husband was employed and this was the sole factor which correlated with a doubling in length of the de jure duration of the marriages of this group (12.2 years compared with 6.2 years for Group 14).

The previous discussion has been largely descriptive, in the sense that it has been concerned with the attempt to identify typologies of those who divorce using multivariate analysis procedures. This next section focuses upon the range of factors which appear to be correlates of divorce, and a possible underlying mechanism is suggested whereby the diversity of the specific correlates of divorce may be related and perhaps better understood. It is suggested that the majority of the correlates of divorce (both from this study and from other studies), may be explained with reference to their influence upon communication between the spouses.

EFFECTIVE COMMUNICATION AND ITS INFLUENCE UPON MARITAL HAPPINESS AND DIVORCE

The notion that effective communication between the spouses may have a fundamental relevance to marital stability may, at first sight, be regarded as relating principally to middle-class marriages and therefore having only a narrow application; this is, perhaps, because several studies have shown that while verbal communication tends to be an important element in marital satisfaction for 'white collar' marriages, it is not so immediately relevant to those marriages which emphasise instrumental roles. Communication in the present discussion, however, is used in a rather wider sense, and is conceived as encompassing the total process whereby husbands and wives learn to understand the needs and expectations of each other; the process thus defined makes use of both verbal and non-verbal cues, and as such would be relevant to both the companionate and the instrumental models of marriage. Effective communication is believed by us to have an increasing relevance to marital stability as opposed simply to marital happiness because the contraction of the extended family into the more focused conjugal family unit of husband, wife and children, has meant a reduction in the number of sources available to an individual for the satisfaction of his emotional needs. In modern marriage, if mutual needs are to be adequately recognised, understood and satisfied, effective communication between the partners seems essential, otherwise marital dissolution may result since the barriers to divorce have diminished and there now exist more options to remaining in an unhappy marriage.

There are perhaps three general points which first need to be made before considering the usefulness of the notion of effective marital communication as an underlying process in terms of which the seemingly diverse and weak correlates of divorce may be better perceived and interpreted. First, effective communication requires that there exists between the partners the opportunity to communicate (either through a physical presence, the willingness to disclose or recognise needs or expectations, or because the spouses each attach a similar meaning to certain cues, verbal or non-verbal). Second, although marital discord seems inevitable in any modern marriage when there is an absence of communication, discord can, of course, still occur in marriages where communication is fully effective between those partners who may be unwilling or unable to meet the needs and expectations which they have accurately perceived in each other. Third, the tendency for the small conjugal family unit increasingly to become a principal source of affectional reward may have greater implications for the wife than for the husband, since a husband at present has potentially more sources of affirmation in his life than has a wife. He has, for example, more continuity of experience in adulthood and fewer abrupt changes of life style; after marriage the bulk of his day is probably spent much as it was prior to it, and parenthood will involve fewer changes for him since he is unlikely to have the main responsibility

for the care of children. Furthermore, his career, his job and work
peers will provide him with an important source of personal affirmation each working day, whereas wives who are mothers may well spend
most of their time at home alone with small children, and are therefore more likely to have to look to their husbands for their identity
confirmation and emotional gratification, which may make undue
demands upon the marital relationship. Communication between the
spouses may, therefore, be of greater importance to women, and may
account for the finding from this study that women report a much
earlier start to their marital difficulties than do men, since it
would be likely that they would be more aware of inadequacies in
interaction.

It has been shown in other studies, and to some extent in this
present one, that partners who are dissimilar in culture, social
background or religion, or too disparate in age, are more prone to
divorce. Such dissimilarity has obvious relevance to communication
difficulties. If there is a high degree of mutuality already
existing between the couple, so that they embark on a marriage
already sharing similar influences, attitudes and values, then it
is very much more likely than if they do not, that there will already
exist a basic framework within which the communication to each other
of their needs and expectations can more easily take place.

Heterogamous couples from very different backgrounds may be
considered as having their marital relationship already at risk
through internal stresses caused by problems such as poor communication, and they may thus be less able to cope with any stresses which
may impinge upon the marriage from outside. The present survey also
suggests that couples who have short courtships are relatively
divorce-prone, and internal stresses within these marriages seem
likely to arise between people who may well be relative strangers
when they marry, since they will have had only a limited period in
which to get to know one another.

Poor communication between a couple may arise for a variety of
reasons: it may be due to the partners' dissimilar backgrounds, or
to an insufficient pre-marital acquaintance, but it seems likely
that it will also be found in marriages where the partners have no
enduring sense of their individual identities, and may even have a
certain instability of personal identity. In this respect, the
divorce-proneness of teenage marriages found in the present study,
may, in part, be interpreted in terms of a greater likelihood of
severe difficulties in communication for couples whose emotional
development may be incomplete, and whose own pressing individual
needs may make them less able to respond to the needs of their
marriage partner.

There are also certain other factors which may cause communication
at some levels between the spouses to be impaired, so that adequate
emotional gratification is prevented. For example, the requirements
of the children of a marriage may be so exacting that their presence
in some ways prevents the formation and development of effective
inter-spousal communication, so that whilst children may be sources
of affectional reward in themselves, their arrival early in a
marriage has been shown in this study to be correlated with divorce.

Similarly, it seems to be the case that there are other external
factors which seem to correlate with divorce, such as low income, or

sub-standard housing, which may in addition to depriving a couple
of environmental benefit, also limit the opportunities they may
have for being able to relax together, thus reducing the likelihood
of effective communication between them. Furthermore, a low level
of education has emerged as a further correlate of divorce, and,
whilst closely related to social factors such as social class and
low pay, it may none the less be an independent element which can
inhibit effective communication between the spouses, through
inadequate development of verbal skills, and hence, perhaps, less
ability to 'self-disclose' to the partner. Since overall there
does appear to be a general shift in our society towards the
companionate type of marriage, it seems likely that verbal skills
will have increasing relevance to marital stability.

Dissatisfaction with the sexual side of the marital relationship,
especially at the beginning of the marriage, is another correlate
of divorce which has been found in this study, and suggests that,
whatever the total causes of the dissatisfaction may have been, the
marriages of many of those who divorce will, from the outset, have
lacked one important source of mutual reassurance and affirmation.

A further strand which has emerged from this study, which seems
to have a direct bearing upon the communication patterns of the
marriage partners, relates to the courtships of those who divorce.
The experience of any pre-marital break-up *per se*, and the greater
number of such break-ups, both of which were more characteristic
of D rather than CM, together with the reasons given by D for
breaking-up may largely be regarded as resulting from communication difficulties. Ineffective communication seems particularly
likely to arise when there is unevenness of pace in the marriage
partners' relationship during the courtship period and this seemed
particularly so for some D as evidenced by only a slender desire
for marriage by one partner, but a firm determination on the part
of the other formally to seal their relationship.

The actual pace of the development of a relationship may well
have important implications for its durability; relationships which
develop relatively slowly, and with a minimum of external stresses
requiring response and adjustment, seem more likely to promote
effective marital communication, since the couple have more
opportunity both to learn about one another and to cope with the
inevitable internal tensions in their relationship. Lack of ritual
preparation for marriage, in the sense of the absence of formal
engagements, church weddings and honeymoons has been shown to be
associated in this study with divorce. It may therefore be that
those who do experience a more ritualised transition from the
single to the married state (and in particular women who do so) are
better equipped to allow their marital relationship to develop at
a slower pace, since they enter marriage with a stronger sense of
their own new marital identity and are less likely to seek confirmation of this from their partners, especially in the earlier stages
of marriage.

Another component of the spectrum of who divorces, which may
also indicate underlying poor communication between the partners,
is the apparent lack of planning evident in the lives of some of
those who divorce, a lack particularly noticeable for D with regard
to patterns of housing. There appeared to be a definite category

of D delineated in this study whose housing pattern seemed erratic
and unplanned. They moved home relatively frequently and invariably
were compelled to leave because of serious discord, either with
their landlord or with relations, and there would seem to be little
likelihood of mutually satisfying marital communication being
fostered by married life in such uncertain environments.

Pre-marital pregnancy is another correlate of divorce, and its
influence upon the marital relationship appears to be greatest when
it is in conjunction with two other factors, namely an associated
courtship disruption and a husband in a low economic position; both
of these would tend to restrict both pre-marital and marital
opportunities for effective 'communication' between the partners.
In this study, the contrasting experiences of D and CM who were
pre-maritally pregnant suggested that the latter would have had both
more opportunity to get to know one another prior to marriage and,
following marriage, would have been more likely to have more parental
support. Whilst the exact nature of the causal relationship between
parental disapproval of a marriage and divorce is unclear, in
marriages where there is both parental approval of the marriage and
good family relations after the wedding, then there will be important
support for the newly-weds, which may make them less compelled to
concentrate all their emotional needs in each other, and their marital
relationship can therefore develop more slowly and may be correspondingly more likely to consolidate.

Expectations which the couple may have of one another regarding
role fulfilment constitute a special aspect of marital communication;
such expectations may vary widely, but the expectation that the
husband will be the principal material provider still seems generally
to hold. In this study, D husbands were more likely than CM husbands
to have been unemployed during the early years of marriage and overall to have been out of work for longer. Research findings from
other studies have shown that marital unhappiness is also correlated
with certain work patterns of the wife; wives who either work full-
time, or work because they are financially obliged to, rather than
through personal choice, tend to have less happy marriages; this may
reflect impaired opportunities for inter-spousal communication due
either to the fatigue of the working wife, or to related economic
disadvantage which may reduce the opportunities for effective
communication. However, it may also be indicative of a barrier to
communication between the couple because of a discontent or resentment between them with regard to basic marital roles.

Barriers to effective communication between the spouses may, it
is postulated, have a generational, social, cultural or educational
origin. Additionally they may result from the personal vulnerability
of one or both spouses, which may militate against their being able
either to receive from, or give to their spouses, adequate affectional rewards. As Winch (1971) notes, 'it is one of the ironies
of inter-personal relationships that the techniques of resolving
marital tension and conflict are least available to those who need
them - the hostile and the insecure.' Clinical and therapeutic
work amongst those with serious marital problems frequently points
to such underlying barriers to emotional gratification between the
spouses. Such barriers are typical of those whose childhoods were
hallmarked by a discordant emotional climate existing either between

their parents or between themselves and their parents. Parental
marital discord does appear from other studies to correlate with
offsprings' emotional difficulties, and in this present study
informants' parental marital unhappiness was associated with marital
unhappiness in the offspring.

On the question of parent-child discord and its implications for
the offspring in terms of their abilities either to receive or give
affectional rewards within marriage, rather less is known. There
are certain data from this study which are indicative of greater
underlying levels of parent-child discord for D relative to CM.
First, parents of D who were opposed to their child's marriage
frequently tended to remain hostile after the wedding, and in many
cases even to break off their relationship with their child
completely. Since intimate relationships are not easily broken,
this behaviour may perhaps indicate rather less parent-child closeness and probably therefore more parent-child conflict for D relative
to CM. Second, the greater experience among D of relatively frequent
and long periods of separation in hospital, whilst in itself liable
to increase the risk both of long-term anxiety and of impeded
emotional development, may also point to inadequate parental
management of illness and to underlying parent-child tensions.
Third, some D clearly used marriage as a means of escape from a home
in which they were unhappy; not only, therefore, was their mate
selection liable to be high risk (because it was not so much a
choice of partner which was made but rather a choice between situations of living), but also, since such parent-child discord was
unlikely to have been short-term, it therefore seems likely that an
unsatisfactory climate for adequate emotional growth had long
existed in their family of origin.

IN CONCLUSION

This study has been an attempt to discover who divorces and the
complex nature of the subject matter has, from the outset, meant
that this question could only at best be answered in part. It is,
however, hoped that some impressionistic and useful lines of
approach have been drawn which may, perhaps, generate future
hypotheses, and give rise to further and more focused research.
In particular, those areas whose exploration was either entirely
precluded from this study or which could only be superficially
dealt with by the survey interview technique might be investigated
in depth. Examples of such future research areas include the
implications which the type and quality of the parent-child
relationship have for offspring marital happiness and stability;
the effect of parental remarriage upon offspring emotional development and offspring marital outcome; the relationship between
preferred parent, parent-child closeness and subsequent mate
selection outcomes; the relationship between differing patterns of
interspousal communication and divorce; the relationship between the
personality traits of the marriage partners and divorce; which
factors reduce the risk of environing disadvantage resulting in
divorce; which factors facilitate the negotiation and resolution
of marital tensions without the resort to marital dissolution and

finally, to what extent, if any, does the relatively easy legal, financial and normative availability of divorce mean that contemporary couples may less readily make a lasting commitment to deep and intimate relationships.

Appendix I

THE SAMPLE

It was not possible to compile a national sampling frame of divorcees
because permission to use the court records in order to do so could
not be obtained. A location in the West Midlands was therefore
chosen as the study area because it was possible to compile for this
area a complete sampling frame of individuals who had been granted a
decree nisi at the local divorce court. Three other local areas,
namely those served by the Gloucester, Derby and Reading divorce
courts were also considered as possible study areas. However, the
one in the West Midlands was finally decided upon because this region
compared well nationally (in comparison with the other three regions),
in terms of its social class distribution (see Table A), and because
it was also administratively the most convenient area to study.

TABLE A

Registrar General's social class	South West %	North Midland %	West Midland %	Southern %	England and Wales %
I	4	3	3	5	4
II	19	14	13	17	15
III	47	52	54	49	51
IV	21	23	21	20	21
V	9	8	8	8	9

THE SAMPLE OF PETITIONERS

It is the practice of certain regional newspapers to publish, after
every sitting of the local divorce court, the names and addresses of
all the petitioners to the divorce case. The sampling frame for the
survey divorced group was constructed from such lists published by
the regional newspaper serving the study area for those divorces
granted between the beginning of September 1970 and the end of March

1972. In order to test the accuracy of the newspaper reporting, a 20% sample of newspaper lists was checked against the equivalent official matrimonial cause lists and found to be complete.

The sampling frame consisted entirely of petitioners, since the name and address of the other party to the divorce, the respondent, was only intermittently reported in the newspaper. The period September 1970 - March 1972 was decided upon for two reasons. First, it is known that divorcees tend to be geographically mobile, and therefore the response rate would be likely progressively to diminish the greater the time lag between the granting of the decree nisi and the start of the survey fieldwork; September 1972 was the date set for the start of the fieldwork, this being six months after the granting of the last decree nisi included in the sampling frame and would, it was intended, allow sufficient time to have elapsed for the decree nisis granted to have been made absolute. A second reason for choosing the period September 1970 - March 1972 was to allow for the investigation of any differences between first, those petitioners divorcing prior to the working of the 1969 Divorce Reform Act (which took effect from January 1971), second, those divorcing in the early months of the operation of this Act, and third, those who petitioned after the period when it was thought that the likely backlog of petitions made eligible by the new law would have been dealt with.

To minimise sample loss due to geographical mobility it was decided to select petitioners from the sampling frame in the following proportions:

Those divorcing Sept. 1970-Dec.1970 to constitute 15% of the sample
Those divorcing Jan.1971-Aug.1971 to constitute 15% of the sample
Those divorcing Sept.1971-Mar.1972 to constitute 70% of the sample

THE SAMPLING FRAME OF PETITIONERS

1,534 petitioners constituted the sampling frame. The vast majority of them lived within a twenty mile radius of the divorce court, as can be seen in the table below:

Petitioner's address	Petitions Sept.-Dec. 1970	Petitions Jan.-Aug. 1971	Petitions Sept.1971- Mar.1972	All Petitions
Within 6 miles of court	194	368	481	1,043
Within 20 miles of court	63	154	196	413
More than 20 from court	17	25	36	78
Total	274	547	713	1,534

Of those divorcing Sept.1970-Dec.1970 34% were male, 66% were female
Of those divorcing Jan.1971-Aug.1971 41% were male, 59% were female
Of those divorcing Sept.1971-Mar.1972 37% were male, 63% were female

The pilot work of the study had indicated that a 70% response rate

would be likely, allowing for refusals and untraceable petitioners.
In order to obtain a final sample of 500 petitioners, it was
estimated that some 716 petitioners should therefore be selected
from the sampling frame, as follows:

	Total Petitioners	Male	Female
Those divorcing Sept.1970–Dec.1970	107	36	71
Those divorcing Jan.1971–Aug.1971	108	44	64
Those divorcing Sept.1971–Mar.1972	501	185	316
Total	716	265	451

SAMPLE SELECTION

The names and addresses of all the petitioners who constituted the
sampling frame (within a 20 mile radius of the divorce court) were
grouped into postal districts according to the sex of the petitioner
and within the three broad petitioning periods under consideration.
The sampling interval was calculated and the starting point determined
by random number procedure. The 78 petitioners who lived outside
this 20 mile radius were scattered about the UK and 25 of them were
selected according to convenience of interviewing. Any slight bias
introduced thereby was regarded as acceptable in the light of the
costs which would have been incurred were the selection procedure
to be totally random.

Towards the end of fieldwork it became necessary to select more
names and addresses from the sampling frame, due to the disappearance
of two interviewer working areas demolished as part of local authority
redevelopment programmes; all efforts at tracing petitioners from
these areas proved abortive. Random selection in line with the
original procedure was again adopted.

In the survey 832 addresses were visited, resulting in 520
successful interviews amongst 336 female petitioners and 184 male
petitioners. The refusal rate for female petitioners was 20%. that
for males was 25%.   12% female petitioners and 20% of male
petitioners could not be traced, due mainly to geographical mobility,
but in some instances to their death.

In order to minimise the refusal rate it was decided to write to
those petitioners who had refused to be interviewed (excluding those
who had been violently opposed) explaining in more detail about the
study and then sending another interviewer to them to try to obtain
an interview. However, this procedure proved unsuccessful since the
number of interviews so obtained was very small with 50 attempts at
interviewing those who had refused resulting in only 2 interviews.

THE SAMPLE OF CONTINUING MARRIED PEOPLE

The electoral registers of the area within a 20 mile radius of the
divorce court (that is the area in which 95% of the petitioners in

the period under review lived) served as the sampling frame for the
continuing married sample. All 314 polling districts within the
chosen area were listed and 100 polling districts were selected by
calculation of the sampling interval, the starting point being
determined by random number procedure.

Informants in the married sample had to be in a primary (i.e. a
first) marriage of at least two years' standing so that certain
comparisons between D and CM could be made, which could take into
account the *de facto* duration of the marriage. It was also felt
necessary to restrict the enquiry to those under 60 years of age
for three reasons. First, since most divorces occur amongst people
under 60 years of age, a younger sample of CM would be more
comparable to the D sample. Second, it was felt that a very long
questionnaire would be too fatiguing for many older informants and
third, because the Eysenck lie score apparently increases markedly
for subjects aged 60 years and over, possibly indicating an increased
desire to present a socially acceptable picture of themselves.

It was decided to select some 2,000 electors in order to guarantee
a minimum of 500 interviews with continuing married people; this
estimation allowed for a 30% refusal rate, divorced and single
electors and those aged 60 years or more. The electors in the chosen
polling districts were listed, the sampling interval calculated and
the starting point determined by random number procedure. In
practice, 1,211 contacts resulted in 570 interviews. Interviews
were, however, conducted in all of the selected polling districts and
although the contact estimation proved inaccurate, since the
selection of electors was done at the research centre and interviewers
were only sent new names and addresses when their previous quota had
been completely followed through, it seems unlikely that an area bias
would have resulted. Interviewing was stopped when 199 men and 371
women had been interviewed. Of those eligible for interview, 69% of
women and 72% of men were successfully interviewed. 4% of women and
7% men proved untraceable. 26% of women, 21% of men refused to be
interviewed and, in many instances, it appeared that the husband of
the eligible female interviewee was instrumental in causing her
refusal, since many appointments with women were subsequently
cancelled, apparently at the husband's directive.

COMPARISON OF SAMPLE STATISTICS WITH OTHER STATISTICS

THE DIVORCED SAMPLE
(a) Marriage cohort

Year of marriage	D	All divorcing in 1971
	%	%
Before 1930	1	2
1930–4	3	2
1935–9	4	4
1940–4	6	5
1945–9	9	9
1950–4	13	11
1955–9	16	17
1960–4	27	26
1965–9	22	23
1970 +	–	–

Comment

The cohorts of sample divorces consisted largely of those divorcing
in 1971 and these compare very well with the Registrar General's
national figures. (Source for the RG figures - 1971 Statistical
Review Part II, p.82, Table P.7(a).)

(b) Bride's age at primary marriage

Bride's age	D	All divorcing in 1971
	%	%
Under 20	44	40
20-4	43	48
25-9	7	9
30-4	3	2
35 +	2	1

(Registrar General - England and Wales. Source as above.)

Comment

The survey sample of divorcees seems slightly over-represented by
the under 20s and slightly under-represented by the 20-4s compared
with the national statistics. This might be reflecting a regional
difference or it may be indicating an age of bride at marriage bias
in the sample. Since there is no access to court registries it will
not be possible to resolve this difference. However, the trend is
in accordance with the national trend and the differences between
the two groups are quite small.

(c) *De jure* duration of marriage

	D	All divorcing in 1971
	%	%
Less than 5 years	12	13
5-9 years	26	30
10-14 years	23	19
15-19 years	12	13
20 years +	27	25

Comment

The sample statistics and the national statistics on *de jure*
duration compare reasonably well. There is a possible small sample
bias/regional difference in the 5-9 and 10-14 year groups. (Source
for the RG figures 1971 Statistical Review Part II, p.76, Table P.4.)

(d) Family size

	D	All divorcing in 1971
	%	%
No children	19	27
1	29	25
2	25	26
3	13	13
4	8	5
5 +	5	4

Comment

The divorced sample appears to under-represent couples without
children. Assuming that an area difference of 8% is unlikely, the
sample bias might be largely accounted for by the 14% of contacts
who were untraceable - the absence of children will facilitate
mobility. (Source of the RG figures - 1971 Statistical Review,
Part II, p.78, Table P.5(a).)

(e) Social class

Four descriptions of social class were derived from the survey data.

(1) The social class of the breadwinner in the informant's and
     spouse's home when he/she was 16 years of age. This is also
     used as a main analysis break.
(2) The social class of the informants and spouses as indicated
     by their first full-time occupation.
(3) The social class of the couple as indicated by the husband's
     occupation at marriage.
(4) The social class of the couple as indicated by the husband's
     occupation at the time of the *de facto* breakdown of the
     marriage.

Considering (1) above. The survey covered marriages taking place
from 1930 to 1969; informants' ages ranged from 20 to 60 years.
Hence, the social classes described could well cover a span of 40-50
years. It is not possible to compare the sample breakdown of breadwinner social class with any official statistics.
Considering (2) above. The age at which the first full-time job
was taken varied from 14 to 23 years and also covered several
decades. Hence, it is not possible to check these figures against
official statistics.
Considering (3) above. The same problems as for (1) and (2).
Considering (4) above. The divorce court rules require that a
husband's current or last occupation be entered on the petition.
Apart from the fact that there is, at present, no access to the
court records, any description of social class thus derived cannot
be directly compared with (4) above since our research enumerates
husband's occupation at the *de facto* breakdown of the marriage
whereas official statistics relate to the husband's occupation at
the *de jure* breakdown of the marriage.
Although direct comparisons between survey divorce social class
statistics and official statistics cannot be made, it can be useful
to see the differences in the various data sources since it seems
unlikely that there would be marked differences between sources.
This can be seen in Table B. It should be noted that the census
enumerates currently divorced males, *not* ever-divorced males. Also,
the divorce noted may be the result of a primary or later marriage,
whereas survey divorces relate to terminations of primary marriages
only. Similarly the Gibson calculations are based upon all marriages
rather than upon primary marriages.
It is, however, possible that survey D over-represents social
class IIIm. This might be a result of the success of interviewers
in gaining the co-operation of this group. Certainly, interviewers
reported that the 'upper' classes and the 'rougher' elements of the

TABLE B

RG Class	Occupation of breadwinner (survey divorced) %	Occupation of husband at marriage (survey divorced) %	Occupation of husband at de facto break-down (survey divorced) %	Occupation of currently divorced males (1971, RG for Great Britain) %	Occupation of those males divorcing in 1961 (Colin Gibson) %
I	Ø	Ø	–	3	3
II	14	5	12	16	14
IIIn-m	7	9	11	11	19
IIIm	53	49	49	38	37
IV	16	13	15	20	16
V	10	10	6	12	11
Armed services/unclassified	–	14	7	–	–
Non-manual	21	14	23	30	36
Manual	79	72	70	70	64

working classes contacted in the survey accounted for the majority
of refusals.
　　Source of RG statistics - Economic Activity Tables 1971 Census
D.T.604.
Source of Gibson statistics - 'British Journal of Sociology', March
1974, Divorce and Social Class in England and Wales, Table II, p.82.

(f)　The presence or absence of pre-marital pregnancy

	All D %	Fertile D %	Those fertile women divorcing in 1966 (RG) %	All legal research unit divorced (fertile & infertile) %
Pmp	32	40	33	20
NoPmp	68	60	67	80

(Source of RG and Legal Research Unit figures - Divorce and Social
Class in England and Wales. C. Gibson, BJS, March 1974, p.85.)

Comment

The MRC sample of divorcees seems to over-represent divorcees who
were fertile at marriage. It will be remembered that the sample also
appears to over-represent brides aged under 20 years, those from
manual worker backgrounds and to under-represent childless couples.
(According to other research findings,* brides aged under 20 are more
likely to be working-class and are the most likely to be pregnant
at marriage.) It may be that RG data relating to those divorcing
in 1971 will show a higher proportion of fertile brides than was
enumerated by the 1966 data - but if there is a survey sample bias
on pre-marital pregnancy, it is possibly accounted for by the three
factors mentioned.
(* Source: C. Gibson, Divorce and Social Class in England and Wales,
'BJS', March 1974, pp.84-5.)

THE CONTINUING MARRIED SAMPLE

(a)　Marriage cohort
Official figures for a given marital cohort include those marriages
which will end in divorce, annulment or death, and, hence, cannot be
directly related to our sample statistics on primary marriages.
　　CM survey marriages are set out below against the Registrar
General's figures for England and Wales. An examination of the
figures for the West Midlands showed there to be very little
variation from the national figures. Also, those at present living
in the West Midlands were not necessarily married there.

	CM %	All primary marriages (Registrar General) %
1930–4	1	10
1935–9	5	12
1940–4	11	12
1945–9	14	13
1950–4	16	12
1955–9	12	11
1960–4	18	11
1965–9	20	13

Comment

The low comparability for the 1930–4 cohort is most likely due to termination of marriages by death with a consequent higher proportion of more recent cohorts in the CM sample.
(Source of RG figures – Statistical Reviews 1930–69 – Usually Table 6.)

(b) Bride's age at primary marriage
There are two problems here which preclude proper comparisons between survey and official statistics.

  (i)   The contamination of the number of official primary marriages by future divorcees.
 (ii) Before 1958, the Registrar General tabulated age at marriage in terms of under 21, rather than under 20. Hence, only cohorts 1960–4 and 1965–9 can be related, and the data is shown in Table C.

(c) Family size

	None CM %	None RG* %	One CM %	One RG %	Two CM %	Two RG %	Three CM %	Three RG %	Four CM %	Four RG %	Five + CM %	Five + RG %
1940–9	4	–	24	–	28	–	25	–	11	–	8	–
1950–9	6	–	19	–	35	–	21	–	12	–	4	–
1960–9	11	–	29	–	45	–	12	–	2	–	1	–

* At present no official data is available. The Office of Population Censuses and Surveys stated (Nov.1974) that the 1971 census fertility analysis would be published in the summer of 1975 but this has not yet been done. The relevant table is 'Women with uninterrupted first marriage, size of family by year of marriage and age at marriage' – Draft table 568 of Fertility Analyses.

TABLE C

	Under 20		20-4		25-9		30-4		35+		All	All
	CM %	RG %	CM %	RG %	CM %	RG %	CM %	RG %	CM %	RG %	CM %	RG %
1960-4	36	32	48	56	12	9	3	2	-	1	105	1,475,382
1965-9	40	31	49	53	8	11	1	3	2	2	116	1,618,674

(Source of RG figures - Statistical Reviews, Part II, 1960-9 (usually Table G, p.53), spinsters who married bachelors).

TABLE D

RG. Class	Occupation of breadwinner (survey CM) %	Occupation of husband at marriage (survey CM) %	Occupation of husband at time of interview (survey CM) %	Occupation married males (1971 census) %	Occupation married males (Colin Gibson 1961 census data) %
I	3	5	5	5	4
II	15	10	14	19	17
IIIn-m	7	11	16	11	13
IIIm	50	49	43	39	38
IV	15	9	14	17	20
V	9	4	55	7	8
Armed services/unclassified	–	12	4	–	–
Non-manual	25	26	34	36	34
Manual	74	62	62	63	66

(Source of RG figures – 1971 Census. Economic Activity Tables, Table D.T.604.
Source of Gibson's figures, Divorce and Social Class in England and Wales, 'BJS', March 1974, Table II,
p.82.)

(d)   The presence or absence of pre-marital pregnancy

	All CM %	All fertile CM %	All married	All fertile married
Pmp	19	20	No data	No data
NoPmp	81	80	No data	No data

(e) Social class
Four descriptions of social class were derived from the survey data and have been listed previously for divorcees; the social class of the husband at the time of the interview was derived from his occupation at that time.

The problems associated with the comparison of survey CM data with official statistics which have already been mentioned apply also to the social class variable as do the limitations 1, 2 and 3 previously listed for divorcees on p.150. Table D shows the comparisons between the various sources.

STATISTICAL SIGNIFICANCE AND SOURCES OF ERROR

The use of significance tests is a strong norm in the social science disciplines and, accordingly, tests involving standardised scores have been applied constantly when looking at the data from this survey.

A large number of tabulations have been drawn up during the course of this study, and many have been commented upon in this book. In general, attention has not been drawn to differences which statistical tests suggest might have occurred by chance five times or more times in 100. However, the point made by Morrison and Henkel (1970) that 'contributions to basic science are often made without the tests, very seldom because of the tests, and sometimes in spite of the tests' has also been borne in mind, and attention has sometimes been drawn to those findings which 'imagination, common sense, informed judgement and the appropriate remaining research methods' indicated were substantially interesting.

According to Morrison and Henkel the conditions for the proper use of significance tests are not and cannot be met in most behavioural research, nor, in their view, should they be, since most behavioural research is implicitly basic in its orientation. Basic science, they point out, 'involves a different scope, form, process, and purpose of inference than statistical inference'. The arguments put forward by Morrison and Henkel in favour of a more restricted use, if not the abandonment, of such tests in most behavioural research, are in many ways persuasive. Essentially, there are four main arguments against the use of such tests upon data derived from survey work. First, such tests assume random sampling, which non-response prevents. Second, since the sample is a local one, inferences may not be extended to the general population. Third, it is bad logic to 'test hypotheses' upon the very tables which generated them, and fourth, because scientific knowledge grows by continuous accumulation and not by dichotomous decisions.

TABULATIONS RELATING TO THE TEXT

A   TABULATIONS RELATING TO CHAPTER 2

TABLE 1   Growing up with sibling(s) of the opposite sex: analysis by age of the bride at marriage for D and CM marriages

	All D n=520 %	All CM n=570 %	Bride under 20yrs D n=230 %	CM n=161 %	Bride 20yrs or more D n=290 %	CM n=409 %
Neither spouse with a sibling of the opposite sex .	11	10	11	7	11	11
One spouse only with a sibling of the opposite sex	44	42	39	39	47	42
Both spouses with a sibling of the opposite sex	45	48	50	53	41	47

TABLE 2   Growing up with sibling(s) of the opposite sex: analysis
by pre-marital pregnancy or not for D and CM marriages

	Pre-marital pregnancy		No pre-marital pregnancy	
	D n=168 %	CM n=352 %	D n=107 %	CM n=463 %
Neither spouse with a sibling of the opposite sex	10	12	11	10
One spouse only with a sibling of the opposite sex	37	47	36	43
Both spouses with a sibling of the opposite sex	53	42	53	47

TABLE 3   Growing up with an older sibling: comparisons between D and
CM marriages

	All D n=520 %	All CM n=570 %
Both spouses with an older sibling	19	19
One spouse only with an older sibling	48	50
Neither spouse with older sibling	32	31

TABLE 4   Growing up with an older sister: comparisons between D and
CM marriages with regard to the bride's age at marriage

	Bride under 20yrs		Bride 20yrs or more	
	D n=230 %	CM n=161 %	D n=290 %	CM n=409 %
Both spouses with older sister(s)	19	20	20	20
One spouse only with older sister(s)	47	47	41	43
Neither partner with an older sister	34	32	39	37

B   LIST OF CONDITIONS WITH A 'PROBABLE' PSYCHOSOMATIC ORIGIN

   Asthma
   Skin trouble
   Hay fever
   Fainting or dizzy spells
   Bilious or vomiting attacks
   Stammer or stutter
   Epilepsy

C   LIST OF CHRONIC OR SERIOUS PHYSICAL AILMENTS

   TB
   Rheumatic fever
   Pneumonia
   Polio
   Sugar diabetes
   Any heart complaint
   Bronchitis

D   TABULATIONS RELATING TO CHAPTER 3

TABLE 5   Attitudes towards divorce for childless couples: social
class differences amongst CM informants

	All CM n=570 %	I n=18 No.	II n=88 %	IIIn-m n=41 %	IIIm n=284 %	IV n=86 %	V n=53 %
In favour of divorce	89	18	91	95	88	88	85
Against divorce	11	-	9	2	12	12	15
Don't know	∅	-	-	2	-	-	-

TABLE 6   Attitudes towards divorce for fertile couples: social class
differences amongst CM informants

	All CM n=570 %	I n=18 No.	II n=88 %	IIIn-m n=41 %	IIIm n=284 %	IV n=86 %	V n=53 %
In favour of divorce	22	4	26	10	22	22	19
Against divorce	74	13	67	83	73	77	76
Don't know	4	1	7	7	5	1	5

TABLE 7 Religious affiliation: social class differences amongst D informants

	All D n=520 %	I n=1 No.	II n=72 %	IIIn-m n=38 %	IIIm n=274 %	IV n=85 %	V n=50 %
Upbringing:							
a religion	91	–	95	94	93	88	90
no religion	9	1	5	6	7	12	10
At marriage:							
a religion	71	–	81	79	71	62	62
no religion	29	1	19	21	29	38	38

TABLE 8 Religious affiliation: social class differences amongst CM informants

	All CM n=570 %	I n=18 No.	II n=88 %	IIIn-m n=41 %	IIIm n=284 %	IV n=86 %	V n=53 %
Upbringing:							
a religion	93	16	99	100	95	90	91
no religion	7	2	2	–	5	9	9
At marriage:							
a religion	77	13	86	90	75	74	72
no religion	22	5	13	10	25	26	28

TABLE 9 Churchgoing during marriage: social class differences amongst D informants

	All D n=520 %	I n=1 No.	II n=72 %	IIIn-m n=38 %	IIIm n=274 %	IV n=85 %	V n=50 %
Informant:							
a churchgoer	30	–	47	50	26	26	28
not a churchgoer	70	1	53	50	75	75	72
Spouse:							
a churchgoer	16	–	25	21	14	16	14
not a churchgoer	83	1	75	79	86	83	86
Partners:							
both churchgoers	13	–	22	18	10	13	10
one a churchgoer	22	–	28	35	20	18	22
neither a church- goer	65	1	50	47	70	69	68

TABLE 10   Churchgoing during marriage: social class differences amongst CM informants

	All CM n=570 %	I n=18 No.	II n=88 %	IIIn-m n=41 %	IIIm n=284 %	IV n=86 %	V n=53 %
Informant:							
a churchgoer	44	10	53	53	40	41	40
not a churchgoer	56	8	47	47	60	59	60
Spouse:							
a churchgoer	34	10	39	54	31	34	23
not a churchgoer	66	8	61	46	69	66	77
Partners:							
both churchgoers	28	9	36	44	25	24	19
one a churchgoer	22	2	19	22	22	24	27
neither a church- goer	49	7	45	34	53	52	54

TABLE 11   Family of origin size: social class differences amongst D informants

	All D n=520 %	I n=1 No.	II n=72 %	IIIn-m n=38 %	IIIm n=274 %	IV n=85 %	V n=50 %
Number of children:							
1	14	1	11	18	15	12	12
2	22	–	40	21	23	18	4
3	18	–	17	13	16	26	26
4	13	–	10	26	12	12	12
5+	33	–	22	21	33	33	46
Mean number	3.96	1.00	3.33	3.50	4.01	4.35	4.36

TABLE 12   Family of origin size: social class differences amongst CM informants

	All CM n=570 %	I n=18 No.	II n=88 %	IIIn-m n=41 %	IIIm n=284 %	IV n=86 %	V n=53 %
Number of children:							
1	15	3	17	22	13	19	13
2	21	6	27	32	19	16	13
3	19	6	18	15	18	17	25
4	16	1	17	15	15	20	13
5+	30	2	20	17	36	27	37
Mean number	3.80	2.61	3.44	2.95	4.05	3.72	4.28

TABLE 13 Type of compulsory education: social class differences amongst D informants

	All D n=520 %	I n=1 No.	II n=72 %	IIIn-m n=38 %	IIIm n=274 %	IV n=85 %	V n=50 %
Selective	11	1	24	13	9	6	6
Non-selective	85	-	67	87	87	92	90
Comprehensive	1	-	-	-	1	-	-
Private	2	-	7	-	2	-	-
Other	2	-	1	-	1	2	5

TABLE 14 Type of compulsory education: social class differences amongst CM informants

	All CM n=570 %	I n=18 No.	II n=88 %	IIIn-m n=41 %	IIIm n=284 %	IV n=86 %	V n=53 %
Selective	18	8	38	32	13	7	8
Non-selective	78	5	55	59	84	93	92
Comprehensive	1	-	2	2	2	-	-
Private	3	5	3	7	2	-	-
Other	-	-	2	-	-	-	-

TABLE 15 Further education: social class differences amongst D informants

	All D n=520 %	I n=1 No.	II n=72 %	IIIn-m n=38 %	IIIm n=274 %	IV n=85 %	V n=50 %
Further education	33	1	51	42	31	26	18
No further education	67	-	49	58	69	74	82

TABLE 16 Further education: social class differences amongst CM informants

	All CM n=570 %	I n=18 No.	II n=88 %	IIIn-m n=41 %	IIIm n=284 %	IV n=86 %	V n=53 %
Further education	35	12	44	54	35	22	13
No further education	65	6	56	46	65	78	87

TABLE 17   Age of bride at primary marriage: social class differences amongst D informants

	All D n=520 %	I n=1 No.	II n=72 %	IIIn-m n=38 %	IIIm n=274 %	IV n=85 %	V n=50 %
Bride aged:							
Under 20	44	–	38	32	43	52	58
20-4	43	–	53	42	42	41	32
25-9	7	1	3	18	7	5	6
30+	5	–	7	8	6	2	4

TABLE 18   Age of bride at primary marriage: social class differences amongst CM informants

	All CM n=570 %	I n=18 No.	II n=88 %	IIIn-m n=41 %	IIIm n=284 %	IV n=86 %	V n=53 %
Bride aged:							
Under 20	28	1	27	22	30	28	36
20-4	57	14	58	61	56	52	51
25-9	12	3	13	15	11	15	7
30+	3	–	2	2	3	5	6

TABLE 19   Unemployment for husbands: social class differences amongst D informants

Unemployment during marriage	All D n=520 %	I n=1 No.	II n=72 %	IIIn-m n=38 %	IIIm n=274 %	IV n=85 %	V n=50 %
Never	67	–	76	68	65	66	60
Less than 3 months overall	9	1	7	8	10	7	10
3 but less than 6 months overall	6	–	6	8	3	6	16
6 but less than 24 months overall	7	–	5	10	8	8	–
More than 2 years overall	11	–	4	5	13	11	14
Can't remember	1	–	1	–	1	2	–
Mean duration (months)	4.4	1.3	2.1	3.2	5.1	4.4	4.9

TABLE 20   Unemployment for husbands: social class differences amongst CM informants

Unemployment during marriage	All CM n=570 %	I n=18 No.	II n=88 %	IIIn-m n=41 %	IIIm n=284 %	IV n=87 %	V n=53 %
Never	78	17	85	83	79	74	55
Less than 3 months overall	7	1	6	12	8	3	9
3 but less than 6 months overall	4	-	5	2	5	6	4
6 but less than 24 months overall	7	-	3	2	6	9	17
More than 2 years overall	4	-	1	-	3	7	11
Can't remember	$\emptyset$	-	-	-	-	-	4
Mean duration (months)	2.2	0.1	0.9	0.4	2.0	3.4	5.7

TABLE 21   Courtship duration: social class differences amongst D informants

Interval between first date and marriage	All D n=520 %	I n=1 No.	II n=72 %	IIIn-m n=38 %	IIIm n=274 %	IV n=85 %	V n=50 %
Less than 6 months	6	-	8	3	7	8	-
6 but less than 12 months	14	-	12	21	11	15	22
1-2 years	39	-	49	26	39	43	30
More than 2 years	41	1	31	50	43	33	48
Can't remember	$\emptyset$	-	-	-	$\emptyset$	-	-
Mean interval (months)	26	84	26	27	24	23	27

TABLE 22   Courtship duration: social class differences amongst CM informants

Interval between first date and marriage	All CM n=570 %	I n=18 No.	II n=88 %	IIIn-m n=41 %	IIIm n=284 %	IV n=86 %	V n=53 %
Less than 6 months	1	-	1	-	2	1	4
6 but less than 12 months	7	1	4	12	6	5	6
1-2 years	34	5	37	27	35	35	28
More than 2 years	57	12	47	61	57	59	61
Can't remember	$\emptyset$	-	1	-	-	-	-
Mean interval (months)	34	37	33	34	33	37	38

TABLE 23 Formal engagement: social class differences amongst D informants

	All D n=520 %	I n=1 No.	II n=72 %	IIIn-m n=38 %	IIIm n=274 %	IV n=85 %	V n=50 %
Engagement	61	1	67	68	57	61	68
No engagement	39	-	33	32	43	39	32

TABLE 24 Formal engagement: social class differences amongst CM informants

	All CM n=570 %	I n=18 No.	II n=88 %	IIIn-m n=41 %	IIIm n=284 %	IV n=86 %	V n=53 %
Engagement	78	16	77	90	78	76	66
No engagement	22	2	23	10	22	24	34

TABLE 25 Place of marriage: social class differences amongst D informants

	All D n=520 %	I n=1 No.	II n=72 %	IIIn-m n=38 %	IIIm n=274 %	IV n=85 %	V n=50 %
Church	69	1	71	84	65	72	72
Registry office	31	-	29	16	35	28	28

TABLE 26 Place of marriage: social class differences amongst CM informants

	All CM n=570 %	I n=18 No.	II n=88 %	IIIn-m n=41 %	IIIm n=284 %	IV n=86 %	V n=53 %
Church	87	14	93	95	86	88	79
Registry office	13	4	7	5	14	12	21

TABLE 27 Taking a honeymoon: social class differences amongst D informants

	All D n=520 %	I n=1 No.	II n=72 %	IIIn-m n=38 %	IIIm n=274 %	IV n=85 %	V n=50 %
Honeymoon	38	1	46	61	35	34	30
No honeymoon	62	-	54	39	65	66	70

TABLE 28 Taking a honeymoon: social class differences amongst CM informants

	All CM n=570 %	I n=18 No.	II n=88 %	IIIn-m n=41 %	IIIm n=284 %	IV n=86 %	V n=53 %
Honeymoon	52	18	70	68	50	35	34
No honeymoon	48	-	30	32	50	65	66

TABLE 29 Serious pre-marital difficulties between the couple: social class differences amongst D

	All D n=520 %	I n=1 No.	II n=72 %	IIIn-m n=38 %	IIIm n=274 %	IV n=85 %	V n=50 %
Serious difficulties	29	1	26	26	29	29	30
No serious difficulties	71	-	74	74	71	71	70

TABLE 30 Serious pre-marital difficulties between the couple: social class differences amongst CM

	All CM n=570 %	I n=18 No.	II n=88 %	IIIn-m n=41 %	IIIm n=284 %	IV n=86 %	V n=53 %
Serious difficulties	19	2	15	12	21	16	21
No serious difficulties	81	16	85	88	79	84	79

TABLE 31 Parental opposition to the marriage: social class differences amongst D informants

	All D n=520 %	I n=1 No.	II n=72 %	IIIn-m n=38 %	IIIm n=274 %	IV n=85 %	V n=50 %
Opposition	43	-	47	45	41	45	50
No opposition	57	1	53	55	59	55	50

TABLE 32   Parental opposition to the marriage: social class
differences amongst CM informants

	All CM n=570 %	I n=18 No.	II n=88 %	IIIn-m n=41 %	IIIm n=284 %	IV n=86 %	V n=53 %
Opposition	13	2	17	22	13	8	13
No opposition	87	16	83	78	87	92	87

TABLE 33   Pre-marital pregnancy: social class differences amongst D
informants

	All D n=520 %	I n=1 No.	II n=72 %	IIIn-m n=38 %	IIIm n=274 %	IV n=85 %	V n=50 %
Pmp	32	-	29	13	33	38	38
No Pmp	68	1	71	87	67	62	62

TABLE 34   Pre-marital pregnancy: social class differences amongst CM
informants

	All CM n=570 %	I n=18 No.	II n=88 %	IIIn-m n=41 %	IIIm n=284 %	IV n=86 %	V n=53 %
Pmp	19	2	19	7	20	20	19
No Pmp	81	16	81	93	80	80	81

TABLE 35   Job changing by husband: social class differences amongst
D informants (in first (5) years of marriage)

	All D n=520 %	I n=1 No.	II n=72 %	IIIn-m n=38 %	IIIm n=274 %	IV n=85 %	V n=50 %
No changes	39	1	50	42	36	41	36
1 job change	22	-	25	16	23	25	12
2 job changes	11	-	8	16	12	9	6
3 job changes	8	-	3	3	9	6	18
4 or more job changes	19	-	14	23	18	18	28
Can't remember	1	-	-	-	1	1	-
Mean number of job changes	2.01	0.00	1.32	1.97	2.15	1.69	2.78

TABLE 36   Job changing by husband: social class differences amongst
CM informants (in first (5) years of marriage)

	All CM n=570 %	I n=18 No.	II n=88 %	IIIn-m n=41 %	IIIm n=284 %	IV n=86 %	V n=53 %
No changes	45	8	42	49	47	48	34
1 job change	26	5	23	17	26	23	36
2 job changes	12	2	13	22	10	14	11
3 job changes	9	1	9	7	10	7	9
4 or more job changes	8	2	14	4	6	7	10
Can't remember	1	-	-	-	1	1	-
Mean number of job changes	1.17	1.22	1.50	1.05	1.09	1.06	1.30

TABLE 37   Family size: social class differences amongst D informants

Number of children in family of origin	All D n=520 %	I n=1 No.	II n=72 %	IIIn-m n=38 %	IIIm n=274 %	IV n=85 %	V n=50 %
1	14	1	11	18	15	12	12
2	22	-	40	21	23	18	4
3	18	-	17	13	16	26	26
4	13	-	10	26	12	12	12
5	8	-	7	5	7	6	18
6	8	-	4	5	8	8	14
7+	17	-	11	11	18	19	14
Mean number	3.96	1.00	3.33	3.50	4.01	4.35	4.36

TABLE 38   Family size: social class differences amongst CM informants

Number of children in family of origin	All CM n=570 %	I n=18 No.	II n=88 %	IIIn-m n=41 %	IIIm n=284 %	IV n=86 %	V n=53 %
1	15	3	17	22	13	19	13
2	21	6	27	32	19	16	13
3	19	6	18	15	18	17	25
4	16	1	17	15	15	20	13
5	10	2	6	10	13	8	6
6	6	-	2	2	7	7	8
7+	15	-	12	5	16	12	23
Mean number	3.80	2.61	3.44	2.95	4.05	3.72	4.28

TABLE 39   Family structure - birth rank: social class differences amongst D informants with siblings

Birth rank of informant	All D n=447 %	I n=0 -	II n=64 %	IIIn-m n=31 %	IIIm n=233 %	IV n=75 %	V n=44 %
Eldest	30	-	33	23	36	19	18
2nd child	29	-	27	39	27	37	27
3rd child	16	-	17	13	13	16	30
4th child	10	-	8	16	10	9	9
5th child	5	-	6	-	5	5	7
6th or later	11	-	10	9	9	13	10
Youngest	32	-	47	32	24	41	36

TABLE 40   Family structure - birth rank: social class differences amongst CM informants with siblings

Birth rank of informant	All CM n=486 %	I n=15 No.	II n=74 %	IIIn-m n=32 %	IIIm n=248 %	IV n=71 %	V n=46 %
Eldest	31	6	32	44	31	30	17
2nd child	27	5	31	38	23	27	28
3rd child	17	2	14	9	18	17	20
4th child	11	2	12	6	12	10	13
5th child	6	-	5	-	6	8	4
6th or later	8	-	5	3	10	8	17
Youngest	30	6	31	28	27	31	43

TABLE 41   Parental preference: social class differences amongst D informants

	All D n=520 %	I n=1 No.	II n=72 %	IIIn-m n=38 %	IIIm n=274 %	IV n=85 %	V n=50 %
Preferred mother	27	1	33	29	27	25	18
Preferred father	19	-	18	18	20	20	14
No preference	44	-	40	45	42	45	58
Inadequate recall due to parental loss or absence	11	-	8	8	12	11	10

TABLE 42 Parental preference: social class differences amongst CM informants

	All CM n=570 %	I n=18 No.	II n=88 %	IIIn-m n=41 %	IIIm n=284 %	IV n=86 %	V n=53 %
Preferred mother	32	8	34	27	31	30	34
Preferred father	14	4	13	17	14	15	11
No preference	45	6	48	51	46	45	38
Inadequate recall due to parental loss or absence	9	-	6	5	9	9	17

TABLE 43 Fertility: social class differences amongst D informants

	All D n=520 %	I n=1 No.	II n=72 %	IIIn-m n=38 %	IIIm n=274 %	IV n=85 %	V n=50 %
Children born to the marriage	81	1	81	74	81	88	68
No children born to the marriage	19	-	19	26	19	12	32
Mean number of children born to the marriage	1.8	1.00	1.6	1.6	1.9	2.2	1.5

TABLE 44 Fertility: social class differences amongst CM informants

	All CM n=570 %	I n=18 No.	II n=88 %	IIIn-m n=41 %	IIIm n=284 %	IV n=86 %	V n=53 %
Children born to the marriage	92	18	92	83	92	94	93
No children born to the marriage	8	-	8	17	8	6	7
Mean number of children born to the marriage	2.1	2.0	2.0	1.6	2.2	2.0	2.8

TABLE 45　Infertility: social class differences amongst D informants in opportunity to conceive

Cohabitation lasted	All D n=520 %	I n=1 No.	II n=72 %	IIIn-m n=38 %	IIIm n=274 %	IV n=85 %	V n=50 %
2 yrs or less	20	–	33	14	18	19	18
3 but less than 4 yrs	6	–	4	3	7	6	10
4 but less than 5 yrs	10	–	4	3	12	9	10
5 but less than 6 yrs	5	1	7	5	4	1	8
6 but less than 7 yrs	6	–	4	11	6	5	10
7 but less than 8 yrs	6	–	4	13	6	1	8
8 but less than 9 yrs	3	–	4	3	3	1	8
9 but less than 10 yrs	5	–	4	5	5	6	6
10 yrs or more	39	–	33	43	39	50	20

TABLE 46　Infertility: social class differences amongst CM informants in opportunity to conceive

Cohabitation lasted	All CM n=570 %	I n=18 No.	II n=88 %	IIIn-m n=41 %	IIIm n=284 %	IV n=86 %	V n=53 %
2 yrs or less	4	2	5	5	3	7	–
3 but less than 4 yrs	4	2	7	5	2	3	4
4 but less than 5 yrs	4	1	3	10	4	3	2
5 but less than 6 yrs	4	2	2	5	4	3	4
6 but less than 7 yrs	3	–	2	2	4	2	5
7 but less than 8 yrs	5	1	7	10	5	3	4
8 but less than 9 yrs	5	1	5	5	6	7	–
9 but less than 10 yrs	3	1	7	5	2	2	2
10 yrs or more	68	8	63	53	72	69	80

TABLE 47 Extra-marital affaires: social class differences amongst D informants

	All D n=520 %	I n=1 No.	II n=72 %	IIIn-m n=38 %	IIIm n=274 %	IV n=85 %	V n=50 %
Extra-marital affaire	19	1	11	24	18	22	28
No extra-marital affaire	80	-	89	76	81	78	72
No answer	∅	-	-	-	1	-	-

TABLE 48 Extra-marital affaires: social class differences amongst CM informants

	All CM n=570 %	I n=18 No.	II n=88 %	IIIn-m n=41 %	IIIm n=284 %	IV n=86 %	V n=53 %
Extra-marital affaire	4	-	3	12	4	3	4
No extra-marital affaire	96	18	97	85	96	97	94
No answer	∅	-	-	2	-	-	2

TABLE 49 Type of accommodation occupied on marriage: social class differences amongst D informants

	All D n=520 %	I n=1 No.	II n=72 %	IIIn-m n=38 %	IIIm n=274 %	IV n=85 %	V n=50 %
Independent housing	26	-	33	21	25	24	26
Semi-independent housing	10	1	11	11	10	8	6
Dependent housing	54	-	43	50	56	56	60
Can't remember	10	-	13	18	9	12	8

TABLE 50   Type of accommodation occupied on marriage: social class differences amongst CM informants

	All CM n=570 %	I n=18 No.	II n=88 %	IIIn-m n=41 %	IIIm n=284 %	IV n=86 %	V n=53 %
Independent housing	39	10	47	56	36	34	26
Semi-independent housing	11	5	10	12	9	14	11
Dependent housing	40	3	34	24	43	45	43
Can't remember	11	-	9	7	12	7	19

TABLE 51   Type of accommodation occupied at the first wedding anniversary: social class differences amongst D informants

	All D n=478 %	I n=1 No.	II n=66 %	IIIn-m n=36 %	IIIm n=150 %	IV n=79 %	V n=46 %
Independent housing	47	-	52	44	46	49	41
Semi-independent housing	8	1	6	17	7	8	2
Dependent housing	43	-	38	36	44	42	54
Can't remember	3	-	5	3	3	1	2

TABLE 52   Type of accommodation occupied at the first wedding anniversary: social class differences amongst CM informants

	All CM n=564 %	I n=18 No.	II n=88 %	IIIn-m n=41 %	IIIm n=279 %	IV n=86 %	V n=52 %
Independent housing	59	16	68	71	56	60	35
Semi-independent housing	5	-	2	7	5	7	10
Dependent housing	32	2	23	17	37	29	52
Can't remember	4	-	7	5	3	3	4

TABLE 53 Type of accommodation occupied at 5th wedding anniversary: social class differences amongst D informants

	All D n=333 %	I n=1 No.	II n=40 %	IIIn-m n=29 %	IIIm n=175 %	IV n=57 %	V n=31 %
Independent housing	81	1	80	72	83	84	77
Semi-independent housing	5	-	-	7	7	4	6
Dependent housing	11	-	20	17	8	9	16
Can't remember	2	-	-	3	2	4	-

TABLE 54 Type of accommodation occupied at 5th wedding anniversary: social class differences amongst CM informants

	All CM n=490 %	I n=11 No.	II n=73 %	IIIn-m n=33 %	IIIm n=250 %	IV n=75 %	V n=48 %
Independent housing	83	10	86	88	82	89	71
Semi-independent housing	5	-	5	3	6	4	6
Dependent housing	7	1	3	-	8	7	15
Can't remember	4	-	5	9	4	-	8

TABLE 55   Wife's work outside the home: social class differences amongst D informants

	All D n=520 %	I n=1 No.	II n=72 %	IIIn-m n=38 %	IIIm n=274 %	IV n=85 %	V n=50 %
During marriage:							
Wife worked	81	1	72	89	84	78	82
Wife always at home	19	-	28	11	16	22	18

	n=423 %	n=1 No.	n=52 %	n=34 %	n=229 %	n=66 %	n=41 %
Phasing of wife's work:							
Throughout marriage	41	1	56	44	39	33	39
Only at start of marriage	26	-	27	24	26	26	27
Intermittently (breaks for children)	31	-	15	29	34	35	34
Only when children were older	2	-	2	3	1	5	-
Type of wife's work:							
Always full time	74	1	87	68	73	68	80
Always part-time	24	-	10	32	25	27	20
Varied	2	-	4	-	3	3	-
Reasons for wife's work:							
Needed the money	84	1	88	88	83	82	83
Needed an outside interest	22	-	15	21	19	26	20
Other	2	-	-	-	2	3	7
Husband's attitude to wife's work:							
Approved	59	1	62	65	57	59	63
Disapproved	14	-	17	15	13	17	7
No strong feelings	27	-	21	21	30	23	29
Wife's attitude to own work:							
Preferred to work	78	1	83	76	79	76	73
Preferred to be at home	22	-	17	24	21	23	27
Mixed feelings	-	-	-	-	-	-	-

TABLE 56 Wife's work outside the home: social class differences amongst CM informants

	All CM n=570 %	I n=18 No.	II n=88 %	IIIn-m n=41 %	IIIm n=284 %	IV n=86 %	V n=53 %
During marriage:							
Wife worked	89	16	80	100	92	87	87
Wife always at home	11	2	20	-	8	12	13

	n=509 %	n=16 No.	n=70 %	n=41 %	n=261 %	n=75 %	n=46 %
Phasing of wife's work:							
Throughout marriage	26	-	29	22	24	35	37
Only at start of marriage	27	9	26	24	27	28	15
Intermittently (breaks for children)	42	6	37	51	43	39	39
Only when children were older	6	1	6	9	2	7	1
Type of wife's work:							
Always full time	56	11	64	66	54	56	43
Always part-time	42	5	36	34	43	43	57
Varied	2	-	-	-	3	1	-
Reasons for wife's work:							
Needed the money	80	10	77	76	80	83	87
Needed an outside interest	32	9	40	34	30	28	26
Other	1	-	1	2	1	3	-
Husband's attitude to wife's work:							
Approved	57	10	69	71	52	60	50
Disapproved	12	3	10	15	12	9	13
No strong feelings	31	3	21	15	36	31	37
Wife's attitude to own work:							
Preferred to work	81	12	81	90	82	77	74
Preferred to be at home	19	4	17	10	18	23	26
Mixed feelings	∅	-	1	-	-	-	-

TABLE 57 Fertility in the early years of marriage: social class differences amongst D informants

	All D n=520 %	I n=1 No.	II n=72 %	IIIn–m n=38 %	IIIm n=274 %	IV n=85 %	V n=50 %
First child in 1st year	45	–	51	26	45	52	45
First child in 2nd year	18	–	10	32	20	15	8
Not fertile in 1st two years of marriage	37	1	39	42	35	33	48

TABLE 58 Fertility in the early years of marriage: social class differences amongst CM informants

	All CM n=570 %	I n=18 No.	II n=88 %	IIIn–m n=41 %	IIIm n=284 %	IV n=86 %	V n=53 %
First child in 1st year	34	3	33	17	35	35	43
First child in 2nd year	22	6	19	7	22	26	26
Not fertile in 1st two years of marriage	44	9	48	76	43	39	31

TABLE 59 Stammering during childhood and adolescence: social class differences amongst D informants

	All D n=520 %	I n=1 No.	II n=72 %	IIIn–m n=38 %	IIIm n=274 %	IV n=85 %	V n=50 %
Stammer	2	–	1	8	1	2	4
No stammer	98	1	99	92	99	98	96

TABLE 60 Stammering during childhood and adolescence: social class differences amongst CM informants

	All CM n=570 %	I n=18 No.	II n=88 %	IIIn–m n=41 %	IIIm n=284 %	IV n=86 %	V n=53 %
Stammer	2	–	2	2	2	–	6
No stammer	98	18	98	98	98	100	94

TABLE 61 Skin trouble during childhood and adolescence: social class differences amongst D informants

	All D n=520 %	I n=1 No.	II n=72 %	IIIn-m n=38 %	IIIm n=274 %	IV n=85 %	V n=50 %
Skin trouble	8	-	10	13	5	9	10
No skin trouble	92	1	90	97	95	91	88

TABLE 62 Skin trouble during childhood and adolescence: social class differences amongst CM informants

	All CM n=570 %	I n=18 No.	II n=88 %	IIIn-m n=41 %	IIIm n=284 %	IV n=86 %	V n=53 %
Skin trouble	5	2	3	2	5	5	9
No skin trouble	95	16	97	98	95	95	91

TABLE 63 Number of hospitalisations: social class differences amongst CM informants

	All CM n=209 %	I n=10 No.	II n=32 %	IIIn-m n=14 No.	IIIm n=105 %	IV n=30 %	V n=18 No.
One hospitalisation	71	6	69	14	81	77	14
Two hospitalisations	16	3	25	-	11	20	4
Three or more hosp-italisations	13	1	6	-	8	3	-
Mean number	1.6	1.5	1.5	1.0	1.4	1.3	1.2

TABLE 64 Age at first hospitalisation: social class differences amongst D informants

	All D n=221 %	II n=30 %	IIIn-m n=13 No.	IIIm n=114 %	IV n=38 %	V n=26 %
Under 5 years	38	40	8	37	24	46
Over 5 years	62	60	5	63	76	54
Mean age (years)	7.5	7.3	6.1	7.4	7.9	7.3

TABLE 65   Age at first hospitalisation: social class differences amongst CM informants

	All CM n=208 %	I n=10 No.	II n=32 %	IIIn-m n=14 No.	IIIm n=105 %	IV n=30 %	V n=17 No.
Under 5 years	30	6	30	4	30	33	4
Over 5 years	70	4	70	10	70	67	13
Mean age (years)	7.6	6.3	7.4	7.6	7.9	7.2	7.5

TABLE 66   Hospitalisation: social class differences amongst D informants

	All D n=520 %	I n=1 No.	II n=72 %	IIIn-m n=38 %	IIIm n=274 %	IV n=85 %	V n=50 %
Hospitalised	43	-	42	34	42	45	52
Never hospitalised	58	1	58	66	58	55	48

TABLE 67   Hospitalisation: social class differences amongst CM informants

	All CM n=570 %	I n=18 %	II n=88 %	IIIn-m n=41 %	IIIm n=284 %	IV n=86 %	V n=53 %
Hospitalised	37	10	36	34	37	35	34
Never hospitalised	63	18	64	66	63	65	66

TABLE 68   Number of hospitalisations: social class differences amongst D informants

	All D n=221 %	I n=0	II n=30 %	IIIn-m n=13 No.	IIIm n=114 %	IV n=38 %	V n=26 %
One hospitalisation	71	-	77	7	72	71	65
Two hospitalisations	16	-	20	2	19	8	11
Three or more	13	-	3	4	9	21	22
Mean number	1.6	-	1.3	2.1	1.4	1.7	2.3

E TABULATION RELATING TO CHAPTER 4

TABLE 69   Marital opposition: comparisons between D and CM marriages
of different generations

	Marriage cohort									
	Before 1940		1940-9		1950-9		1960-9		1970 or later	
	D n=41 %	CM n=38 %	D n=75 %	CM n=142 %	D n=149 %	CM n=159 %	D n=255 %	CM n=221 %	D n=0 -	CM n=16 No.
Opposition	34	13	40	13	40	17	48	11	-	1
No opposition	66	88	60	87	60	83	52	89	-	15

F   TABULATIONS RELATING TO CHAPTER 5

TABLE 70   Hospitalisation: comparisons between D and CM informants
according to the age of the bride at marriage

	Bride under 20 years		Bride 20 yrs or over					
	D n=230 %	CM n=161 %	D n=290 %	CM n=409 %	DW n=336 %	DM n=184 %	CMW n=371 %	CMM n=199 %
Hospitalised	48	41	38	35	47	34	36	38
Never hospitalised	52	59	62	65	53	66	64	62

TABLE 71   Fears and difficulties before 11 years of age: comparisons between D and CM informants according to sex of informant and the age of the bride at marriage

| Mean scores | Bride under 20 years | | Bride aged 20-4 years | | All DW | All DM | All CMW | All CMM |
	D n=230	CM n=161	D n=226	CM n=322	n=336	n=184	n=371	n=199
1 Fear of school	4.08	3.96	4.11	4.06	4.05	4.19	4.05	4.07
2 Inability to concentrate in school	3.57	3.53	3.67	3.76	3.59	3.72	3.78	3.63
3 Fear of the dark	3.71	3.61	3.73	3.70	3.43	4.25	3.57	4.08
4 Fear of animals	4.42	4.25	4.34	4.34	4.27	4.61	4.25	4.39
5 Fear of strangers	3.90	3.86	4.07	4.07	3.75	4.45	3.84	4.34
6 Shy with other children	3.90	3.86	3.99	4.12	3.84	4.07	4.03	4.05
7. Bedwetting	4.49	4.52	4.57	4.60	4.51	4.61	4.64	4.50
8 Nightmares	3.93	3.96	4.02	4.12	3.90	4.23	4.11	4.11
9 Nerves	4.31	4.47	4.42	4.43	4.25	4.46	4.41	4.51
10 Difficulty in sleeping	4.52	4.55	4.56	4.63	4.44	4.66	4.66	4.56
11 Homesickness	4.46	3.96	3.94	3.90	3.71	4.37	3.85	4.16
12 Depression	3.86	4.32	4.40	4.31	4.29	4.55	4.37	4.30
13 Difficulty in making friends	4.32	4.14	4.20	4.26	4.04	4.41	4.24	4.23
14 Quick-tempered	4.15	3.46	3.59	3.34	3.32	3.44	3.47	3.40
15 Lacking in confidence	3.13	3.01	2.92	2.98	2.73	3.46	2.82	3.31

TABLE 72 Fears and difficulties during adolescence (12-16 years): comparisons between D and CM informants according to sex of informant and the age of the bride at marriage

Mean scores	Bride under 20 years		Bride aged 20-4 years		All DW	All DM	All CMW	All CMM
	D n=230	CM n=161	D n=226	CM n=322	n=336	n=184	n=371	n=199
1 Dislike of school	3.59	3.58	3.65	3.82	3.58	3.85	3.76	3.75
2 Inability to concentrate in school	3.76	3.84	3.86	4.04	3.77	4.01	4.06	3.86
3 Worries about appearance	3.03	3.02	3.13	3.07	2.95	3.37	2.98	3.35
4 Shyness with opposite sex	3.13	3.26	2.94	3.11	2.98	3.18	3.25	3.04
5 Nerves	4.16	4.24	4.39	4.39	4.18	4.42	4.35	4.36
6 Bedwetting	4.74	4.77	4.77	4.78	4.76	4.80	4.88	4.63
7 Quick-tempered	3.33	3.38	3.62	3.43	3.44	3.50	3.51	3.48
8 Lacking in confidence	3.37	3.27	3.15	3.26	3.01	3.74	3.07	3.59
9 Difficulty in making friends	4.10	4.24	4.16	4.23	4.04	4.30	4.26	4.23
10 Depression	4.08	4.02	4.27	4.24	4.04	4.46	4.15	4.32

TABLE 73 Relationship with those opposing the marriage: comparisons between D and CM according to the age of the bride at marriage

	Bride under 20 years		Bride 20 years or over	
	D n=123 %	CM n=31 %	D n=103 %	CM n=45 %
On good terms	20	55	34	44
Not on good terms	80	45	66	56

TABLE 74   Home moves during marriage: comparisons between D and CM
informants according to the age of the bride at marriage

	Bride under 20 years		Bride 20 years or over	
	D n=230 %	CM n=161 %	D n=290 %	CM n=409 %
Never moved	16	7	22	17
Moved once	22	30	29	30
Moved twice	27	28	22	26
Moved 3 or more times	35	35	26	26

TABLE 75   Accommodation on marriage: comparisons between D and CM
informants according to the age of the bride at marriage

	Bride under 20 years		Bride 20 years or over	
	D n=230 %	CM n=161 %	D n=290 %	CM n=409 %
Independent housing	18	27	32	43
Semi-independent housing	10	12	9	11
Dependent housing	60	51	49	35
Can't remember	12	11	9	11

TABLE 76   Home moves during the first year of marriage: comparisons
between D and CM informants according to the age of the bride at
marriage

	Bride under 20 years		Bride 20 years or over	
	D n=211 %	CM n=159 %	D n=267 %	CM n=405 %
Never moved	48	50	63	70
Moved once	36	41	28	25
Moved 2 or more times	16	9	9	5

185 Appendix III

TABLE 77 Accommodation at the first anniversary: comparisons
between D and CM informants according to the age of the bride at
marriage

	Bride under 20 years		Bride 20 years or over	
	D n=211 %	CM n=159 %	D n=267 %	CM n=405 %
Independent accommodation	43	53	50	62
Semi-independent accommodation	8	4	7	5
Dependent accommodation	45	37	41	30
Can't remember	3	6	2	3

TABLE 78 Friction between sharing parties in first accommodation:
comparisons between D and CM informants according to the age of the
bride at marriage

	Bride under 20 years		Bride 20 years or over	
	D n=151 %	CM n=99 %	D n=155 %	CM n=192 %
A lot of friction	26	11	17	7
A little friction	28	23	28	15
No friction	46	65	54	78
Can't remember	-	1	1	Ø

TABLE 79 Friction between sharing parties in second accommodation:
comparisons between D and CM informants according to the age of the
bride at marriage

	Bride under 20 years		Bride 20 years or over	
	D n=60 %	CM n=31 %	D n=63 %	CM n=55 %
A lot of friction	22	10	16	9
A little friction	23	13	22	7
No friction	55	74	60	78
Can't remember	-	3	2	5

TABLE 80   Number of children of the marriage: comparisons between D and CM informants according to the age of the bride at marriage

| | Bride under 20 years | | Bride 20 years or over | |
	D n=230 %	CM n=161 %	D n=290 %	CM n=409 %
No children	13	4	25	10
One child	27	24	30	26
Two children	26	39	25	34
Three or more children	35	34	20	30
Mean number	2.1	2.4	1.6	2.0

TABLE 81   The timing of the first child: comparisons between D and CM informants according to the age of the bride at marriage

| | Bride under 20 years | | Bride 20 years or over | |
	D n=230 %	CM n=161 %	D n=290 %	CM n=409 %
In 1st year of marriage	59	44	35	30
In 2nd year of marriage	15	26	20	20
In 3rd year of marriage	13	26	20	39
No children	13	4	25	10

TABLE 82   The timing of the second child: comparisons between D and CM informants according to the age of the bride at marriage

| | Bride under 20 years | | Bride 20 years or over | |
	D n=230 %	CM n=161 %	D n=290 %	CM n=409 %
In 1st year of marriage	1	–	–	1
In 2nd year of marriage	17	9	4	4
In 3rd year of marriage	14	17	10	10
In 4th year or later	27	47	30	49
Not applicable	40	28	55	36

TABLE 83   Job changing by husband (in first (5) years of marriage): comparisons between D and CM informants according to the age of the bride at marriage

	Bride under 20 years		Bride 20 years or over	
	D n=230 %	CM n=161 %	D n=290 %	CM n=409 %
No changes	37	40	41	47
1 job change	20	25	24	26
2 job changes	12	13	10	11
3 job changes	9	11	8	8
4 or more job changes	21	9	17	7
Can't remember	1	1	-	Ø
Mean number of job changes	2.24	1.31	1.84	1.10

TABLE 84   Unemployment for husbands: comparisons between D and CM informants according to the age of the bride at marriage

Unemployment during marriage	Bride under 20 years		Bride 20 years or over	
	D n=230 %	CM n=161 %	D n=290 %	CM n=409 %
Never	67	73	66	79
Less than 3 months overall	7	10	11	6
3 but less than 6 months	7	2	5	8
6 but less than 24 months	6	8	7	3
More than 2 years overall	13	6	10	2
Can't remember	1	-	1	1
Mean duration (months)	4.8	2.9	4.1	1.9

TABLE 85   Courtship duration: comparisons between D and CM informants according to the age of the bride at marriage

Interval between first date and marriage	Bride under 20 years		Bride 20 years or over	
	D n=230 %	CM n=161 %	D n=290 %	CM n=409 %
Less than 6 months	5	2	7	2
6 but less than 12 months	16	11	12	7
1 - 2 years	43	44	37	30
More than 2 years	36	43	44	61
Can't remember	-	1	Ø	-
Mean interval (months)	23	27	29	37

TABLE 86   Formal engagement: comparisons between D and CM informants according to the age of the bride at marriage

	Bride under 20 years		Bride 20 years or over	
	D n=230 %	CM n=161 %	D n=290 %	CM n=409 %
Engagement	61	72	62	80
No engagement	39	28	38	20

TABLE 87   Serious pre-marital difficulties between the couple: comparisons between D and CM informants according to the age of the bride at marriage

	Bride under 20 years		Bride 20 years or over	
	D n=230 %	CM n=161 %	D n=290 %	CM n=409 %
Serious difficulties	31	22	26	14
No serious difficulties	69	78	74	86

TABLE 88   Place of marriage: comparisons between D and CM informants according to the age of the bride at marriage

	Bride under 20 years		Bride 20 years or over	
	D n=230 %	CM n=161 %	D n=290 %	CM n=409 %
Church	66	78	72	91
Registry office	35	22	28	9

TABLE 89   Taking a honeymoon: comparisons between D and CM informants according to the age of the bride at marriage

	Bride under 20 years		Bride 20 years or over	
	D n=230 %	CM n=161 %	D n=290 %	CM n=409 %
Honeymoon	30	37	44	59
No honeymoon	70	63	56	41

TABLE 90 Pre-marital pregnancy: comparisons between D and CM informants

	All D n=520 %	All CM n=570 %
Pmp	32	19
No Pmp	68	81

TABLE 91 *De facto* duration of marriage: comparisons between D informants according to the presence or absence of pre-marital pregnancy

	All D	
Cohabitation lasted	Pmp n=168 %	No Pmp n=352 %
Less than 5 years	46	31
5-9 years	18	29
10-14 years	17	19
15-19 years	9	9
20 years +	8	13

TABLE 92 Husband's unemployment: comparisons between D and CM informants according to the presence or absence of pre-marital pregnancy

	All D		All CM	
	Pmp n=168 %	No Pmp n=352 %	Pmp n=107 %	No Pmp n=463 %
No unemployment	60	69	73	79
Unemployment				
Less than 3 months	8	10	12	6
3 but less than 12 months	15	6	9	9
12-24 months	3	3	2	3
More than 2 years	14	9	5	4
Can't remember	1	2	-	Ø
Mean total period of unemployment (months)	5.7	2.9	2.4	2.1

TABLE 93   Job changing by husband in the first (5) years of marriage: comparisons between D and CM informants according to the presence or absence of pre-marital pregnancy

	All D		All CM	
	Pmp n=168 %	No Pmp n=352 %	Pmp n=107 %	No Pmp n=463 %
No job change	37	40	49	44
1 job change	17	25	23	26
2 job changes	15	9	14	11
3 job changes	32	25	15	17
Can't remember	1	1	-	1
Mean number	2.26	1.89	1.05	1.20

TABLE 94   Duration of any post-puerperal depression (followed birth of 1st child): comparisons between D and CM according to the presence or absence of pre-marital pregnancy

	D		CM	
	Pmp n=43 %	No Pmp n=60 %	Pmp n=25 %	No Pmp n=115 %
Less than 3 months	51	53	68	58
3-12 months	35	43	32	35
More than 1 year	14	3	-	7
Mean duration (months)	7.7	5.1	3.8	5.7

TABLE 95   Mean number of children of the marriage: comparisons between D and CM according to the presence or absence of pre-marital pregnancy

	D		CM	
	Pmp n=168	No Pmp n=352	Pmp n=107	No Pmp n=463
Mean number of children	2.2	1.6	2.7	2.0

TABLE 96   Pre-marital affaire: comparisons between D and CM informants according to the presence or absence of pre-marital pregnancy

	D		CM	
	Pmp n=168 %	No Pmp n=352 %	Pmp n=107 %	No Pmp n=463 %
Pre-marital affaire	35	32	21	13
No pre-marital affaire	65	68	79	87
No reply	1	Ø	-	Ø

TABLE 97 Extra-marital affaire: comparisons between D and CM informants according to the presence or absence of pre-marital pregnancy

| | D | | CM | |
	Pmp n=168 %	No Pmp n=352 %	Pmp n=107 %	No Pmp n=463 %
Extra-marital affaire	21	18	9	3
No extra-marital affaire	79	81	91	97
No reply	–	1	–	∅

TABLE 98 The importance attached to the sexual side of marriage: comparisons between D and CM informants according to the presence or absence of pre-marital pregnancy

| Sexual side of marriage
regarded as | D | | CM | |
	Pmp n=168 %	No Pmp n=352 %	Pmp n=107 %	No Pmp n=463 %
Very important	58	55	48	42
Fairly important	38	41	50	53
Fairly unimportant	4	2	2	4
Not at all important	1	2	1	1
No answer	–	–	–	–

TABLE 99 Sexual satisfaction at the start of marriage: comparisons between D and CM informants according to the presence or absence of pre-marital pregnancy

| | D | | CM | |
	Pmp n=168 %	No Pmp n=352 %	Pmp n=107 %	No Pmp n=463 %
Sexual side satisfactory	83	77	94	86
Sexual side unsatisfactory	17	23	6	14
No reply	–	∅	–	∅

TABLE 100   Type of accommodation occupied on marriage: comparisons
between D and CM informants according to the presence or absence of
pre-marital pregnancy

	D		CM	
	Pmp n=168 %	No Pmp n=352 %	Pmp n=107 %	No Pmp n=463 %
Independent housing	18	29	21	43
Semi-independent housing	11	9	16	10
Dependent housing	62	51	50	37
Can't remember	9	11	12	10

TABLE 101   Type of accommodation occupied at the first wedding
anniversary: comparisons between D and CM informants according to
the presence or absence of pre-marital pregnancy

	D		CM	
	Pmp n=155 %	No Pmp n=323 %	Pmp n=105 %	No Pmp n=459 %
Independent housing	46	47	51	60
Semi-independent housing	6	8	5	5
Dependent housing	46	41	41	31
Can't remember	1	3	3	4

DESCRIPTION OF AID
(Automatic Interaction Detector)

The basic strategy employed by AID is to divide the total sample into the most homogeneous groupings in terms of the dependent variable. The earliest form of dependent grouping was undertaken by mechanical or hand sorting techniques which gave cross distributions of each independent variable against the criterion. For the sample under consideration at any particular stage (often called the candidate group) the independent variable which gave the 'best' discrimination with respect to the dependent was used to divide that group into two further groups, which themselves may be candidates for further division.

This technique gives a 'tree-like' structure of groups, with successive divisions, increasing the number of groups by one at each separation stage. It is also usually true of this approach that any 'root' or 'branch' (depending which way up the tree is displayed) of the tree is exclusive of any other in terms of the individuals within it, and will remain so for all successive divisions. In short, retrospective merging of groups or of individuals across groups is not permitted.

The Belson segmentation was an early type of this approach and its basis for the 'best' discrimination was a chi squared test on each cross tabulation against the criterion variable. Operational forms allowed some subjective influence, as it involved successive cross tabulations and the 'best' could be chosen by use of both the significance of the chi square and the preconceptions of the researcher. This approach has two drawbacks which may counteract its flexibility, those being that it is both laborious and often time-consuming in terms of input to final solution.

A comparatively recent American program (AID) has been able to overcome these problems to a large extent. It automatically studies the candidate groups at each stage and selects that division which brings about the best discrimination in the criterion. The mechanics of the test are sums of squares of the criterion as opposed to the chi square of Belson:

$$\text{Test} = \frac{BSS_{ij}}{TSS_k}$$

Where BSS_{ij} = Sum of squares between
resultant (i and j)
split-groups from group k
   TSS_k = Sum of squares of group k
before splitting
(and k has become the candidate for splitting)

   The k th group becomes a candidate when (subject to constraints on size and proportion of total variance set by the user) it has the largest TSS of all existing groups.
   It therefore chooses that division on a given variable which best divides the criterion. The resulting groups are defined *totally* by these divisions, in that the groups contain discrete values of the predictors used at this stage coupled with any values of predictors used at any previous division. Variables not used for any divisions are not defined for the groups unless further analysis is undertaken. The advantages of this type of segmentation are that each group is simply defined in terms of the predictors used for splitting. The value of the criterion is known for each group and it is further known that a 'good' discrimination in the criterion across groups has been made.
   AID can handle as predictors two major types of variable, FREE and MONOTONIC. The former are treated as nominal classifications and during the division process *any* combination of classes within such is permitted in order to most efficiently divide the sample. The latter are scales and therefore only a limited type of grouping of classes is permitted, namely those which divide the variable above and below a trial position along the scale. That is combinations of the form High and Low VERSUS Medium are not permitted on monotonic variables.
   The division process is contained to operate in the mode described in 1.0, namely that the test value is maximised (BSS/TSS). However there are a number of other influences on the analysis which operate as follows:
   Candidate Groups are nominated at each stage of splitting such that they contain the largest TSS of all groups currently intact. (In the first split this means the universe.) Constraints may be placed on this selection based on (a) the number of objects in the candidate and (b) the proportion of the universe variation.
   Extent of division is simply constrained by setting an upper limit to the number of final groups required.
   Each of the above are defined by the user prior to the analysis.

LIMITATIONS OF AID

The Automatic Interaction Detector which was proposed by Morgan and Sonquist in 1963 has become widely used in the analysis of survey data but, like most multivariate analysis techniques, it has considerable limitations. For example, a problem which frequently occurs in the application of AID analyses is the presence of highly inter-correlated predictor variables. In this study, for example, differential opportunities to conceive produce an overall correlation between the age of the bride and the number of children born to the

marriage; in situations such as this, one of these inter-correlated
factors will normally be chosen for a split at some branching point,
but the other factors will rarely determine subsequent splits,
giving the mistaken impression that they are not important contributing factors. Furthermore, in the presence of inter-correlated
variables, AID may also be sensitive to sampling error. Some form
of validation (such as split sample analysis or discriminant
analysis) is desirable. Useful too would be a 'control' AID analysis
of the CM survey group; this would clarify the correlation structure
of the explanatory variables as present in the continuing married
group, lending a sense of perspective to the analyses of the D group
presented in Chapter 10. Regrettably, for a variety of reasons,
further treatment of the survey groups by AID could not take place.

Suggested reading

MORGAN, J.N. and SONQUIST, J.A., Problems in the analysis of survey
data and a proposal, 'Journal of the American Statistical Associa-
tion', 58 (September 1963), pp.415-34.
DOYLE, P., The use of AID and similar search procedures, 'Operational
Research Quarterly', 24 (September 1973), pp.465-7.
DOYLE, P. and FENWICK, I., The pitfalls of AID, 'Journal of
Marketing Research', (November 1955), pp.408-13.
HEALD, G.T., The application of AID and multiple regression
techniques to the assessment of store performance and site selection,
'Operational Research Quarterly', 23 (June 1972), pp.445-54.
STAELIN, R.A., Another look at AID, 'Journal of Advertising
Research', 11 (October 1971), pp.23-8.

VARIABLE LIST FOR THE AID ANALYSIS

Marriage cohort
Courtship duration
Other serious girl/boy friends prior to spouse or not
Timing of first child
Timing of second child
Timing of third child
Bride's social class
Groom's social class
Husband's job changing
Unemployment for husband in first (5) years of marriage
Groom's personality traits
Bride's personality traits
Age of bride
Age of groom
Age differences between couple
Formal engagement or not
Marital opposition or not
Who opposed the marriage
Reconciliation with opposition after marriage or not
Serious pre-marital problems or not
Place of marriage

Honeymoon or not
Type of first accommodation
Type of second accommodation
Rented/bought accommodation (1st)
Rented/bought accommodation (2nd)
Shared accommodation or not (1st)
Shared accommodation or not (2nd)
Friction in any shared accommodation or not
People with whom 1st accommodation was shared
People with whom 2nd accommodation was shared
Pre-marital pregnancy or not
Number of children born to the marriage
Problems during adolescence
Hospitalisation
Bride an only child
Groom an only child
Couple only children
Parental preference
Age at leaving school
Further education or not
Wife worked during marriage or not
Phasing of wife's work
Husband's attitude to wife's working
Type of wife's work
Reasons for wife's work
Wife's attitude to own work
Religion at marriage
Bride's religion
Groom's religion
Churchgoing during marriage
Frequency of churchgoing during marriage
Importance of sexual side of marriage
Sexual difficulties at start of marriage
Improvement in initial sexual problems
Sexual difficulties later into marriage
Gender differences in obtaining pleasure from sex

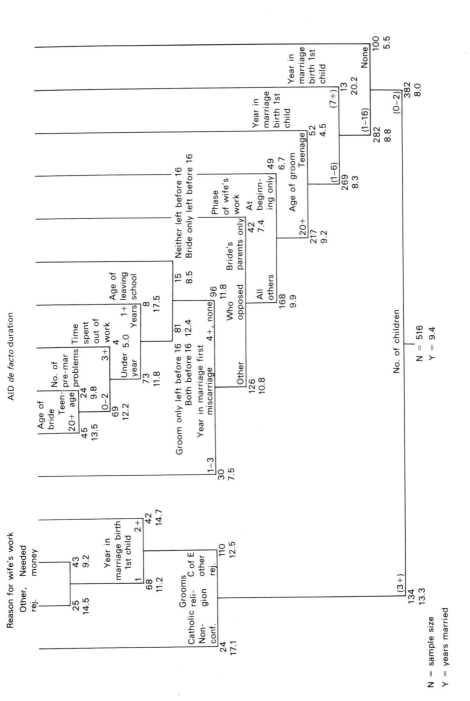

AID *de facto* duration

Reason for wife's work

N = sample size

Y = years married

N = 516
Y = 9.4

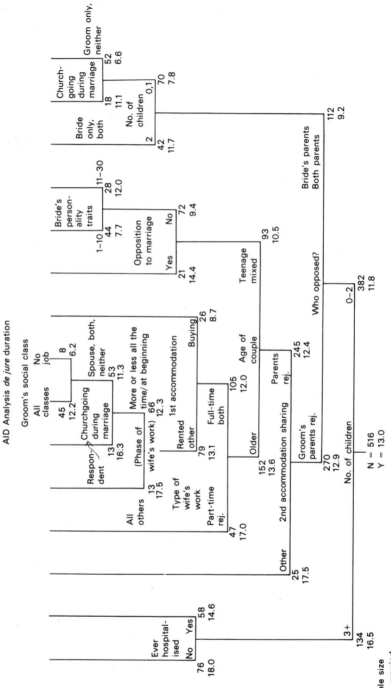

AID Analysis *de jure* duration

N = sample size
Y = years married

CONTENT OF THE INTERVIEW SCHEDULE

I COURTSHIP, ENGAGEMENT, MARRIAGE

Date of marriage
Age at marriage (informant and spouse)
Closeness of living in relation to spouse at first meeting
Age at 'going out' with spouse
Length of time 'going out' with spouse before marriage
Whether formal engagement
Length of time between engagement and marriage
Length of time between decision to marry and marriage
Opposition to the marriage, and outcome
Steady boy/girl friends and engagements prior to spouse
Church or Registry Office wedding

II ACCOMMODATION DURING MARRIAGE

Types, and length of time in each
Any sharing, and if so, whether friction
Reasons for moving to different accommodation

III CHILDREN IN THE MARRIAGE

Dates of birth
Post-puerperal depression following any birth
Miscarriages/still-births, and any subsequent depression

IV CHILDHOOD AND ADOLESCENT HEALTH

Whether any of these illnesses: (a) TB; rheumatic fever; pneumonia; polio; diabetes; heart complaint; bronchitis
(b) asthma; skin trouble; hay fever; dizzy spells; bilious attacks; stammering; epilepsy

Whether experienced any 'common
fears or difficulties' 7-11 years: Fear of school
                                                  Difficulty in concentrating in
school
                                                  Fear of the dark

Whether experienced any 'common
fears or difficulties' 7-11 years:

- Fear of school
- Difficulty in concentrating in school
- Fear of the dark
- Fear of animals
- Fear of strangers
- Shy with other children
- Bed-wetting
- Nightmares
- Suffered with nerves
- Homesick
- Feelings of misery and depression
- Difficulty in making friends
- Quick temper
- Lacking in confidence

Whether experienced any of these
problems commonly found in
teenagers:

- Dislike of school
- Inability to concentrate in school
- Worry about personal appearance
- Shy with opposite sex
- Suffered with nerves
- Bed-wetting
- Quick temper
- Lacking in confidence
- Difficulty in making friends
- Feelings of misery and depression

Hospitalisation before 16 (age and duration)
Age at puberty

V FAMILY OF ORIGIN

Siblings and own position in family
Marital outcome of siblings (happily married, separated, divorced)
Informants' parents' marriage: date of marriage (if married)
Whether parents remained married, separated, divorced, or died (until
   informants 16 years)
(if parents remained married):   whether or not parents happily
married
which parent preferred by
informant

(if parent/s separated, divorced,
dead):   age of informant when this took
place
guardianship arrangements (until
informant 16)
whether or not parents happily
married (if dead)
which parent preferred by informant (if both remembered well)
any parental remarriage

VI   EDUCATION

Type of last school attended by informant
Schooling 5-7; 8-11; 12-16
Age at leaving school
Further education; apprenticeship; training; higher education

VII   SOCIAL CLASS AND OCCUPATION

Occupation of main breadwinner in informant's family (when informant 16)
Occupation of informant after school/university/college
Occupation of informant at marriage
Husband's job changes in first (five) years of marriage
Amount of time unemployed during marriage (husband)
Pattern of wife's work (if any) during marriage
Husband's response to wife working
Wife's response to going out to work

VIII RELIGION

Religious affiliation at marriage
Religious affiliation in upbringing
Church attendance during marriage

IX   BACKGROUND OF SPOUSE

(a) Spouse family background

Siblings and own position in family
Marital outcome of siblings
Spouse parents' marriage: whether parents remained married, separated, divorced, died
(if remained married): whether or not happily married
(if separated, divorced, died): guardianship arrangements (before spouse 16)

(b) Spouse education

Type of school last attended
Age at leaving school
Further education; apprenticeship; training; higher education

(c) Spouse social class

Occupation of main breadwinner in spouse's family (spouse aged 16)
Occupation of spouse after leaving school/university/college
Occupation of spouse at marriage
Husband's job changes in first (five) years marriage
Amount of time unemployed during marriage (husband)

(d)   Spouse religion

Religious affiliation at marriage
Religious affiliation in upbringing
Church attendance during marriage

(e)   Spousal personality traits and temperament (5 point bi-polar scale)

30 items: e.g. optimistic/pessimistic
                  not talkative/talkative

X   CONTINUING MARRIED INFORMANTS ONLY

Whether ever any difficulties in their own marriage serious enough
   to make either partner contemplate breaking up the marriage
Whether these difficulties caused (temporary) separation
If a marriage were unhappy and no children involved, whether or not
   the couple should seek divorce
If a marriage were unhappy and there were children involved, whether
   or not the couple should seek divorce
Rating of own marital happiness (5 point scale)

Divorced informants only

Date of start of difficulties in the marriage
Date of first separation
Date of reconciliation (if any)
Date of final separation
Date of decree absolute

XI   SEXUAL BEHAVIOUR

Initial satisfaction/dissatisfaction with the sexual side of
   marriage
Reasons for any dissatisfaction, and outcome
Later satisfaction/dissatisfaction with the sexual side of marriage
Importance of sexual side of marriage
Whether man or woman derives more pleasure from love-making
Pre-marital sexual relationships
Extra-marital sexual relationships

THE EYSENCK PQ FORM

In 1972, when the fieldwork of this study began, it was not possible to obtain a short personality inventory which would provide measurements of individuals with regard to neuroticism, psychoticism and extraversion and which had been standardised on a UK population. Fortunately, however, Dr Sybil Eysenck working at the Institute of Psychiatry was in the process of finishing the development* of such an inventory (then called the PQ form, and which also provided a lie score); she agreed to let us use it in our research and also to calculate for us the scores for the survey divorced and continuing married populations of men and women. The format and the item list of the PQ form (scores were finally based upon 90 items instead of 101) are contained at the end of this Appendix. Four scores were derived: P (Psychoticism); N (Neuroticism); E (Extraversion); L (Lie Score).

RESULTS

Divorced men had consistently higher scores than continuing married men and, in particular, appeared both more extraverted and more neurotic, as Table A shows.

TABLE A   P, E, N and L scores of men

	n*	P		E		N		L	
		Mean	SD+	Mean	SD	Mean	SD	Mean	SD
DM	215	3.54	2.83	13.25	4.64	10.71	5.09	10.62	5.18
CMM	519	2.83	2.44	12.00	5.17	9.25	5.17	9.97	4.66

* includes informants and spouses
+ Standard Deviation

* Published in 1975 as the Eysenck Personality Questionnaire by Hodder & Stoughton Educational.

The differences between divorced and continuing married women were particularly marked for neuroticism and more marked than DM-CMM differences for psychoticism. DW and CMW appear to be remarkably similar in terms of extraversion, as Table B shows.

TABLE B   P, E, N and L scores of women

	n	P Mean	P SD	E Mean	E SD	N Mean	N SD	L Mean	L SD
DW	345	2.90	2.25	11.89	5.05	14.67	5.06	11.94	4.69
CMW	550	2.07	1.83	11.91	4.67	12.67	5.08	11.40	4.67

The data from the PQ form also indicated that women may be more neurotic than men and also more inclined to lie on personality tests; conversely they appear to be both less psychotic and less extraverted than men. As can be seen, the differences between men and women are far more marked for the divorced group.

PERSONALITY QUESTIONNAIRE

OCCUPATION   AGE   SEX

INSTRUCTIONS

Please answer each question by putting a circle around the 'YES' or the 'NO' following the question. There are no right or wrong answers, and no trick questions. Work quickly and do not think too long about the exact meaning of the question.

PLEASE REMEMBER TO ANSWER EACH QUESTION

1   Do you have many different hobbies?   YES   NO
2   Do you stop to think things over before doing
    anything?   YES   NO
3   Does your mood often go up and down?   YES   NO
4   Have you ever taken the praise for something you knew
    someone else had really done?   YES   NO
5   Are you a talkative person?   YES   NO
6   Would being in debt worry you?   YES   NO
7   Do you ever feel 'just miserable' for no reason?   YES   NO
8   Were you ever greedy by helping yourself to more than
    your share of anything?   YES   NO
9   Do you lock up your house carefully at night?   YES   NO
10 Are you rather lively?   YES   NO
11 Would it upset you a lot to see a child or an animal
    suffer?   YES   NO
12 Do you often worry about things you should not have
    done or said?   YES   NO

13	If you say you will do something, do you always keep your promise no matter how inconvenient it might be?	YES	NO
14	Would you enjoy parachute jumping?	YES	NO
15	Can you usually let yourself go and enjoy yourself at a lively party?	YES	NO
16	Are you an irritable person?	YES	NO
17	Have you ever blamed someone for doing something you knew was really your fault?	YES	NO
18	Do you enjoy meeting new people?	YES	NO
19	Do you believe insurance schemes are a good idea?	YES	NO
20	Are your feelings easily hurt?	YES	NO
21	Are *all* your habits good and desirable ones?	YES	NO
22	Do you tend to keep in the background on social occasions?	YES	NO
23	Would you take drugs which may have strange or dangerous effects?	YES	NO
24	Do you often feel 'fed-up'?	YES	NO
25	Have you ever taken anything (even a pin or button) that belonged to someone else?	YES	NO
26	Do you like going out a lot?	YES	NO
27	Do you enjoy hurting people you love?	YES	NO
28	Are you often troubled about feelings of guilt?	YES	NO
29	Do you sometimes talk about things you know nothing about?	YES	NO
30	Do you prefer reading to meeting people?	YES	NO
31	Do you have enemies who want to harm you?	YES	NO
32	Would you call yourself a nervous person?	YES	NO
33	Do you always say you are sorry when you have been rude?	YES	NO
34	Do you have many friends?	YES	NO
35	Do you enjoy practical jokes that can sometimes really hurt people?	YES	NO
36	Are you a worrier?	YES	NO
37	As a child did you do as you were told immediately and without grumbling?	YES	NO
38	Would you call yourself happy-go-lucky?	YES	NO
39	Do good manners and cleanliness matter much to you?	YES	NO
40	Do you worry about awful things that might happen?	YES	NO
41	Have you ever broken or lost something belonging to someone else?	YES	NO
42	Do you usually take the initiative in making new friends?	YES	NO
43	Can you easily understand the way people feel when they tell you their troubles?	YES	NO
44	Would you call yourself tense or 'highly-strung'?	YES	NO
45	Do you throw waste paper on the floor when there is no waste paper basket handy?	YES	NO
46	Are you mostly quiet when you are with other people?	YES	NO
47	Do you think marriage is old-fashioned and should be done away with?	YES	NO
48	Do you feel self pity now and again?	YES	NO
49	Do you sometimes boast a little?	YES	NO
50	Can you easily get some life into a rather dull party?	YES	NO
51	Do people who drive carefully annoy you?	YES	NO

52	Do you worry about your health?	YES	NO
53	Have you ever said anything bad or nasty about anyone?	YES	NO
54	Do you like telling jokes and funny stories to your friends?	YES	NO
55	Do most things taste the same to you?	YES	NO
56	Do you sometimes sulk?	YES	NO
57	As a child were you ever cheeky to your parents?	YES	NO
58	Do you like mixing with people?	YES	NO
59	Does it worry you if you know there are mistakes in your work?	YES	NO
60	Do you suffer from sleeplessness?	YES	NO
61	Do you always wash before a meal?	YES	NO
62	Do you nearly always have a 'ready answer' when people talk to you?	YES	NO
63	Do you like to arrive at appointments in plenty of time?	YES	NO
64	Have you often felt listless and tired for no reason?	YES	NO
65	Have you ever cheated at a game?	YES	NO
66	Do you like doing things in which you have to act quickly?	YES	NO
67	Is (or was) your mother a good woman?	YES	NO
68	Do you often feel life is very dull?	YES	NO
69	Have you ever taken advantage of someone?	YES	NO
70	Do you often take on more activities than you have time for?	YES	NO
71	Are there several people who keep trying to avoid you?	YES	NO
72	Do you worry a lot about your looks?	YES	NO
73	Are you always polite even to unpleasant people?	YES	NO
74	Do you think people spend too much time safeguarding their future with savings and insurances?	YES	NO
75	Have you ever wished that you were dead?	YES	NO
76	Would you dodge paying taxes if you were sure you could never be found out?	YES	NO
77	Can you get a party going?	YES	NO
78	Do you try not to be rude to people?	YES	NO
79	Do you worry too long after an embarrassing experience?	YES	NO
80	Have you ever insisted on having your own way?	YES	NO
81	When you catch a train do you often arrive at the last minute?	YES	NO
82	Do you suffer from 'nerves'?	YES	NO
83	Have you ever deliberately said something to hurt someone's feelings?	YES	NO
84	Do you hate being with a crowd who play harmless jokes on one another?	YES	NO
85	Do your friendships break up easily without it being your fault?	YES	NO
86	Do you often feel lonely?	YES	NO
87	Do you always practise what you preach?	YES	NO
88	Do you sometimes like teasing animals?	YES	NO
89	Are you easily hurt when people find fault with you or the work you do?	YES	NO
90	Would life with no danger in it be too dull for you?	YES	NO

91	Have you ever been late for an appointment or work?	YES	NO
92	Do you like plenty of bustle and excitement around you?	YES	NO
93	Would you like other people to be afraid of you?	YES	NO
94	Are you sometimes bubbling over with energy and sometimes very sluggish?	YES	NO
95	Do you sometimes put off until tomorrow what you ought to do today?	YES	NO
96	Do other people think of you as being very lively?	YES	NO
97	Do people tell you a lot of lies?	YES	NO
98	Are you touchy about some things?	YES	NO
99	Are you always willing to admit it when you have made a mistake?	YES	NO
100	Would you feel very sorry for an animal caught in a trap?	YES	NO
101	Did you mind filling in this form?	YES	NO

PLEASE CHECK TO SEE THAT YOU HAVE ANSWERED ALL THE QUESTIONS

BIBLIOGRAPHY

ACKERMAN, K. (1963), Affiliations: structural determinants of differential divorce rates, 'American Journal of Sociology', vol.69, pp.13-20.

AINSWORTH, K.D. (1962), The effects of maternal deprivation: a review of findings and controversy in the context of research strategy, in 'Deprivation of Maternal Care: a reassessment of its effects', Public Health Papers no.14, World Health Organisation, Geneva.

ANDRY, R.G. (1960), 'Delinquency and Parental Pathology', Methuen.

BANE, M.J. (1975), 'Economic Influence on Divorce and Remarriage', Cambridge Centre for the Study of Public Policy.

BARRY, W.A. (1970), Marriage research and conflict: an integrative review, 'Psychological Bulletin', vol.73, pp.41-54.

BEAUCHAMP, D. (1969), reported in S. Jacoby, Transition to parenthood: a reassessment, 'Journal of Marriage and the Family', vol.31, pp.720-7.

BERENT, J. (1954), Social mobility and marriage, in D. Glass (ed.), 'Social Mobility', Routledge & Kegan Paul, pp.321-8.

BERNARD, J. (1964), The adjustments of married mates, in H.T. Christensen (ed.), 'Handbook of Marriage and the Family', Rand McNally, Chicago.

BIRTCHNELL, J. (1974), Some possible early family determinants of marriage and divorce, 'British Journal of Medical Psychology', vol.47, pp.121-7.

BLAU, P.M. (1956), Social Mobility and Interpersonal Relations, 'American Sociological Review', vol.21, pp.290-5.

BLOOD, R.C. and WOLFE, D.M. (1960), 'Husbands and Wives: The Dynamics of Married Living', Free Press, Chicago.

BOWLBY, J. (1969), 'Attachment: Attachment and Loss Vol.I', Hogarth Press.

BOWLBY, J. (1973), 'Separation: Anxiety and Anger: Attachment and Loss Vol.II', Hogarth Press.

BOWLBY, J., AINSWORTH, M.D. and ROSENBLUTH, D. (1956), The effects of mother-child separation: a follow-up study, 'British Journal of Medical Psychology', vol.29, pp.211-47.

BRADBURN, N.M. and CAPLOVITZ, D. (1965), 'Reports on Happiness', Aldine.

BRANDEWEIN, R.A., BROWN, C.A. and FOX, E.M. (1974), Women and children last: the social situation of divorced mothers and their families, 'Journal of Marriage and the Family', vol.36, pp.498-514.

BRIM, O.G., GLASS, D.C., LAVIN, D.E. and GOODMAN, N. (1962), 'Personality and Decision Processes', Stanford University Press.

BROWN, C.A., FELDBERG, R., FOX, E.M. and KOHEN, J. (1976), Divorce: chance of a new life-time, 'Journal of Social Issues', vol.32, pp.119-33.

BROWN, G.W., BHROLCHAIN, M.M. and HARRIS, T.O. (1975), Social class and psychiatry: disturbance amongst women in an urban population, 'Sociology', vol.9, pp.225-54.

BUMPASS, L. and SWEET, J. (1972), Differentials in marital stability, 'American Sociological Review', vol.37, pp.754-66.

BURCHINAL, L.G. (1959), Adolescent role deprivation and high-school age at marriage, 'Marriage and Family Living', vol.21, pp.378-84.

BURCHINAL, L.G. (1964), Characteristics of adolescents from unbroken homes and reconstituted families, 'Journal of Marriage and the Family', vol.26, pp.44-5.

BURGESS, E.W. and COTTRELL, L.S. (1939), 'Predicting Success or Failure in Marriage', Prentice-Hall, New York.

BURGESS, E.W. and WALLIN, P. (1953), 'Engagement and Marriage', Lippincott, Chicago.

BURR, W.R. (1970), Satisfaction with various aspects of marriage over the life cycle, 'Journal of Marriage and the Family', vol.32, pp.26-37.

BUSFIELD, J. and PADDON, M. (1977), 'Thinking about Children', Cambridge University Press.

CAMPBELL, A. (1975), The American way of mating: Marriage si, children only maybe, 'Psychology Today', May, pp.37-43.

CARTWRIGHT, A. (1976), 'How Many Children?', Routledge & Kegan Paul.

CHESSER, E. (1957), 'The Sexual, Marital and Family Relationships of the English Woman', Roy, New York.

CHESTER, R. (1970), Sex differences in divorce behaviour, 'J urnal of Biosocial Science', supplement 2, p.122.

CHESTER, R. (1971a), The duration of marriage to divorce, 'British Journal of Sociology', vol.22, pp.172-82.

CHESTER, R. (1971b), Health and marriage breakdown: experience of a sample of divorced women, 'British Journal of Social and Preventive Medicine', vol.25, pp.231-5.

CHESTER, R. (1971c), Contemporary trends in the stability of English marriage, 'Journal of Biosocial Science', vol.3, pp.389-402.

CHESTER, R. (1972a), Divorce and legal aid: a false hypothesis, 'Sociology', vol.6, pp.205-16.

CHESTER, R. (1972b), Current incidence and trends in marital break-down, 'Post-graduate Medical Journal', vol.48, pp.529-41.

CHESTER, R. (1972c), Is there a relationship between childlessness and marriage breakdown?, 'Journal of Biosocial Science', vol.4, pp.443-54.

CHESTER, R. (1972d), Some characteristics of marriages of brief duration, 'Medical Gynaecology and Sociology', vol.6, pp.9-12.

CHESTER, R. (1978), (with collaboration of Gerrit Kooy), England and Wales in 'Divorce in Europe', pp.69-95, Martinus Nijhoff, Leyden.

CHRISTENSEN, H.T. (1960), Cultural relativism and pre-marital sex norms, 'American Sociological Review', vol.25, pp.31-9.
CHRISTENSEN, H.T. and MEISSNER, H.M. (1953), Studies in child spacing: III - pre-marital pregnancy as a factor in divorce, 'American Sociological Review', vol.18, pp.641-4.
CHRISTENSEN, H.T. and RUBINSTEIN, B.B. (1956), Pre-marital pregnancy and divorce: a follow-up study by the interview method, 'Marriage and Family Living', vol.18, pp.114-23.
COOMBS, R.H. (1966), Value consensus and partner satisfaction among dating couples, 'Journal of Marriage and the Family', vol.28, pp.166-73.
COOMBS, L.C. and ZUMETA, Z. (1970), Correlates of marital dissolution in a prospective fertility study: a research note, 'Social Problems', vol.18, pp.92-101.
COOPER, D. (1972), 'Death of the Family', Penguin Books.
CUBER, J.F. and HARROF, P. (1962), The more total view, 'Marriage and Family Living', vol.25, pp.140-5.
CUTRIGHT, P. (1971), Income and family events: marital stability, 'Journal of Marriage and the Family', vol.33, pp.291-306.
CUTRIGHT, P. and SCANZONI, J. (1973), 'Income supplements and the American family. The Family Poverty and Welfare Programs: factors influencing family stability' (Studies in Public Welfare, Paper no.12, part 1), US Government Printing Office, Washington DC.
DAVIS, K., BREDEMEIER, H.C. and LEVY, M.J., Jnr (1950), 'Modern American Society: Readings in the problems of order and change', Holt, Rinehart & Winston, New York.
DESPERT, J.L. (1953), 'Children of Divorce', Doubleday, New York.
DOMINIAN, J. (1968), 'Marital Breakdown', Penguin Books.
DOMINIAN, J. (1977), What future for marriage? 'Sunday Telegraph', 10 April.
DOMINIAN, J. (1978), Verbal communication.
DOUGLAS, J.W.B. (1964), 'The Home and the School', MacGibbon & Kee.
DOUGLAS, J.W.B. (1975), Early hospital admissions and later disturbances of behaviour and learning, 'Developmental Medicine and Child Neurology', vol.17, pp.456-80.
DOUGLAS, J.W.B., ROSS, J.M. and SIMPSON, H.R. (1968), 'All Our Future', Peter Davies.
DRISCOLL, R., DAVIS, K.E. and LIPETZ, M.A. (1972), Parental interference and romantic love, 'Journal of Personality and Social Psychology', vol.24, pp.1-10.
DURKHEIM, E. (1952), 'Suicide', Routledge & Kegan Paul.
DYER, E.D. (1963), Parenthood as crisis: a re-study, 'Marriage and Family Living', vol.25, pp.196-201.
FAGIN, C.M.R.N. (1966), 'The effects of maternal attendance during hospitalisation on the post-hospital behaviour of young children: a comparative study', F.A. Davis, Philadelphia.
FLETCHER, R. (1973), 'The Family and Marriage in Britain', Penguin Books.
FINER, M. (ed.) (1974), 'Report of the Committee on One-parent Families', HMSO.
FREEDMAN, R., WHELPTON, P.K., CAMPBELL, A.A. (1959), 'Family Planning, Sterility and Population Growth', McGraw-Hill, New York.
FURSTENBERG, F.F., Jnr (1976), Pre-marital pregnancy and marital instability, 'Journal of Social Issues', vol.32, pp.67-86.

GENERAL REGISTER OFFICE (1964), 'The Registrar-General's Statistical Review of England and Wales', HMSO.
GENERAL REGISTER OFFICE (1965), 'The Registrar-General's Statistical Review of England and Wales for the year 1965', Part III, HMSO.
GIBSON, C. (1974), The association between divorce and social class in England and Wales, 'British Journal of Sociology', vol.25, pp.79-93.
GLICK, P.C. (1957), 'American Families', Wiley, New York.
GLICK, P.C. and LANDAU, E. (1950), Age as a factor in marriage, 'American Sociological Review', vol.15, pp.517-29.
GOLDEN, J. (1954), Patterns of negro-white intermarriage, 'American Sociological Review', vol.19, pp.144-7.
GOODE, W.J. (1956), 'After Divorce', Free Press, Chicago.
GOODE, W.J. (1966), Family disorganisation, in R.K. Merton and R.A. Nisbet (eds). 'Contemporary Social Problems', Harcourt, Brace & World, New York.
GOODE, W.J. (1971), A sociological perspective on marital dissolution, in M. Anderson (ed.), 'Sociology of the Family', Penguin Books.
GOODY, E.N. (1962), Conjugal separation and divorce amongst the Gonja of Northern Ghana, in M. Fortes (ed.), 'Marriage in Tribal Societies', Cambridge University Press.
GORER, G. (1971), 'Sex and Marriage in England Today', Nelson.
GOVE, W. (1972), The relationship between sex roles, mental illness and marital status, 'Social Forces', vol.51, pp.34-44.
GOWER, L.B.C. (1952), 'Minutes of Evidence taken before the Royal Commission on Marriage and Divorce', First Day, 20 May.
GREER, S., GUNN, J.C. and KOLLER, K.M. (1966), Aetiological factors in attempted suicide, 'British Medical Journal', vol.2, pp.1352-5.
GUNTER, B.G. (1977), Notes on divorce filing as role behaviour, 'Journal of Marriage and the Family', vol.39, pp.95-8.
GURIN, G., VEROFF, J. and FELD, S. (1960), 'Americans View Their Mental Health', Basic Books, Monograph Series no.4, Joint Commission on Mental Illness and Health.
HART, N. (1976), 'When Marriage Ends: a study in status passage', Tavistock.
HAVIGHURST, R.J. (1961), Early marriage and the schools, 'The School Review', Spring, pp.36-47.
HEILPERN, E.P. (1943), Psychological problems in step-children, 'Psychoanalytic Review', vol.30, pp.163-76.
HEISS, J. (1972), On the transmission of marital instability in black families, 'American Sociological Review', vol.37, pp.82-92.
HERSOV, L. (1977), Emotional disorders, in M. Rutter and L. Hersov (eds), 'Child Psychiatry: Modern Approaches', Blackwell, Oxford.
HERZOG, E. and SUDIA, C.E. (1971), 'Boys in Fatherless Families' (US Dept of Health Education and Welfare), Children's Bureau, No.72-83, US Government Printing Office, Washington DC.
HILLMAN, K.G. (1962), Marital instability and its relation to education, income and occupation: an analysis based on census data, in R.F. Winch, R. McGuiness and H.R. Barringer (eds), 'Selected Studies in Marriage and the Family', rev. edn, Holt, Rinehart & Winston, New York.
HOBBS, D.F., Jnr (1965), Parenthood as crisis: a third study, 'Journal of Marriage and the Family', vol.27, pp.367-72.

HMSO (1966), 'Reform of the Grounds of Divorce: The Field of Choice', Cmnd 3123.

HMSO (1967), Figures produced by the Registrar General for 'The Committee on the Age of Majority', Appendix 8, Cmnd 3342.

HMSO (1968), 'Committee on Statutory Maintenance Limits', Cmnd 3587.

INEICHEN, B. (1977), Youthful marriage: the vortex of disadvantage, in R. Chester and J. Peel (eds), 'Equalities and Inequalities in Family Life', Academic Press, London and New York.

ISR (1974), 'Measuring the quality of life in America', Newsletter, Institute for Social Research (2).

JACOBSON, P.H. (1959), 'American Marriage and Divorce', Holt, Rinehart & Winston, New York.

JOHNSON, W.B. and TERMAN, L.M. (1940), Some highlights in the literature of psychological sex differences published since 1920, 'Journal of Psychology', vol.9, pp.327-36.

KAGAN, J. and MOSS, H.A. (1962), 'Birth to Maturity', Wiley, New York.

KEPHART, W.M. (1972), 'The Family, Society and the Individual', 3rd edn, Houghton Mifflin, Boston.

KERCKHOFF, A.C. (1974), The social context of interpersonal attraction, in T.L. Huston (ed.), 'Foundations of interpersonal attraction', Academic Press, London and New York.

KINSEY, A.C. et al.(1953), 'Sexual Behaviour in the Human Female', Saunders, Philadelphia.

KOMAROVSKY, M. (1967), 'Blue Collar Marriage', Vintage Books, New York.

KUBIE, L.S. (1956), Psychoanalysis and marriage, in V.W. Eisenstein (ed.), 'Neurotic Interaction in Marriage', Tavistock.

LAING, R.D. and ESTERSON, A. (1970), 'Sanity, Madness and the Family', Penguin Books.

LANDIS, J.T. (1946), Length of time required to achieve adjustment in marriage, 'American Sociological Review', vol.11, pp.666-77.

LANDIS, J.T. (1960), The trauma of children whose parents divorce, 'Marriage and Family Living', vol.22, pp.7-13.

LANDIS, J.T. (1962), A comparison of children from divorced and non-divorced unhappy homes, 'Family Life Coordinator', vol.11, p.61.

LANDIS, J.T. (1963), Some correlates of divorce or non-divorce among the unhappily married, 'Marriage and Family Living', vol.25, pp.178-80.

LANGNER,T.S. and MICHAEL, S.T. (1963), 'Life Stress and Mental Health', Collier-Macmillan.

LAPOUSE, R. and MONK, M. (1959), Fears and worries in a representative sample of children, 'American Journal of Orthopsychiatry, vol.29, pp.803-18.

LE MASTERS, E.E. (1957), Parenthood as crisis, 'Marriage and Family Living', vol.19, pp.352-5.

LEACH, E. (1968), 'A Runaway World', Oxford University Press.

LEETE, R. (1976), Marriage and divorce, 'Population Trends', no.3, pp.3-8.

LEVINGER, G. (1966), Marital dissatisfaction amongst divorce applicants, 'American Journal of Orthopsychiatry', vol.36, pp.803-7.

LEVINGER, G. (1976), A social psychological perspective on marital dissolution, 'Journal of Social Issues', vol.32, no.1, pp.21-47.

LEVINGER, G, and MOLES, O.C. (1976), In conclusion: threads in the fabric, 'Journal of Social Issues', vol.32, pp.193-207.

LIPSET, S.M. and BENDIX, R. (1959), 'Social Mobility in an
Industrial Society', Heinemann.
LLOYD, G.C. (1977), Psychological reactions to physical illness,
'British Journal of Hospital Medicine, vol.18, pp.352-8.
LOCKE, H.J. (1951), 'Predicting Adjustment in Marriage, a comparison
of a divorced and a married group', Holt, New York.
LOCKWOOD, D. (1958), 'The Black-coated Worker', Allen & Unwin.
LOWRIE, S.H. (1965), Early marriage: pre-marital pregnancy and
associated factors, 'Journal of Marriage and the Family', vol.27,
pp.49-56.
McCANN-ERIKSON (1977), 'You Don't Know Me: a survey of youth in
Britain', McCann-Erikson.
McGREGOR, O.R. (1957), 'Divorce in England', Heinemann.
McGREGOR, O.R. (1960), The stability of the family in the welfare
state, 'Political Quarterly', vol.31, pp.132-41.
McGREGOR, O.R. (1967), Towards divorce law reform, 'British Journal
of Sociology', vol.18, pp.91-9.
McGREGOR, O.R. (1970), with L. BLOM-COOPER and C. GIBSON, 'Separated
Spouses', Duckworth.
MARTINSON, F.M. (1955), Ego deficiency as a factor in marriage,
'American Sociological Review', vol.20, pp.161-4.
MEAD, M. (1971), Anomalies in American post-divorce relationships,
in P. Bohannan (ed.), 'Divorce and After', Doubleday, Garden City,
New York.
MERTON, R.K. (1957), 'Social Theory and Social Structure', Free
Press, Chicago.
MOLES, O.C. (1976), Marital dissolution and public assistance
payments: variations among American States, 'Journal of Social
Issues, vol.22, pp.87-101.
MONAHAN, T.P. (1953), Does age at marriage matter in divorce? 'Social
Forces', vol.32, pp.81-7.
MONAHAN, T.P. (1960), Premarital pregnancy in the United States,
'Eugenics Quarterly', vol.7, p.140.
MONAHAN, T.P. (1962), When married couples part: statistical trends
and relationships in divorce, 'American Sociological Review', vol.27,
pp.625-33.
MORGAN, G.A. and RICCIUTI, H.W. (1969), Infants' responses to
strangers during their first year, in B.M. Foss (ed.), 'Determinants
of Infant Behaviour', vol.4, Methuen.
MORRISON, D.E. and HENKEL, E. (1970), Significance tests in
behavioural research: sceptical conclusions and beyond, in 'The
Significance Test Controversy', Butterworth.
MOSS, J.J. and GINGLES, R. (1959), The relationship of personality
to the incidence of early marriage, 'Marriage and Family Living',
vol.21, pp.373-7.
MUELLER, C.W. and POPE, H. (1977), Marital instability: a study of
its transmission between generations, 'Journal of Marriage and the
Family', vol.39, pp.83-92.
MURCHISON, N. (1974), Illustration of the difficulties of some
children in one-parent families, in M. Finer (ed.), 'Report of the
Committee on One-parent Families', HMSO.
NORTON, A.J. and GLICK, P.C. (1976), Marital instability: past,
present and future, 'Journal of Social Issues', vol.32, pp.5-20.

NYE, F.I. (1957), Child adjustment in broken homes, 'Marriage and Family Living', vol.19, pp.356-61.

NYE, F.I. and BERARDO, F.M. (1973), 'The Family: its structure and interaction', Macmillan, New York.

OFFICE OF POPULATION CENSUSES AND SURVEYS (1976), Marriage and Divorce: R. Leete in 'Population Trends' no.3, Spring 1976, HMSO.

OTTERSTROM, E. (1952), The social outlook for children of divorcees, 'Acta Genetica et Statistica Medica', vol.3, p.72.

PIERCE, R.M. (1963), Marriage in the fifties, 'Sociological Review', vol.11, pp.215-40.

PODOLSKY, E. (1955), The emotional problems of the step-child, 'Mental Hygiene', vol.39, pp.49-53.

POHLMAN, E.H. (1969), 'Psychology of birth planning', Schenkman, Cambridge, Mass.

POPE, H. and MUELLER, C.W. (1976), The intergenerational transmission of marital instability: comparison by race and sex, 'Journal of Social Issues', vol.32, pp.49-66.

QUINTON, D. and RUTTER, M. (1976), Early hospital admissions and later disturbances of behaviour: an attempted replication of Douglas' findings, 'Developmental Medicine and Child Neurology', vol.18, pp.447-59.

RADLOFF, L. (1975), Sex differences in depression: the effects of occupation and marital status, 'Sex Roles: a Journal of Research', vol.1, pp.249-65.

RHEINSTEIN, M. (1960), The stability of the family: a report to the Director General of UNESCO on the colloquium on a comparative study of the legal means to promote the stability of the family, 'Annales de la Faculté de Droit d'Istanbul', 8th year, vol.IX, no.13, part II, pp.1-14.

RICHMAN, N., STEVENSON, J.E. and GRAHAM, P.J. (1975), Prevalence of behaviour problems in 3 year old children: an epidemiological study in a London borough, 'Journal of Child Psychology and Psychiatry', vol.16, pp.277-87.

ROBERTSON, J. and ROBERTSON, J. (1971), Young children in brief separation: a fresh look, 'The Psychoanalytic Study of the Child', vol.26, pp.264-315.

ROLLINS, B.C. and CANNON, K.L. (1974), Marital satisfaction over the family life cycle: a re-evaluation, 'Journal of Marriage and the Family', vol.36, pp.271-82.

ROSSI, P.H., SAMPSON, W.A., BOSE, C.E., JASSO, G. and PASSEL, J. (1974), Measuring household social standing, 'Social Science Research', vol.3, pp.169-90.

ROWNTREE, G. (1965), Some aspects of marriage breakdown in Britain during the last 30 years, 'Population Studies', vol.18, pp.147-63.

ROWNTREE, G. and CARRIER, N.H. (1958), The resort to divorce in England and Wales 1857-1957, 'Population Studies', vol.ii, pp.188-233.

RUTTER, M. (1971), Parent-child separation: psychological effects on the children, 'Journal of Child Psychology-Psychiatry, vol.12, pp.233-60.

RUTTER, M. (1972a), Relationship between child and adult psychiatric disorders: some research considerations, 'Acta Psychiatry Scandin-avia', vol.48, pp.5-21.

RUTTER, M. (1972b), 'Maternal Deprivation Reassessed', Penguin Books.

RUTTER, M. (1977), Separation, loss and family relationships, in
M. Rutter and L. Hersov (eds), 'Child Psychiatry: Modern Approaches',
Blackwell, Oxford, ch.3, pp.59-62.
RUTTER, M. and MADGE, N. (1976), 'Cycles of Disadvantage', Heinemann.
SAWHILL, I. (1975), Marriage, divorce and re-marriage (unpublished
manuscript), Urban Institute, Washington DC.
SCANZONI, J. (1965), A re-inquiry into marital dis-organisation,
'Journal of Marriage and the Family', vol.27, pp.483-91.
SHEPHERD, M., OPPENHEIN, A.N. and MITCHELL, S. (1966), Childhood
behaviour disorders and the child-guidance clinic: an epidemiological
study, 'Journal of Child Psychology - Psychiatry, vol.7, pp.39-52.
SLATER, E.and ROTH, M. (1969), 'Clinical Psychiatry', 3rd edn,
Cassell.
SMITH, C.E. (1966), Negro-white intermarriage: forbidden sexual
union, 'Journal of Sex Research', vol.2, pp.169-73.
STENGLER, E. (1964), 'Suicide and Attempted Suicide', Penguin Books.
THOMAS, M.M. (1968), Children with absent fathers, 'Journal of
Marriage and the Family', vol.30, pp.89-96.
TOMAN, W. (1961), 'Family Constellation', Springer.
US BUREAU OF CENSUS (1972), '1970 Census of Population: Marital
status (Final Report PC (2) 4c)', US Government Printing Office,
Washington DC.
US BUREAU OF CENSUS (1975), Money, income and poverty status of
families and persons in the US., 'Current Population Reports,
Series p-60, No.99', US Government Printing Office, Washington DC.
UDRY, J.R. (1966), Marital instability by race, sex, education and
occupation using 1960 census data, 'American Journal of Sociology',
vol.72, pp.203-9.
WALLIN, P. (1960), A study of orgasm as a condition of women's
enjoyment of intercourse, 'Journal of Social Psychology', vol.51,
pp.191-8.
WALLIN, P. and CLARK, A.L. (1958), Marital satisfaction and husbands'
and wives' perception of similarity in their preferred frequency of
coitus, 'Journal of Abnormal and Social Psychology', vol.47,
pp.370-3.
WEDGE, P. and PROSSER, H. (1973), 'Born to Fail?', Arrow Books in
association with National Children's Bureau.
WEISS, R.S. (1976), The emotional impact of marital separation,
'Journal of Social Issues', vol.32, pp.135-45.
WINCH, R.F. (1971), 'The Modern Family', Holt, Rinehart & Winston,
New York.
WINCH, R.F. and GREER, S.A. (1964), The uncertain relationship
between early marriage and marital stability: a quest for relevant
data, 'Acta Sociologica', vol.8, pp.83-96.
WOLFF, S. (1973), 'Children under Stress', Penguin Books.
YOUNG, M. and WILLMOTT, P. (1957), 'Family and Kinship in East
London', Routledge & Kegan Paul.
YOUNG, M. and WILLMOTT, P. (1973), 'The Symmetrical Family: a study
of work and leisure in the London region', Routledge & Kegan Paul.
ZELDITCH, M. (1964), Family, marriage and kinship, in R.E.L. Farris
(ed.), 'Handbook of Modern Sociology', Rand McNally, Chicago.

SUBJECT INDEX

AUTHOR INDEX

Ackerman, K., 61
Ainsworth, K.D., 33
Andry, R.G., 33

Bane, M.J., 3
Barry, W.A., 50, 61
Beauchamp, D., 89
Bendix, R., 49
Berardo, F.M., 5
Berent, J., 49
Bernard, J. 119
Bhrolchain, N.M. (with Brown,
    G.W. et al.), 89
Birtchnell, J., 27
Blau, P.M., 49
Blom-Cooper, L. (with McGregor,
    O.R. et al.), 126
Blood, R.C., 119
Bose, C.E. (with Rossi, P.H.
    et al.), 50
Bradburn, N.M., 119
Brandewein, R.A., 7
Bredemeier, H.C. (with Davis, K.
    et al.), 91
Brim, O.G., 119
Brown, C.A. (with Brandewein,
    R.A. et al.) 7; (with Feldberg,
    R. et al.), 8
Brown, G.W., 89
Bumpass, L. 15, 50, 53
Burchinal, L.G., 7, 72
Burgess, E.W., 61, 119
Burr, W.R., 88
Busfield, J., 88

Campbell, A., 88
Cannon, K.L., 88
Caplovitz, D., 119
Carrier, N.H., 38, 90
Cartwright, A., 79
Chesser, E., 54
Chester, R., 2, 5, 6, 73, 90, 91,
    118, 123, 124, 125, 126, 128,
    129
Christensen, H.T., 72, 77
Coombs, L.C., 77
Coombs, R.H., 47
Cooper, D., 13
Cottrell, L.S., 61, 119
Cuber, J.F., 50
Cutright, P., 3, 50

Davis, K., 91
Davis, K. (with Driscoll, R. et
    al.), 62
Despert, J.L., 16
Dominian, J., 4, 12, 72, 89, 92,
    97, 131
Douglas, J.W.B., 7, 29, 33
Driscoll, R., 62
Durkheim, E., 49
Dyer, E.D., 89

Esterson, A., 13

Fagin, C.M.R.N., 33
Feld, S. (with Gurin, G. et al.),
    15
Feldberg, R. (with Brown, C.A.
    et al.), 8